Unstoppable

The Story of George Mikan, the First NBA Superstar

George L. Mikan
and Joseph Oberle

MASTERS PRESS

A Division of Howard W. Sams & Company

Published by Masters Press
A Division of Howard W. Sams & Company
2647 Waterfront Pkwy E. Dr, Suite 100, Indianapolis, IN 46214

97 98 99 00 01 02   10 9 8 7 6 5 4 3 2 1

Library of Congress Cataloging-in-Publication Data Pending

Every reasonable effort has been made to obtain photo permissions.
If there has been an error, please notify the publisher. We will gladly
correct any inadvertant errors or omissions in subsequent editions.

For my wife, Pat.
G.L.M.

For my children, Seth, Tessa and Paige —
to teach the future about the past.
J.O.

Table of Contents

Credits:

Edited by Kim Heusel
Proofread by Bryan Banschbach
Cover designed by Suzanne Lincoln
Front cover photo, George Mikan in his first game as a Minneapolis Laker, 1947 (Courtesy of AP/Wide World Photos)
Back cover photo, George cleans the marquee at Madison Square Garden (Courtesy of AP/Wide World Photos)

Acknowledgments

The authors would like to thank the following people for their generosity in time, effort and talent in the compilation of this book.

അ

Bill Erickson – *for his belief in the project and sticking to his guns when it mattered*

Lora Oberle – *for her flawless judgment and selfless effort in editing the manuscript*

Jim LaBumbard – *for his expertise and hustle in proofing it on a tight deadline*

The staff of the Minnesota Timberwolves – *for their flexibility and support*

Dick Jonckowski – *for his contributions of valuable research material*

Mr. Basketball of the first half-century, George Mikan.*(Courtesy of NBA Photos)*

Introduction

You almost don't notice former Minneapolis Lakers' great George Mikan as he watches Minnesota Timberwolves NBA basketball in Target Center. Mikan sits on the end of a row about halfway up the bleacher seats under one basket, his long, slender legs — too long to fit behind the seat in front of him — stretching out into the aisle. Dressed in a warm winter sweater, his now-silver mane combed above his trademark large-rimmed glasses, Mikan waits patiently for the game to start. In the aisle in front of him, fans and officials buzz about in pregame activity. Inches away, young autograph hounds hug the bleachers' end rail, jockeying for position, just a few feet above the walkway where the Timberwolves' opponents will enter to take the court.

Suddenly, a black-and-white image comes across the giant scoreboard above the arena floor. The grainy, 1950s-era footage grabs the audience's attention. On the screen, a basketball team is working the ball down court, taking a shot and scoring. Timberwolves broadcast host Tom Hanneman's voice introduces the subject of the film: "Mr. Basketball of the first half-century, George Mikan. In his eight years with the Minneapolis Lakers, Mikan led the league in scoring four times and rebounding once. His teams captured seven pro championships in the 1940s and '50s, and he was one of the first players to be elected to the Basketball Hall of Fame . . ."

Mikan cranes his neck upward to watch the black-and-white images of himself and his old Lakers teammates. Slowly, a magnificent smile emerges across his face, the same smile now appearing on the screen above him. On the scoreboard, the young Mikan is sitting on a locker room bench as one of his old teammates throws an arm around him and then tousles the curly locks hanging with sweat over his smiling face. Simultaneously in the Target Center seats below, one of Mikan's friends pats him on the shoulder as the scoreboard piece ends.

A Timberwolves beat reporter from press row spies Mikan in his seat. Word of the NBA legend spreads among the media, and soon a camera crew is dragging its setup to that end of the floor to grab a shot of the old cager for the evening sports highlight show. As the camera trains on Mikan, several of the youngsters nearby turn to see where it's pointing. One of them puts it together and tells his buddy, "That's George Mikan." Instantly, those with the worst position for the players' autographs are in a great spot to get Mikan's.

As several of them surround Mikan, jockeying for a place in line, Mikan grabs a pen and program and starts signing — his smile reaching its broadest peak. Mikan knows how great an autograph makes a young fan feel — he learned that feeling when he was very young.

In 1934, long before George Mikan played professional basketball, two champions of another sort met on a ballfield in Chicago. One was the immortal Babe Ruth, already the greatest legend of baseball history. The other was Mikan himself — but at the time, he was only ten years old and the marbles champion of Will County, Illinois.

By winning that marbles tournament, young Mikan had won the right to attend a New York Yankees-Chicago White Sox baseball game, to meet the Babe and receive an autographed baseball. At the time, no one knew that Ruth was signing a baseball for the future original superstar of professional basketball, a seven-time league champion, Hall of Famer, record holder and pioneer of his own sport. And no one knew that the young Mikan, standing and watching his baseball hero, would eventually become the "Babe Ruth" of basketball.

Today, all that remains of that meeting is a photo in Mikan's scrapbook showing the Babe signing the ball, with a young, lanky Mikan smiling at his side. The ball itself lies somewhere in the grassy area behind Mikan's former suburban Minneapolis home. Years after Mikan met Ruth, when Mikan's living room was growing crowded with his own championship trophies and basketball mementos, two of his young sons took the Babe Ruth baseball down off the mantle to play with it. Outside, they lost the ball in the weeds.

And while years of growth have buried the ball, they haven't dimmed the influence that the baseballer had on Mikan.

"He was my hero," said Mikan of Ruth. "I always appreciated how he took time to sign autographs and spend time with the kids. I made sure that I always did the same."

To look at the photo now, it's easy to imagine that Mikan was destined for greatness. Like the picture of a young Bill Clinton meeting President John Kennedy, the picture of Mikan's encounter with Ruth seems to foreshadow Mikan's own sports greatness. But the story of how Mikan became a legend could not be more different from Ruth's. The Babe was a gifted natural athlete who seemed at times to excel despite himself, but Mikan had to overcome physical obstacles — including poor eyesight — as well as the opinion of some experts that, at 6 feet, 10 inches, he was "too awkward" to play. But overcome them Mikan did, with a dogged determination that propelled him to the pinnacle of his sport.

Mikan was linked to Ruth's legend again in 1950, when both were honored as the best athletes of the first half of the century in their respective sports (as determined by an Associated Press poll of national sportswriters and broadcasters). "Mr. Basketball" is the title that was awarded to Mikan to celebrate his illustrious sports career. Besides Ruth, the honor put Mikan in the company of such sports immortals as Bobby Jones (golf), Jesse Owens (track and field), Jim Thorpe (football), Johnny Weismuller (swimming), Bill Tilden (tennis), Jack Dempsey (boxing) and Man O' War (horse racing). And at the time, Mikan was only halfway through his playing career.

But basketball is a sport that seems to exist in an eternal present. At the end of the twentieth century, Babe Ruth's legend is still strong as baseball's most storied player, but Mikan's legend is a bit like that long-lost baseball of his, buried under years of growth and change in the National Basketball Association.

Today, the NBA — which turned a mere fifty years old in 1996 — is just beginning to discover its history, and people are finding 'Big George' Mikan is every bit as essential to the history of basketball as the Bambino was to baseball. Many of the NBA's original scoring records were set by Mikan — he led his league in scoring for five of his eight full pro seasons and in rebounding for another season. Shooting smooth hook shots with either hand, Mikan was an unstoppable offensive force. He also played tough defense: his dominating play under the basket led to several rules that shape modern basketball, such as the ban on goaltending and the wider (12-foot) lane — rules that were made in an attempt to neutralize his play. Mikan's strong rebounding, deadly inside hook shots, and powerful elbows changed the game into a power and muscle game and sent the NBA on an upward spiral to where it is played today, above the rim.

As a member of the Minneapolis Lakers, Mikan was the NBA's first superstar in the league's first dynasty. Teamed with the 6-foot, 7-inch Vern Mikkelsen and 6-foot, 5-inch Jim Pollard, he showed both coaches and the public the advantages of having a big man in the lineup: the trio became the first and one of the most dominating front lines in NBA history. Mikan was the focal point of every opponent's game plan, often being guarded by two or even three players. In an era when the game was played rough, Mikan paid a physical price for his stardom — broken bones, broken teeth, cuts, bruises, elbows in the face. He played one league championship with a broken arm, another with a broken ankle.

Mikan led the Minneapolis Lakers to six league championships. (He had a total of seven championships in his pro career, which spanned ten seasons, four professional leagues and two teams.) Mikan is a charter member of the NBA Hall of Fame, and his unselfish passing helped teammates Pollard, Mikkelsen and Slater Martin, as well as Lakers coach John Kundla, to also attain that place of honor.

Big George was the most popular player of his time, the first marquee name in the NBA. Fans all over the country crowded arenas to see the Minneapolis Lakers' big man play. One night, the marquee at Madison Square Garden read "Geo Mikan vs. Knicks" — a testament to his popularity and his prowess. A fierce competitor on the court, he was a smiling and gentle giant off of it, and he often travelled into a town ahead of the rest of the team, just to meet with reporters.

Mikan played in an era of competing basketball leagues, when the NBA was just getting its start. Mikan was the biggest name in the game, and his popularity was crucial to the infant NBA as it struggled to find its identity. Like Michael Jordan of today, Mikan's presence alone affected the league. Mikan put the fledgling NBA on the map, stabilized it and gave it credibility. Jordan, Magic Johnson and Larry Bird might have taken the NBA's popularity to its pinnacle; George Mikan set the NBA on its modern-day course of worldwide popularity.

But Mikan's influence on the game didn't end with his playing days. When the American Basketball Association was formed in the mid-1960s, Mikan was named its first commissioner. At the time, Mikan was brought in to give the new league credibility, and he did — many claimed that the ABA would not have been as successful as it was without Mikan. But Big George was more than just a name.

As ABA commissioner, Mikan was responsible for many innovations in the game of professional basketball, including the three-point shot, expanded halftime entertainment and a red light behind the basket to show who scored. It was Mikan who insisted that the ABA differentiate itself with the legendary red, white and blue basketball. He wanted the game to be widely accessible: fans in the higher reaches of the arena could see the brightly colored ball more easily, and families were attracted to the carnival-like atmosphere.

When the ABA disbanded and four of its teams joined the NBA, many of Mikan's innovations were adopted by the NBA. Once again, Mr. Basketball had changed the shape of professional basketball.

But Mikan's legacy was not yet complete. In the 1980s, he was named to chair a committee to bring professional basketball back to the state of Minnesota, which had been without a team since the Lakers moved to Los Angeles in 1960. And on November 8, 1989, the NBA did return, when the Minnesota Timberwolves played their first game in the Hubert H. Humphrey Metrodome, just blocks from the Minneapolis Armory, where Mikan had thrilled audiences some thirty-five years before. It was a symbolic closure for the circle of his basketball legacy.

Today, Mikan is a living legend. But he's more than just a name on an old championship trophy — he was a pioneer in the beginning of professional basketball, an innovator in its tough, growing middle years, and a resource today, as the league keeps expanding and changing.

As the NBA rediscovers its past, it's almost as if someone is clearing away years of growth around that old ball signed by Mr. Baseball, looking for the connection to Mr. Basketball. Because there they will find the pivotal figure of the early history of the NBA — George Mikan. And now the autograph seekers in Target Center are beginning to figure that out.

Part I

Before Basketball

Ten-year-old George Mikan of Joliet, Illinois, meets his hero, Babe Ruth, at a New York Yankees/Chicago White Sox game at Comisky Park. Mikan won the Will County marble tournament for the right to meet the Sultan of Swat in 1934.
(Courtesy of George Mikan)

೫ 1 ೫

A Croatian-American Childhood

A t some point, I must have been able to see fairly well. After all, in 1934, at age ten, I won the marbles tournament of Will County, Illinois, without glasses on. I'm sure I was squinting, down on my knees with a big shooter clenched between my thumb and forefingers. But I still had to be able to see straight to knock those marbles out of the big circle and keep my shooter in the ring. You can't do that with blurred vision — those cat's-eyes would all run together.

Playing marbles was a big deal when I was growing up in Depression-era Joliet, a town just outside of Chicago. We played whenever we could, to pass the time, and it wasn't very expensive. You didn't need a lot of equipment or a court, just a flat spot of earth and a sackful of marbles. And before I got my quarter-inch thick glasses a couple of years later, I, George Lawrence Mikan, was pretty good at knocking marbles around.

So there I was, a spry young marbles champion from Joliet, at Comiskey Park in Chicago looking to watch a ballgame and get an autograph. Along with winning the Will County tournament had come the right to meet Babe Ruth at a Chicago White Sox-New York Yankees baseball game. I already stood nearly as tall as the legendary baseballer, which probably emboldened me when the other county winners and I met Ruth before the game. I guess I was flush with the moment and bravely asked the Babe a question.

"Mister Ruth," I said sheepishly, "will you hit a home run for us?"

Without a second thought, Ruth replied, "Sure, kid, I'll hit one for you."

For a moment, I thought he could perform on command. The surety with which he responded made me believe I would see a home run that afternoon.

3

And I did — the Babe hit a home run just as he had promised. When our group of kids met Ruth again after the game to get our pictures taken together and receive an autographed baseball, a fellow walked up with a baseball in his hand.

"Mister Ruth," he said. "This is the ball you hit into the stands for a homer. It hit me on the head. Will you autograph it for me?"

Before anyone could ask whether he wanted his head or the ball autographed, Ruth grabbed the ball, replied, "Sure, kid," and winked at me. Ruth signed the ball and then quickly palmed it, giving the fellow one of the autographed balls meant for us. When the man left, Ruth patted me on the head and handed me the home run ball with his name on it. He was truly a man of his word.

That trip home from the ballpark was the longest that I can remember — waiting to show off my prize to my family and friends. Years later, when kids were seeking my autograph, I remembered the kindness of Babe Ruth, not only to me, but to all his young fans. I was determined to treat my fans the same way. In 1950, when I was honored as Mr. Basketball of the first half-century right alongside Ruth, who was named Mr. Baseball, I figured that the Babe had touched me in more ways than just with a pat on the head. He inspired to me strive to be the best basketball player I could be and to never forget the people who care the most about it — the fans.

ᘓ

Thrills such as meeting the Sultan of Swat were rare in the depressed Illinois town of Joliet. It wasn't every day that you met a legend of the baseball diamond. Mostly, every day you worked, and worked hard. But there were still a lot of games being played. Ballgames — either on the baseball diamond or on the basketball court — were at first a diversion and then a passion for the Mikan family. For me, I guess, basketball would become an obsession.

I was born on June 18, 1924, and grew up with my two brothers, Joe (older) and Ed (younger), and a sister, Marie (the baby), on the second floor of an old tavern near the industrial part of town. My hard-working parents were named Joseph and Minnie Mikan. We were poor, like everyone back then, but we all pulled together in every way that we could. The lessons I learned while growing up, about hard work and sacrifice, have stuck with me all my life.

My folks ran Mikan's Tavern, a restaurant owned by my Croatian grandparents. My grandfather was also named George Mikan, and

Mikan's Tavern (above) on Elsie Avenue and Broadway in Joliet — George's boyhood home is on the second floor and his first job was located on the main floor. Inside the tavern (above left) George's grandfather, George, visits with the locals, Monkey Joe and the Crazy Serbian, et. al. George's parents, Joseph and Minnie Mikan, on their wedding day (lower left). *(Courtesy of George Mikan)*

my grandmother, Mary, was known affectionately as Blondie. My grandparents had immigrated to the United States in the early 1900s and still spoke Croatian at home sometimes, even though they insisted that we grandkids speak nothing but English. Gramps had left their town of Vivodina in Croatia by himself, leaving Blondie behind to wait for him. He settled in Pittsburgh and went to work in the steel mills. Within three weeks, Gramps had made enough money to send for Blondie.

My dad was born in Pittsburgh; shortly thereafter the family moved to Chicago, where Gramps eventually bought our combination tavern and restaurant at the corner of Elsie Avenue and North Broadway in Joliet. Elsie Avenue was a poor neighborhood, just one block from the edge of town. My dad would meet my mom, Minnie Blinstrup, in Joliet and there they would be married, eventually to bear the staff of Mikan's Tavern.

My parents were of above-average height for the time — my dad was 6 feet, 1 inch, and my mom was 5 feet, 11 inches — so they must have assumed that their children would be on the tall side. However, when I hit the 6-foot mark at age eleven, they must have known something was up. My mom still kept me in short pants, though, a common practice of the time for young boys. As you can imagine, I cut a rather ridiculous figure.

My height made me somewhat self-conscious as a child. Of course, the neighborhood kids teased me, something kids always do. But sometimes even the neighbors would lean out their windows and call at me, "For gosh sakes, George, stop eating! Do you want to reach the moon?" I tended to stoop a little bit, so people wouldn't think I was so tall.

But we were a close-knit community, and the neighbors would watch out for us as often as they'd rib us. At the heart of our community was Mikan's Tavern. Gramps and Dad took care of the tavern business and tended bar until the three of us boys were old enough to see over the bar and do it ourselves (which was at a young age for the fast-growing Mikan boys). Mom was the restaurant's cook, and a great one at that — her 35-cent fried chicken became a staple for the community. I know she was a great cook because whatever she made for the restaurant was what we had for dinner, as well. We kids did everything else at Mikan's Tavern, from waiting on tables and cleaning the place up to cleaning the fish for the weekly fish fry.

I came to hate fish very much because of the fish fry we had every Friday night. Every Thursday, Dad would drive to Chicago and get some fresh Lake Michigan perch from the market, and we had to scale the fish and clean them. Then on Friday, Mom would put out a big cauldron of oil, and we'd fry them up.

Mother would have us dressed up like little sailors with sailor caps on, and we'd carhop. It cost you 10 cents to get a fish fry. And a glass of beer was 10 cents. If you ordered fried chicken with it, the cost was 75 cents an order.

Since Mom spent all day in the tavern kitchen, Blondie was left to pretty much raise us. Blondie spent much of her child-rearing time back behind the tavern, where Joe and I had constructed a basketball hoop out of a wooden backboard and the rim from an old beer-barrel hoop. I was about eleven when we started playing basketball. Originally, our ball was a plastic beach ball with the air tube taped down — it served us for many years.

Blondie didn't know much about the game of basketball, but she knew when something wasn't right. She decided all the court squabbles with the end of her broom and a rule of mandatory courtwide free throws. If there was an argument brewing into a fight, Blondie awarded all the players a free throw — which usually took long enough for everyone to cool down.

Probably because she refereed us so much, Blondie became a real fan of our games and would come to watch Joe and me — and later, Ed — play wherever we were playing. I went to seven years of grammar school at St. Mary's Croatian school in Joliet and played some basketball there. While I didn't know anything about the intensity of basketball fans at the time, I learned a bit about it from my grandmother at one of those games.

Our grammar-school games were organized, yet somewhat informal, but the desire to win was there just the same. We had homemade uniforms — T-shirts with hand-painted numbers — which made us feel like it was more than just a pickup game in the backyard. I remember one basketball game in particular because a guy kicked me right in the groin. As I lay on the ground, writhing in pain, I heard an uproar from the crowd. I looked down the court and could see my grandma with her umbrella going after the guy who hit me.

As soon as I was on my feet, I said, "Grandma, you can't do that."

But Blondie would hear nothing of it. "They shouldn't do that," she replied. I was about twelve years old, and it was really embarrassing for me. But the Mikans have always stood up for one another, no matter what.

Since our family lived and worked so closely together, that attitude came by us naturally. In times as tough as the 1930s, people all over were pulling together to get by. Our neighborhood was surrounded by the dankness of industrial smokestacks — the Texaco refinery and coke plant were within smelling distance — and the factories really dominated people's lives. Over the years, we Mikan boys had a variety of jobs at the local factories. Another way we'd make ends meet is to go down to the coke piles at the factories where they made the brick and dumped the ashes. We'd pick the useable coke out of the pile and bring it home and use it in the fire. Every dime counted.

The community we lived in was a small melting pot of immigrant America: predominantly Catholic, but ethnically Croatians, Serbs, Slovaks, Italians and Spaniards. The men worked either at the local factories, making roofing shingles or silicon bricks for high-heat ovens, or at the nearby railroad yard. But they all came to Mikan's Tavern to relax.

ᗺ

ED MIKAN: George and I helped Mother in the restaurant. George tended bar and helped Mother in the kitchen. Our mother was a great cook. During the war years, they had stamps for food, and all the people in the community used to come to Mother's place. And she fed them like there was no tomorrow. She didn't care about the price of anything. All the construction workers used to come see Ma for their food. No one ever walked out of there hungry.

ᗺ

Mikan's Tavern was the meeting place of the local gentry, the characters, the Damon Runyon people. They were hard-working folks — real people, with strange nicknames like Monkey Joe and the Crazy Serbian. They'd stop in on their way to work in the morning and have their kannuppers — a shot of booze — and beer. That's all Gramps allowed us to serve.

After work, the men would stop on their way home from the factories, tired and dirty, but smiling when they came through the door. They would have a couple more kannuppers and a few more beers, and then they would load up their lunch pails with beers to take home. When I was young, I went to sleep many a night with the jukebox playing downstairs.

It was not all play at Mikan's Tavern, however. I saw plenty of fights started by patrons who had a few too many drinks. Their way of fighting was a lot different than you might see today. Back then, you would defend yourself more than anything. One guy would take a swing and whack the other guy. And while his hands were down, the other guy would take a swing and whack him back. This went on until one of them would quit — usually the one who was quite bloody.

Still, the community protected each other. One night when I'd come home from college, I was tending bar and two men no one knew walked in. I was working my way up and down the aisles between the six checkerboard cloth-covered tables serving drinks. One of the men stopped me and said, "From now on, we're going to collect protection money from you." They were trying to muscle us.

Slightly startled, I said, "What are you talking about?"

Right then, Monkey Joe, the Crazy Serbian, and another guy all ordered bottles of beer. These were guys who never drank beer from a bottle. The next thing I knew, they'd broken the bottoms of the beer bottles off on the bar rail. They turned, glared at the two strangers, and said, "You'd better get out of here, because you're going to need protection."

The pair took off, and we never heard from them again. Like I say, we were a close-knit group of people. Anybody outside that group was a stranger.

The community certainly adopted us Mikan boys, and they were always very supportive of our basketball careers. As the trophies and awards started to pile up, Gramps built a case behind the bar and collected them there for all of our friends, neighbors and patrons to see.

Gramps was fairly determined about my publicity. Whenever I received a write-up in the paper, Gramps wouldn't serve anyone until they read the article. He made sure that our neighbors and

friends were well aware of what Joe, Ed and I were doing. But Gramps had a sense of humor about it, too. He liked to tell everyone that he was the one winning the trophies with the name of George Mikan on them.

But George Mikan wasn't the only name on the awards in my grandfather's case. My brothers, Joe and Ed, brought home their share, as well. Like me, they both later played college ball and had pro careers. Joe, who eventually stood 6 feet, 5 inches, was a superb athlete, able to excel at any sport he picked up. During World War II, Joe spent some time in the service, which shortened his professional career to only one year with the Chicago American Gears. Ed, at 6 feet, 9 inches, was my backup at DePaul. He was just two years behind me and played in the pros for six seasons. When we were growing up, the Mikan boys played together on several different teams, and we formed a pretty tough nucleus for a lot of championships.

The Mikan brothers also played baseball together in our early years. My dad, who was a justice of the peace for four years, was a friend of the local prison warden and set up baseball games between our team and the prisoners. The prisoners took a liking to the Mikans, and when we were younger, they built a bed for us that was 8 feet long, 6 feet wide, and 4 feet off the floor. My mother's jaw almost dropped through the floor when she saw it. It was too big to fit in any of our bedrooms, so Mom transformed our living room into a bedroom just for that incredible bed. It's one of the few beds I've slept in which my feet didn't stick out the end.

The prisoners followed my basketball career as I got older, and I would always get a Christmas card from "The Boys at Joliet State Penitentiary."

CB

ED MIKAN: We had an old Model A Ford, a delivery truck with the doors in the back. It had only one seat in it for the driver. Every couple of days, mother would send George and me to the store with a big order of groceries to fill for the restaurant.

One Saturday night, George was driving home. At that time, they had road blocks where the state patrol would check out cars. Well,

---

Opposite page: Joseph Mikan and his three sons (l to r) George, Ed and Joe, Jr., enjoy an Independence Day parade in front of Mikan's Tavern. *(Courtesy of George Mikan)* *a policeman was bending over a car in front of our car, facing the same direction we were going. The flares were burning, but George, who was fourteen or fifteen at the time and had bad peripheral vision, didn't see the policeman. All of sudden, I heard a loud thump.*

"George," I said, "what did you hit?"

"Ed, I think I hit a cop," he said.

Right away, the police stopped us and grabbed us. Of course, we didn't have too good of brakes on that old Model A. They took us in for interrogation. The head of the commission running the road check was my dad's associate, and we had to go before him. George had put the cop in the hospital, but he ended up all right. The commissioner penalized George by making him write a several-thousand word essay on why not to hit a policeman. We were lucky both the cop and the commissioner knew Dad.

CS

Certainly, all these things — the town and the times I grew up in — helped shape my attitudes and feelings about my own loyalties in later life. Our life was tough and spare, yet we never felt like we wanted anything. These are lessons that everyone who has gone through the Depression carries with them for the rest of their life. Some are overt, like a knee in the groin on a grammar-school basketball court. And some are more subtle, like the one I learned as a waiter in our restaurant.

I don't remember ever finding a lost dime on the floor of our tavern because people hung onto their money tightly when I was growing up. But one afternoon, the promise of extra money in the form of a tip had me excitedly flying through the tavern.

"Give me an extra special chicken for this order, will you, Mom?" I asked her in the kitchen.

"Why, son, what's so special about Mister Cerljan today?" she replied.

"He said he'd give me a tip," I told her.

My mom, well aware of what was coming, kindly obliged me with a huge plate of chicken. I set it before Mr. Cerljan with the most fawning service I had ever performed. After he'd finished eating, I waited tableside with a hopeful look on my face. As Cerljan paid the 35 cents for the chicken and then put away his pocketbook, my heart dropped into my stomach.

"I promised you a tip, and this is a good tip," he said, preparing to leave. "Get out of this business. Go to school; get an education."

He grabbed his weather-beaten hat off the chair and left.

I had been taken in. I was crestfallen and had to be consoled by my mom.

"We don't get tips here," she explained. "Tips are for people who can afford to eat well and drink well. They are for people who have more money than we have. And tips are not for friends. Here we do things for our customers that we do for our friends — because they are our friends. And friends don't pay for favors."

The tears I cried over that tip were the last ones I ever shed over anything like that. I learned that you get what you work for and that impressing someone with a favor and a smile does not guarantee the same in return. Hard work alone is rewarded.

Besides, Mr. Cerljan was right. School was my way out of the restaurant business, which wasn't the business for me.

ငၗ2ౠ
Doctor, Priest or Pianist?

Every athlete has roadblocks to overcome on the way to fulfilling his or her dreams. In my case, I had to overcome a lot. My eyesight was an obvious hurdle — without my glasses, my vision was like driving through a rainstorm without windshield wipers. And ironically enough when looked at from today's perspective, my size was another hurdle. Basketball is a game of speed and agility, and back then a lot of people perceived tall men as gangly, awkward rubes, maybe not too bright. And I was uncommonly tall. I even overheard one of my high school teachers say, "That Mikan will never amount to anything — when a boy is oversized, all his strength goes into his height, and there's nothing left for his brain."

So I took a rather circuitous route to my basketball career. I never even considered basketball as a career option — even though I'd played all my life — until I was offered a basketball scholarship to DePaul University in 1941. Of course, professional basketball was neither a high-paying or prestigious career back in the '30s. Growing up in a poor family, I wanted a job that would get me ahead, and at first I thought about being a doctor. I sure didn't want to spend my life doing the kind of work I was doing then.

Even though Depression-era jobs never paid much, there was usually work nearby for an able-bodied young lad. As teenagers, my brothers and I were always juggling two or three jobs, trying to help the family get by. One of my first summer jobs outside Mikan's Tavern came at age fourteen, working on the railroad for 7 cents an hour. I carried rails, laid them and then spiked them down with sledgehammers. It was hard work, but we needed the money.

At the time, my dad had a side job selling coal, and my brothers and I would help him by removing the coal from the coal cars at the railroad yard and shoveling it into coal bins. We used to walk along the railroad tracks and pick up coal that had been dropped off the cars and take it home — we could always use some extra coal at home.

At age fifteen, I went down the street to the Joliet Ruberoid plant and asked for a job. I was a fairly tall kid, and the man hiring workers told me I was too big to work there. I was slightly startled at his response, but it was something I was starting to hear more and more often. I was once even told that I was too big to play baseball. (I wonder what the Seattle Mariners' 6-foot, 10-inch Randy Johnson would have to say about that.)

Well, I never accepted it when people tried to tell me I couldn't do something — not even back then at the Ruberoid.

"What is the toughest job that you've got?" I replied to the man.

Skid loading, he said, which was taking the bundles of roofing off the conveyor and putting them on a skid so they could then be hauled and stored by a forklift. You'd have to work as fast as the bundles came down the line.

"You give me that job," I said, "and if I can't handle it, I'll let you know." It was a tough job, mainly bull work, but I stuck it out.

It was while I was at the Ruberoid that I decided to get an education, because I didn't want to be a skid loader the rest of my life. I worked with a bunch of great guys, though, who all became my friends. One fellow who worked the tying machine — a machine that wrapped the bundles up with wire for the conveyor belt — taught me to do that job, and we would trade off. Eventually, I worked my way up the ladder to the job of stacking the roofing sheets.

CB

ED MIKAN: Perhaps George was too big to stack roofing sheets. His co-workers used to holler when he would stack the shingles. George would stack them so high, the shorter guys couldn't reach them off the top. "That goddamn Mikan is stacking the sheets too high," they'd say.

CB

I worked at the Ruberoid factory for a couple of years. All during that time, as soon as I received my check, I'd take it home and sign it over to the family. My dad would take it and give me some walking-around money, a dollar or two, when I needed it.

As much as I yearned for something else to do with my life, my family was thinking along the same lines. In fact, my mother's first idea was that I'd make a great piano player. My mom admired the size of my hands and signed me up to take piano lessons. Now, I lived in a fairly rough neighborhood to be taking piano lessons. Many of our neighbors worked in the nearby factories and lived in company-owned houses. A lot of the kids didn't continue in school beyond the elementary grades. I tried to beg off the piano, but Blondie insisted that I take the lessons.

I started out by studying piano with the nuns at St. Mary's Croatian school; after getting my diploma there, I went on to take lessons at a nearby music conservatory. When I returned home, I would put the music in my pants so that the guys in the neighborhood wouldn't rib me. But they knew where I'd been and would ride me about it — inevitably, there would be a fight. Sometimes, the kids picking the fights were bigger than me, and sometimes they were smaller. I did pretty well in those fights; I learned to be a competitor.

I learned to play the piano, too. Blondie had me practice one hour every day, and it was a lot of fun. Eventually, the guys would be on the front step waiting for me as I finished my lesson so that we could continue playing ball outside. I did have good hands for the piano — my teacher was amazed at how many keys I could reach. I firmly believe that playing piano actually made me a better basketball player. The strength and touch I built up in my hands had to be a direct result of running scales day after day. All those hours on that old piano must have contributed greatly to my ability to control the ball. In fact, one sportswriter, Oscar Farley of the United Press, later agreed and put it down in print:

> *"Go out and get yourself some piano lessons, son, if you want to be an All-American basketball player.*
> *George Mikan, the great DePaul college center with one of the greatest finger-touches in basketball, has a couple of piano conservatory degrees in piano.*
> *George's coach, Ray Meyer, says there isn't any question that his years of piano lessons helped to develop his fingers to the point where George can control a basketball on the very tips of them."*

Ultimately, eight years of piano lessons would give way to time on the basketball court. I had wanted to play jazz music, but at the conservatory you had to play classical. I didn't really like the classical stuff — I liked the beer-barrel polka. I played more of my style with family and friends in later years.

And that was how I spent most of my time when I was growing up: going to school, working in the tavern or at another job, taking piano lessons or playing basketball. For the first seven years of my education, I attended St. Mary's Croatian school. While I was there, I played ball in the grammar-school league.

My older brother, Joe, also played basketball at St. Mary's. As is true with any older brother, his example helped to increase my interest in the sport. Joe played guard and was an excellent ballplayer. He had good hands, which made him a great playmaker on the court and a very good end for the Joliet Catholic football team. It also made him a pretty fair whittler, something that would have a dramatic effect on me.

One day when I was about twelve, Joe and I were in the tavern kitchen and Joe was whittling. I guess I must have been nosier than usual that day and sitting too near him. A piece of wood got stuck, Joe pried at it with his knife, and then suddenly it flew from his knife and hit me in the corner of the eye. I bled like a stuck pig.

Mom and Dad rushed me to the hospital, and our family doctor sewed the injury up. The prognosis was that some nerve tissue had been cut.

It didn't hurt too bad. In fact, the worst part about it was that I had to wear a bandage over my eye for four or five days. When the bandage came off, I could see just as well as ever, but from then on it seemed like my eyes became weaker. I've worn glasses ever since.

Joe blamed himself for my glasses, but my dad wore a strong prescription as well, so my eyes would probably have needed correcting anyway. When I first got the glasses, I stubbornly refused to wear them. Being taller than most kids was bad enough without being teased for wearing thick glasses on top of it. But my reluctance to wear them would get me into hotter water than a bit of razzing.

After graduating from St. Mary's Croatian in 1936 at age twelve, I went on to Joliet Catholic High School. Joe was going there, as well, and we both went out for the basketball team. I was only a freshman, but I was still on the team after the initial cutdowns to the roster. Then, on the day before the first game, our coach, Father Gilbert Burns, discovered that he had only twelve uniforms but still had fourteen players on the team. Father Burns chose the top eleven players, and there was only one roster spot left for the remaining three of us.

As Burns was talking to us about the coming game, he noticed me squinting while I listened.

"You, George," he said suddenly, "what're you squinting at?"

"The light's in my eyes," I explained. Well, he didn't buy that, because none of the other players was squinting.

"I guess it's because I'm not wearing my glasses," I admitted.

Of course, this was just the opportunity the coach needed. He told me that my glasses were going to be a problem. I explained to him that my dad was making me a cage to wear over them, but he didn't buy that, either.

"You just can't play basketball with glasses on," he said. "You better turn in your suit, son."

☞

ED MIKAN: Father Gilbert told George, "Why don't you go home and play your piano?" So George told him to go to hell. Then Father Gilbert chased him, and George ran out the door and out of the school — Father Gilbert could never catch George with those long legs of George's.

Later in life, Father Gilbert was transferred out East. Every time George and the Lakers played out there, Father Gilbert would call George and George would get him and his team tickets to sit on the Lakers' bench during the game. Whether there was one player or ten tagging along, whenever the Lakers were close by, George got Father Gilbert's team seats on the bench. That's just the kind of guy George was — he never held grievances against anyone.

☞

Since I had played all kinds of baseball and basketball games with my glasses on the previous summer, I should have just worn them at the Joliet Catholic practices and then I probably would have made the team. I vowed never to take them off again. When I left that gym, my heart broke. That's when I made up my mind that I didn't want to go to Joliet Catholic anymore — I finished out the year and transferred to Quigley Prep Seminary the following fall.

Quigley was a training ground for future priests. I got there thanks to my mom and Father Violich, the parish priest from St. Mary's. Father Violich thought I would make a good priest, and Mom and Blondie agreed. In fact, Father Violich felt so strongly about it that he set up a scholarship fund at Quigley and wanted me to be the first to use it.

George's grandfather, George Mikan, in the barn out back of Mikan's Tavern. George's grandmother, Mary ("Blondie") Mikan, visits with her grandson Ed. *(Courtesy of George Mikan)*

Well, there wasn't much I could say. My basketball dreams seemed to have been cast into the dustbin, it didn't seem like I'd make it as a pianist, and my early thoughts of being a doctor had gone nowhere. When I was twelve, I'd had an inkling toward politics thanks to one day spent as the boy mayor of Joliet, but that was only an inkling. The scholarship would certainly help finance my education and it would get me out of Joliet Catholic. Besides, Father Violich said I was not bound to anything by accepting the scholarship. So I did.

Quigley was not just the next school down the road. It was actually located fifty miles away, on the north side of Chicago — a bus, train and streetcar away from Elsie Avenue. Later, the three of us boys who were heading to Quigley from Joliet made a deal with the Joliet Bluebird Bus Lines that took us straight into Chicago on the bus. Still, it meant almost an hour and a half on the bus, one way. A lot of travel for a thirteen-year-old.

Quigley did not immediately solve my lack of basketball. The travel schedule made playing impossible — I didn't have the time. Every morning, my grandparents would get me up and make sure I was ready to catch the bus out on U.S. Highway 66 in front of the tavern. Gramps would sit out front with his watch, where he could see down the road about a half-mile, while Blondie would make everyone breakfast. As soon as Gramps saw the bus, he'd sing out, "Here comes the bus," and Blondie would send me off.

By the time I got home, it was five-thirty and time for supper, studying and helping in the restaurant. Had I gone out for the Quigley school team, I would have gotten home about three hours later. I did play a bit of intramural ball that first year, and I played with Ed and Joe in the backyard, but basketball suddenly dropped way down on my list of daily priorities.

Gramps and I had a pact. Every day as he packed me off to school, he would check to see if I had a dollar. If I spent anything out of that dollar, I was to tell him and he would replace it. That motivated me to try to save some money. Instead of taking the streetcar, which cost about 14 cents at the time, I would run the two-and-a-half miles from the station to school. At night, I would run back. That way, I would save a quarter.

Quigley was a five-year prep school. In my second year, I was fourteen years old and growing like mad. I was still shorter than

Joe but taller than most of the kids at Quigley. People started asking me why I didn't play for the high school basketball team. But this tall guy wore glasses, and Father Burns' credo never left the back of my mind. So I told them no.

Still, I didn't stop playing basketball, either. Joe persuaded me to join him in the Catholic Youth Organization games down at St. Mary's. As the two tallest players in the league, Joe and I took it by storm. The CYO was well-organized, but we played most of our games at home, at Joliet Catholic. Traveling was not a regular occurrence for CYO teams. So we were real excited one Sunday in 1938 when our team traveled to Waukegan to play St. Anne's in a game. I brought along a new pair of what were called "cushion bottom gym shoes."

Before the game I noticed the guys from St. Anne's drinking booze in the locker room. It kind of went against my grain. Different places, different faces, I guess. I just put on my new gym shoes and went out to play.

The game was barely minutes old when I tried to make a quick move in my new shoes. I stopped quickly in front of an opponent, and the shoe bottoms, acting like a vacuum, held my foot fast. The guy I faked didn't stop — he ran into my leg and broke it.

I struggled to get back to my feet but luckily couldn't. A doctor on the scene put a temporary cast on my leg, and he told me it was a compound fracture. If I had put any weight on it, I would have shortened the leg permanently.

In those days, our team travelled in a converted hearse, and they brought me home to our tavern in Joliet in the back of it. It was about midnight by the time we got there. Mom came running out to see what was going on, and she immediately fainted. We reassured her that I was all right. In the morning, my folks took me down to the hospital to set my leg.

That leg laid me up in the hospital for almost three weeks, which was tough on a fourteen-year-old, but I kept busy anyway. During that stretch while I was on crutches, I put on about six or seven inches. I outgrew the bed, I outgrew my brother Joe, and I outgrew everyone at Quigley.

A 6-and-a-half foot kid on crutches is hard to miss. When I got back to Quigley, the basketball coach approached me about playing for the team.

"I can't see anything without these glasses," I said.

"Well, come on out to practice and we'll try it," he replied.

I was delighted. Finally, someone who thought a fellow with bad eyes could play basketball. I guess my height allowed him to see past the glasses. So I showed up for the practice. In the CYO, I was so much taller than the other kids that I didn't have to worry about my glasses being knocked off. The Quigley coach solved that problem by taping the glasses to my head. He was also kind enough to give me a little tutoring.

By this time, though, it was nearly the end of the basketball season. Since my leg was still stiff, I decided to try out for the Quigley team the next fall. Unfortunately, something in my schedule had to give — high school basketball meant the official end to my piano lessons.

As it turned out, my schedule prevented me from joining the team that fall. I didn't play for Quigley until my fourth year there, when I was sixteen. Even then, I had to make room in my schedule for games in the CYO league and also in the Joliet City League, where I played with a team called the Joliet Moose. The Quigley team wanted me to play every game, but the long trip home to Joliet made it hard to practice every night. So in my fourth year I practiced some and played a select number of games.

It so happened that one of those Quigley games was against a Chicago high school called St. Leo's. St. Leo's had a real fine team, and they had a kid by the name of Beronoski, who ended up going to Notre Dame. But at this particular game, Beronoski was being scouted by DePaul University athletic director Paul Mattei and coach Paul Wendt.

I was pretty tall at the time, about 6 feet, 7 or 7-and-a-half inches, so I was pretty noticeable. Also, we beat St. Leo's. After the game, Mattei approached me.

"George," he said, "if you ever want to go to college, come to DePaul and we'll give you a scholarship."

"Well," I said, "I'm studying to become a priest. I really don't know." But when I got to thinking about it, I didn't believe that I really had a true vocation.

So I finished out my fourth year at Quigley. That fall, the fall of 1941, I went over to DePaul, which was also in Chicago, and took them up on their offer. They gave me a scholarship, books, tuition, everything I needed to get started, and told me I was going to play with the freshman squad. I was all set to go, except for one thing: I had failed to tell my parents that I had transferred schools.

So here I was, going to DePaul, and my folks thought I was still going to Quigley. After all, it was still the same bus ride into Chicago every day. All summer long, I'd agonized over the decision, but hadn't known how to spoil my mom's dreams of a priest in the family.

One day that fall, my dad called me into the kitchen, where he was reading the *Chicago Tribune*. "You know," he said, "it's funny. I never knew we had any relatives in Chicago, but there's a George Mikan playing for DePaul University."

"Well, Dad, that's me," I said.

He just started to laugh and said, "Well, why didn't you tell me?"

So I told him the whole story about how I ended up at DePaul and explained that I didn't want to hurt Mom's and Blondie's feelings. Dad was great about it — he straightened everything out with Mom and Blondie. Mom was disappointed to lose her pianist, doctor and priest in one fell swoop, but she was relieved to hear that I intended to use my education to earn a law degree. For me, I was thinking about basketball with renewed determination and growing confidence. All that remained was making the varsity team at DePaul — and with that scholarship in hand, I was certain that height, glasses and short-sighted coaches were not going to stand in my way.

Part II

School Days

George Mikan corrals a rebound for DePaul University, where he became a three-time All-American. *(Courtesy of George Mikan)*

Ꮕ3ᏋᏏ
Laying a Hardcourt Foundation
1941-1943

By deciding to go to DePaul in 1941, I had basically decided to make basketball a serious career move. Although I planned to study law while I was there, I'd been given a basketball scholarship, and I decided I was going to earn that scholarship by playing the best damn ball that I could.

DePaul University was a fairly young college when I arrived there in the fall of 1941 — it had been founded only about forty years before by the Vincentian Fathers, a Catholic religious order. It was not someone's romantic vision of college, with huge oak trees lining the campus and coeds hustling to class amidst falling autumn leaves. No, DePaul was a small, urban campus on the north side of Chicago, scraping by on tuitions and whatever money the priests could raise. Most of the students came from Chicago itself and were the sons and daughters of working-class families. The Depression had just ended, but money was still tight for most folks, so there were no dormitories — all the students commuted to class.

For me, that meant living at home and taking that fifty-mile bus ride to school each day. I rose with the early birds to hop the Joliet Bluebird bus every morning, and I still made it home each night by five-thirty, to have dinner with my family and then tend bar at Mikan's Tavern. Maybe because I had so much time on the bus to study, I managed to pull down some decent grades in my pre-law studies.

My classes at DePaul were done each day by one o'clock, so I had plenty of time for basketball. I was a member of the freshman team, which meant being on the "pig squad" for the varsity — we were their guinea pigs, and they tried out new plays on us. Day after day, we battled the varsity, usually having our hats handed to us.

The varsity center at the time was big Frank Wiscons. At 6 feet, 6½ inches, he was an inch-and-a-half shorter than I was at the time. (I was 6 feet, 8 inches and 215 pounds that first year at DePaul, but I was just a seventeen-year-old kid, and still growing.) I might have been bigger, but Wiscons was more experienced. Frank and I developed a pretty good rivalry that first year. We went toe-to-toe at a number of scrimmages, but the varsity generally came out on top.

Practice took place in an aging theater building we called the "Old Barn," which had been refurbished as our gym. Games with major opponents were played in Chicago Stadium, but as freshmen we didn't have to worry about those. Coach Paul Wendt was too busy with the varsity squad to take much time with the freshmen, and he didn't have any assistants. So we were left on our own — used for the varsity scrimmages and then left alone to practice or pull together whatever games we could against other freshman squads, junior colleges or independent teams. We even earned a little respect on campus by winning the St. Sabina tournament for independents.

I was gaining basketball success outside of the DePaul gym, as well. I still played along with my brother Joe on the Joliet Moose team in the Joliet City League, and I'd joined the St. Anthony's team in the Catholic Youth Organization league. All three Mikan brothers were earning plenty of basketball "hardware" to fill up my grandfather's tavern trophy case. But playing on so many teams made for some busy days of basketball for me — occasionally, I had to practice and then play a game or two all in the same day. Yet I still couldn't get enough basketball.

It was on one of those busy fall afternoons in 1941, after a scrimmage with the varsity squad, that my basketball fortunes almost took a huge detour.

Frank Gaglioni, a former captain of the Notre Dame basketball team, was coaching at Joliet Catholic High School, and he stopped in at DePaul to check on our scrimmage with the varsity. From the sidelines, he intently watched as Wiscons and I battled up and down the court. Gaglioni must have seen something he liked because after the practice he presented me with a surprising offer.

"George, why don't you go to a school that is known for basketball?" he said. "Why don't you go to Notre Dame? With your height, a little good, sound coaching will make a real basketball player out of you."

"Notre Dame?" I replied, thinking it over. Sure, it was a power-house basketball school, but I was happy at DePaul. Besides, I had a scholarship there, and Notre Dame wasn't offering me any financial help. I explained as much.

Gaglioni said that he could set up a tryout with Notre Dame if I was interested. At that time, schools could give kids tryouts before they gave them scholarships. He was heading down to South Bend for a visit over Christmas, and he invited me to come along.

I agreed to go only if my brother Joe could go with me — I figured we'd give them a two-for-one deal. I wasn't that interested because they hadn't offered me anything, but I figured Joe might have a chance to play there.

So it was all set — I'd go visit the nationally renowned campus of Notre Dame and let them take a look at me. Unfortunately, a couple of weeks before we got there, I hurt my right foot during practice. I didn't know at the time that the arch was broken, so I just had it taped and continued playing on it, figuring it would heal. Since I'd made the commitment to go to Notre Dame, I went anyway.

Joe and I made the couple of hours' drive down to South Bend with Gaglioni. It was Christmas vacation, but the Notre Dame coach, George Keogan, had kept the players at school for a couple of holiday games. Joe and I joined their freshman squad in a scrimmage against the varsity.

The way I remember it, Keogan kept having the other players throw the ball at my ankles to see how, being a big guy, I'd react to a low pass. Well, I was having a bad day — a lot of balls bounced off my feet and I wasn't moving very well on my broken arch. I like to joke that I kicked more three-pointers that day than the Notre Dame football team's field-goal kicker. I pretty much blew the tryout.

When the scrimmage was over, we went into Keogan's office and Ray Meyer, an assistant with Keogan at the time, was sitting there.

ଔ

RAY MEYER: The first time I ever met George Mikan was when I was working with George Keogan at Notre Dame. Mikan had come down for a tryout, and they just threw him on the floor with the varsity kids. Some of those kids didn't like to see him do well. He had a rough day.

I was standing next to Keogan when he was watching the boys scrimmage. Mikan didn't look as good as those varsity kids because he didn't fit in with them. Those kids were all individual stars, and they'd get you the ball when they felt like it — which was about once a year. Those guys had big names. Some of them would have been All-Americans.

In his office after the scrimmage, Keogan told Mikan he should go to a small school where they could give him a bunch of attention and a chance to make the ball team.

℃

Keogan looked at me and said, "George, I recommend that you go back to DePaul. You'll make a better scholar than a basketball player."

"That's your opinion," I replied, "I've been fighting that battle all my life. But you'd be wrong on two counts." Which meant I'm not a great scholar, but I am a pretty good basketball player.

So we left. I never told Keogan about my foot, but the Notre Dame trainer, Scrapiron Young, noticed it. He was the one who told me the arch was broken. "Kid," he said, "you're crazy to try to play basketball on that foot!"

It was nice to know why I wasn't playing well, but I wasn't too broken up about not making it at Notre Dame. Like I said before, I was happy at DePaul. Later, when I started winning all kinds of awards and fame for being a great basketball player, people liked to trot out that story, how the Notre Dame coach thought I couldn't play. And it was part of the big man's syndrome, I guess, that I had to overcome in my early life — someone always telling me, 'you can't do that.'

Keogan was interested in Joe, however, but Joe passed on his offer, saying, "The Mikans are a package deal." We Mikans were used to some tough times (like everyone else during the Depression), and we always stuck together first and foremost, especially when things were going against us.

When I returned to DePaul, my freshman teammates gave me a rough time about my performance in South Bend. I finished out the season at DePaul, convinced that I would be spending my remaining college career there. But then, after the last varsity game, coach Wendt announced that he was resigning. Here was a coach who saw something in me, and he was leaving the program before I really got started in it.

Naturally, I was curious about who our new coach would be. To my shock and dismay, Ray Meyer, the former Notre Dame assistant who'd witnessed one of my lowest moments on the basketball court, was hired as the new DePaul coach. My first thought was, "Oh, my gosh, here comes Ray Meyer, and he didn't like me at Notre Dame. Where am I going to go to school now?"

Ray called a special spring practice to get a look at his new team. This was the spring of 1942, and that was allowed back then. DePaul was Ray's first crack at being a head coach — he'd been hired for just a one-year contract — and I guess he wanted to make sure he did a bang-up job. So he walked onto the gymnasium floor and had us all sit in a group in front of him. It was me, Wiscons, Mel Frailey, Johnny Jorgenson, Tony Kelly, Cliff Lind, Bill Ryan and Jim Cominsky.

Then Ray took off his suit coat, looking like he really meant business, and said, "No one on this team has a starting position. We're all going to work hard, and the cream will come to the top."

So we practiced and scrimmaged for nearly four hours. Ray ran us all through a series of drills. It didn't matter whether we played forward, guard or center, we ran fast-break drills and weaves and wind sprints and pivot plays, all those kinds of things. When we were done, I hobbled down into the training room to have my ankle wrapped and my blisters taken care of. I thought right then and there we were in for something. In fact, it was only the beginning of the hard work to come.

Ray gave us all some advice on how to stay in shape over the summer, swimming, skipping rope, exercising. I didn't have any problem with that. Besides working full time loading skids at the Ruberoid factory, I was playing baseball in the Joliet City League, pitching for the West Side Grocers. One day, I pitched a no-hitter against the Joliet Moose team, which prompted calls from several major-league baseball teams. But if it was a choice between going to school or playing baseball, I opted to get my education and play basketball. That scholarship was a powerful incentive — in baseball, you have to grind it out in the minors for a number of years and you never know if you're going to make it. I felt I had a better chance of playing basketball, despite what George Keogan thought.

That fall, Ray was as good as his word, giving everyone a chance at a position. He worked us all out to evaluate everybody on the squad, and I was given every opportunity to beat out Wiscons.

C♂

RAY MEYER: Frank Wiscons, the big left-hander, had been DePaul's center the prior year. I knew I would have a good team with Wiscons at center. But I felt we had a chance at having a great team with Mikan at center. I knew after a few days of watching him, that George had something that was inherent — he was a winner. He worked harder to accomplish what he wanted.

When you look at athletes, you can measure their talent, but you can't measure what's in their heart or in their head. There was something about George that stood out — he had great heart. I liked to work with people who have that kind of disposition or that innate [characteristic] because that's the way I felt when I played. I was not the greatest player, but I had the heart to do just what had to be done.

C♂

Ray really worked us. He called practice the first day of class that fall of 1942, and we scrimmaged every day after that. Our training drills would go on for a long time. We boxed, jumped rope and ran track to build up our stamina. I don't know how many laps we did in the gym. Ray wanted to develop his own team concept and needed to know who would play together the best. And then after practice, Ray and I would work out some more.

Ray saw the potential in me, and he kind of took me under his wing. Every day we had an individual practice, working on conditioning, coordination, agility, shooting, offensive tactics, defensive tactics, all kinds of stuff. I skipped rope, did calisthenics, ran. Some days, Ray brought in one of the other players to work with me, one-on-one. With Wiscons, I worked on defensive movements; 5-foot, 4-inch guard Billy Donato ran circles around me until I learned how to guard a smaller, faster player and increase my quickness and agility.

C♂

RAY MEYER: After we scrimmaged, I'd spend all my time with George and let the other guys go, because my whole future was in how well he developed. I always knew the value of the big man. I knew that the big men get more baskets by accident than the little guys get on purpose. They dominate the game. They eliminate the extra shots for the opposing team. And since basketball games are games of percentages,

*the big guy is going to get the easy shots underneath the basket. When
you look at the shooting percentages, it's always the centers that have
the best percentages.*

∞

Ray and I worked on my pivot shot — I put up thousands of
shots, refining them over time. We worked on the right hook first
and then just a little bit on the left hook. In my second year working
with Ray, the other teams would try to stop me from throwing my
right-hand hook, so Ray taught me the left-hand hook. In the long
run, my left became more proficient than my right.

Ray said, "The object of this game, George, you see this round
ball, you see that hoop. The idea is to put this round ball in that
hoop." He liked to needle me.

I think Ray made me. Everything I've done, I owe to him. He
gave of himself so much. When we weren't working on hook shots,
we'd be doing rebound drills and put-back drills, ultimately developing what they call the George Mikan drill. The Mikan drill is a
figure eight of little hook shots from right and left of the basket.
First, the right hand puts up the shot and then the left. When the
ball comes through the hoop, you catch it and put it up with the
other hand.

Ray did everything he could to develop my speed, my agility
and my grace. He even went so far as to hire some of the cheerleaders to teach me how to dance. I had to learn to avoid stepping on
their toes, and that made me more nimble on my feet.

∞

*RAY MEYER: One thing that impressed me from the beginning is
that George did everything I asked him to do. And a lot of the things I
asked him to do, a lot of other players would have rebelled against,
would never have done. By today's standards, had George come into
the game now, with the attitude that some players have, he would have
never become George Mikan. But his attitude was he would do whatever it takes. We had him jumping over benches and taking a hook
shot. How many kids would do that today? Little things . . . I used to
shoot the ball and I would make George jump up and bat it away —
never believing that someday we would use [that tactic].*

∞

Ray and I worked together right up to the season opener on
December 2, 1942, when I made my first start, as a forward, for the

The DePaul basketball team. George is number 99 (middle-front) and his brother
Ed is number 32 (middle-back). Coach Ray Meyer is located front row, right.

(Courtesy of George Mikan)

DePaul University varsity. I scored 10 points, respectable for the times, en route to a 51-28 win over Navy Pier. It felt great to get that first game, and a win to boot, under my belt.

We rolled over the opposition that December; by the end of the month, after seven games, we were still undefeated. In our fifth game, against Purdue, I started at center for the first time. I played nearly the entire game, putting in 16 points.

 C8

RAY MEYER: We were 4-0 when George moved into the pivot against the Boilermakers. Ward "Piggy" Lambert coached Purdue at the time, and he gave Mikan a lot of guff from the sidelines as George prepared to shoot a free throw in front of the Purdue bench. George turned to him, pointed a finger, and said, "This one's for you, Piggy." He put it right in. We won, 45-37.

C8

My confidence was growing in proportion to my height, but apparently my size was about all that was getting noticed. Six-foot, eight-inch basketball players don't warrant a second glance today, but back then, my height made me a media sensation. There were only three notable big men in college ball: me, Bob Kurland of Oklahoma A&M, at 7 feet, and Don Otten of Bowling Green, also at 7 feet. Following the Purdue game, Wilfrid Smith of the *Chicago Tribune* wrote, "All [Mikan's] points were the result of his physical advantage over his opponents." He gave me no credit for my skills nor for the hard work that Ray and I had put in. I became determined to prove Smith wrong.

A few nights later, it seemed like the *Tribune* reporter was vindicated when we lost by three points at Notre Dame to Ray's former boss, George Keogan. It was a game that Ray and I both wanted, for obvious reasons, but we lost it nonetheless. The following season, we avenged the loss in Chicago. I had a pretty good game that night and felt pretty satisfied about winning. But Keogan was no longer around to witness it — he'd passed away early in 1943.

We finished the 1942-43 regular season with an 18-4 record, which surprised many people around the country. Late in the season, we'd knocked off the powerhouse Kentucky Wildcats, and even the *Tribune's* Smith had to say something nice about me: "The 6'-8" center never played a better game, using his height to advantage and yet moving as nimbly as a forward."

For lowly DePaul University to have compiled such a winning record was a big shock to the basketball world, and when Illinois decided not to accept an invitation to the NCAA Tournament, we got the bid and were determined to shake a few cages. In the first round, we knocked off Dartmouth, and I was able to pour in 18 points, something to brag about in 1943. But what made an even greater impact was the fact that I knocked 17 Dartmouth shots out of the basket. Ray Meyer's old shot-blocking drill worked to perfection that night — for the first time acquiring for me the derogatory moniker of "goaltender."

Now, granted that by today's rules I was doing just that: goaltending, which is now illegal. When the shot came up and then arced down towards the basket, I would jump up and either knock the ball out of the cylinder, or grab it and start a fast break up the other way. At the time, the move was perfectly legal, and as Ray told me, until they make a rule against it, we were best served to use it.

Dartmouth coach Ozzie Cowles was livid about how my goaltending disrupted his ball team. But he wasn't the only coach upset about goaltending, and I wasn't the only player doing it. Others — particularly Bob Kurland — were doing the same thing. But I do believe it was that 1943 game DePaul played against Dartmouth that prompted the NCAA National Rules Committee to pass an experimental rule the following season that prevented players from interfering with the ball in its downward arc — another in a long line of rules created to thwart the big man.

At any rate, DePaul was knocked out by Georgetown in the next round of the NCAA, but we had already gotten the attention of basketball people around the country. And we were just preparing to put our mark on the game.

∞4∞
Playing in Wartime
1943-1944

O ver the summer of 1943, I grew another inch, to 6 feet, 9 inches. Meat, sugar and other foods had been rationed due to World War II, but my mother always managed to find enough to feed her growing sons. To show her patriotism, Mom always gave a free meal to anyone in uniform who came into the tavern.

The war had changed my world in a lot more significant ways, though: My brother Joe was drafted shortly after our trip to Notre Dame. At the time, he had been going to school at St. Joseph's in Indiana, where he played baseball and was future Dodger baseball great Gil Hodges' roommate. After he was drafted, Joe joined the Air Force and served four years. Joe saw action in Guam, which caused a lot of worry for our family, and he later became a military police officer.

Fortunately for my mother that summer, my brother Ed was too young for the draft. I was nineteen, but ineligible to serve because the Army thought I was too tall and my eyesight was poor. Like the rest of my countrymen, I was ready to serve, but the good Lord hadn't equipped me with the best body to do so.

I was certainly tall enough to goaltend, however, and that's what was on people's minds in the basketball world. The NCAA had passed an experimental rule banning goaltending for the 1943-44 season. As an experimental rule, it wasn't leaguewide and didn't affect us at DePaul. So we would play a large role in the goaltending fracas to come.

Another big concern among basketball folks that summer was the shortage of good players because of the war. I watched as all around me guys I'd played either with or against the previous season had volunteered or been drafted. Just as the country was getting used to the idea of rationing raw materials and goods for the

Dad and the boys (left): George, Joe, Jr. and Ed (from l to r). Twin towers (below): DePaul centers George and Ed Mikan. *(Courtesy of George Mikan)*

war effort, basketball players were going to have to be rationed as well.

Coach Ray Meyer had his work cut out for him that season. The country's at-war need for young men in their prime had decimated DePaul's squad. Only three of us remained from the team's nucleus: me; Dick Triptow, who became the team captain and was 4-F because he had a double hernia; and Ray, who had a bad knee. Ray needed some bodies fast or he would have had to cancel our schedule, so he went to the local Catholic high schools to find them.

St. Philip's sent us Ernie DeBenedetto, whose eyesight kept him out of the service, and Ed "Whitey" Kachan, who had a perforated eardrum. Gene Stump, who came to us from St. Rita's, was too young for the draft — he was a real character who later became my friend and roommate. Jack Allen and Jack Dean, two more teenagers, also joined the team. We were a ragtag group of very young players, but we were eager to build on the past season's success.

DePaul also picked up another good ballplayer that season: Ed Mikan. Ed had a good high school career at Joliet Catholic, and he was still too young for the draft. So he came to DePaul as a freshman, to play backup center. I was reunited with my brother on the practice court, which was good for both of us. We always pushed each other to play better.

Ray put Ed through the same rigorous training he put us all through, sometimes pitting Ed and me against each other. At one practice, Ray accused me of nearly knocking Ed senseless with an elbow; another day I actually loosened a few of Ed's teeth, but we were both used to playing the game hard.

Another time, Ray had Ed and me box each other at a practice. Boxing was used to improve our hand quickness and footwork, and to toughen us up for play underneath the basket. So there Ed and I were in the Old Barn, decked out in our practice uniforms and boxing gloves. I was having a hard time of it because I didn't want to hurt my little brother, so we kept dancing around one another.

"C'mon," Ray said, encouraging us to spar, "hit him!"

I still held back. Then Ed hit me in the nose, so I whacked him a good one back. I felt bad about it, though.

ᘓ

ED MIKAN: I never faced anyone tougher than George. He was a hard-nosed ballplayer, not a dirty ballplayer. But he was out there for one purpose: to win.

I used to tell Blondie, "You know, you've got a very mean grandson. He beats me up all the time — every time I play him." Blondie just said, "Georgie, don't you hit your little brother."

ᘓ

Ed was drafted during his first year at DePaul, so he didn't get to play the whole season. He went into the Army, in a communications unit, where he hurt his knee climbing down a telephone pole. The injury wouldn't stop his later basketball career, but it was enough to earn him an honorable discharge after only three months in the service. He rejoined DePaul's squad the following fall.

Ed was a good center — he came close to breaking a lot of my records at DePaul. He was also good at rebounding and blocking opponents' shots, like I was. After I graduated, he went on to be co-captain of the team, and he helped Ray win quite a few ballgames in those years.

ᘓ

RAY MEYER: Ed was a good ballplayer, probably the second-best center I ever had at DePaul, but unfortunately, he was always compared to George. I can always remember after George graduated, we came to New York for the NIT tournament and Ed played. Joe Lapchick and Nat Holman came over and said, "Where the hell was he all year, we never heard of him?" He was the best center they'd seen all year.

Ed was always being compared to George. It's like a good coach, whoever replaces him is in trouble. Like John Wooden. Every one of those guys who coached UCLA after Wooden, was fired almost immediately or within a year or two. They couldn't last. Everyone was compared to Wooden. If they lost a game, Wooden never would have lost it.

And it was the same way with Adolph Rupp at Kentucky. The next coach, Joe B. Hall, won the NCAA. But after the tournament, I was walking through the hotel lobby, and someone said, "Hey, coach, when are you going to come over to Kentucky?" Apparently Hall didn't win by enough, by comparison.

And that's what happened to Ed Mikan. If we could put Ed in today, he'd be the regular center at DePaul. And he'd do very well.

 C&

This was Ray's second year coaching us. Ray wasn't even sure he wanted to stay in basketball before he came to DePaul. He'd had some experience as head coach for Notre Dame in 1941, when George Keogan had a heart attack and Ray had to take over temporarily. So Ray saw what coaching could do to a person. When he got to DePaul, he must have seen some potential in us. Ray once said, "Then I saw George Mikan play and I've been associated with basketball ever since."

Ray appreciated the benefits of a big man on the basketball court. He saw the big man as the focal point of a strong offense and the anchor of a tough defense. "It's just like the quarterback on a football team or the pitcher on a baseball team," he'd say. "You secure a good center, and you can build a team around him." What he saw in me was a raw ability that he could build up and build around. And the center that we built was different from the way the position had typically been played.

C&

RAY MEYER: Back then, centers were basically like robots. Then, they had the jump ball at the center position, and the center mainly just did the jump ball and then stood under the basket. They weren't agile. The big centers were thought to be like posts out there. That's why they called them posts. Centers didn't move.

I'd say George was the forerunner of all big men being a rounded ballplayer. When big guys came in back then, they were either a defensive ballplayer or they stood around the basket. Don Otten mostly played the post, not much offense. Bob Kurland was a defensive ballplayer. He could score, but not like Mikan. Kurland couldn't run the floor like George. Mikan was a complete basketball player. He could do almost anything.

C&

Nothing that Ray taught me caused a bigger stir than the use of my height as a goaltender. Thanks to all those drills with Ray, I could jump up and swat the ball away from the basket or grab it out of its downward arc and pass it up court. Ray taught Ed this skill, as well, and as the 1943-44 season progressed and we kept winning, the complaints about our then-legal maneuver began to snowball. Pretty soon, there were more coaches who wanted goaltending banned permanently than those who wanted to keep it. You see, there weren't a lot of teams with players big enough to do it like we did at DePaul, and the complaint of Dartmouth's Ozzie Cowles that it was unfair seemed to be the prevailing sentiment.

That issue of goaltending became such a big deal that there is still discussion about who did more to help get it finally banned: me or Bob Kurland.

Kurland was a 7-foot center for Oklahoma A&M and a very good defensive player. Over the years that I was at DePaul, the Blue Demons had a number of battles with the Oklahoma A&M Aggies, and Kurland and I were always at the center of it. In fact, we developed quite a rivalry. The Aggies were a very good defensive team, they always played tough, and goaltending was a big part of their defense.

ᘓ

BOB KURLAND: Well, there were other guys who could do it [goaltending], but it depends on who you talk to. In terms of the actual team that caused the [ban on goaltending], I think it was ours. We instituted a defense that incorporated goaltending, and goaltending was a bad thing for the game. Other people could knock the ball down, but they couldn't do it consistently. If you could convince the opposing team that you could knock their shots down by knocking down two or three of them in the fore part of the game, when you got to the middle of the game, you'd broken a practice habit. And when you did that, you had your opponents beat psychologically.

There were a lot of guys who could do that, but no one put the defense into play like we did, where the other team knew what we were going to do on every damn shot they put up. We never did [goaltend every shot]. But they thought we would, and we broke them. That was a bad thing for the game of basketball.

ᘓ

It's true that a *Saturday Evening Post* piece on goaltending from about this time featured the Aggies, in particular a picture of an NCAA official sitting in a chair above the basket to watch for Kurland's hand in the cylinder. But no one received more publicity about goaltending than DePaul and the Mikans. Every time we played a team without a goaltender of their own, there were complaints about my ability to pick the ball out of the basket before it went through. When we went to New York early in the season, there was a caricature of me in the *World-Telegram* that showed me with an oversized hand swatting a ball out of the hoop.

And then there was the incident with Adolph Rupp. The previous season, the 'Baron of Basketball,' as he was called, had brought his powerful Kentucky team up to Chicago Stadium and gotten soundly beaten by us. This was a team that had walked all over Notre Dame the week before.

Rupp was not happy about the way we played. Kentucky had a guard named Milton Ticco, who could shoot well from the outside. Ray told me to watch out for him, so I did. Ticco took 21 shots, and I blocked 19 of them. The guy just plain refused to shoot anymore. Of course, DePaul kicked Kentucky's fanny.

ɔ₃

RAY MEYER: Ed Krause was coaching Notre Dame, and they had recently played Kentucky. Ed called me and said Kentucky had two guards — Ticco and Marvin Akers — who would score two points every time they got set. Every time. So I put George under the basket, and I wanted him to bat the ball away. The game started, and he didn't bat it, he caught it. He threw that ball down the floor, and we were quickly winning by 22-2. It was no contest.

ɔ₃

After the game, Rupp said to Ray, "We won't play your team again until Mikan's out of college." And he didn't — even after the experimental goaltending rule was made permanent. Rupp had a lot of influence in the basketball world. Not only did he take us off his schedule, he and some of our other opponents probably helped convince the NCAA to make the goaltending rule leaguewide.

When you look at all the rules put in college basketball, for years they were aimed at us big men. Everything. The three-second rule was put in to hurt the big guy, so we couldn't stand in the lane. Then the rulemakers took out the center jump after each basket, to keep the big man from monopolizing possession of the ball. And then they put in the rule where you couldn't interfere with the ball on its downward arc, to stop tall players from goaltending.

Later on, when big guys like Wilt Chamberlain came along and started disturbing the ball on offense, a rule was made that you couldn't interfere with a ball in the cylinder (basically the area above the rim). They stopped the practice of throwing the ball over the backboard when coming in from out-of-bounds — big men were the ones scoring on those plays. And all of these rules against the big man, all they did was make us better players. When big players weren't valuable just because of their size, they had to have other skills. They had to adjust.

With the help of Ray's drills, I adjusted. And in adjusting, we made the big man into a player instead of a statue.

While my defensive play under the basket was causing such a ruckus, my extra work with Ray on my other skills was rounding me into a more complete ballplayer. I was probably a better all-around ballplayer than some folks suspected at the time. More than anything, Ray was teaching me to think about my opponents and about the game itself. Everything he taught me was beginning to make sense on the court. I believe I was becoming a better ballplayer as Ray continued to work with me. If anyone thought that just banning goaltending would stop DePaul, well, they weren't paying attention.

ᑲ

RAY MEYER: When George first started playing ball at DePaul, he was a raw talent, but he was clumsy, awkward. He needed some work, and he and I set out to do it. The hours working with George were very enjoyable because it was like watching a flower blooming. I could see him getting better everyday. I could see the agility.

We had a little guy of about 5 feet, 4 inches named Billy Donato — very quick. And I made George guard him at the top of the free-throw line. It was like an elephant chasing a fly for a long time, but you could see the improvement every day. Gradually, George was catching up with him. First, George would be blocking one shot from behind, and then Donato couldn't go by him that easily. Then, Donato had to work like hell to get by him. Sure, [speed was] a tremendous advantage, but those drills helped George to be quicker.

Probably George's greatest asset is that he was a very intelligent ballplayer, he had the ability to make adjustments. You don't get that every day, where all you had to do was tell [a player something]. Some games, for instance, I'd say, "They're overplaying your right side, your right hand." I never had to tell him twice. He'd go immediately to his left hand and walk right by them. He could do things by being told.

One time, we were playing that big center, Zowalik from St. John's. Zowalik would dribble out to the free-throw line and lure his defender to follow him, but he wouldn't shoot from there. Instead, he

The Teacher and the Pupil. DePaul coach Ray Meyer and George Mikan. Says Meyer: "My whole future was in how well George developed." Says Mikan: "Ray made me the player I became." *(Courtesy of AP/Wide World Photos)*

would whirl around and go to the basket. I told George to step back three feet and wait. He said no problem, he'd do it. And he did.

There was a carryover value in everything we told him. That's very rare in athletes today. Most athletes do what comes naturally, and they practice the things they do best. In George's case, he worked on the things that made him a better ballplayer. And it wasn't what I did for him, it was what he did for himself.

○

As 1943-44 wore on, we were becoming harder to stop. We won our first thirteen games, until Valparaiso tripped us up. We evened the score with them later in the season, beating them by more than 30 points. But we received some rough treatment that game, and shortly after that I noticed some pain in my ankle that would bother me the rest of the season. The doctors had it X-rayed, but they couldn't tell what it was — they thought it might be bone chips.

It was my second basketball injury, and it hurt like heck, but I didn't have time to worry about it. At the end of that week, we were playing Big Ten champ Ohio State with its tough center Arnie Risen. It was a big game. We were 17-3, and a victory over the Buckeyes might mean another trip to the NCAA Tournament. Ohio State was also thinking about the NCAA bid because it had just won the Big Ten. But if we didn't win, we wouldn't be going anywhere.

That game was my first against Arnie Risen. Risen was highly touted for his size (6 feet, 8½ inches) and ability, and he was pretty well-known because he played in the Big Ten. My bad ankle slowed me, and DePaul struggled the whole ballgame.

○

GENE STUMP: We're down seven or eight points with about two minutes to play, and Ray calls a timeout. He's all excited and he's saying, "Let's run this, and let's run that." And George says to Ray in the huddle, "Hold the phone!"

Well, Ray starts saying the "Hail Mary" — every time Ray got a little rattled, he would start praying.

"Look here," says George, "prayers aren't going to get us to New York. Get me the goddamn ball!"

Ray just looked up at him, and George turned and went back to the court.

We threw George the ball, and he went out there and fouled out

Arnie Risen. Inside of two minutes, George scored six or eight points all by himself — physically, one-on-one beating these guys.

ᘓ

The game went into overtime, and we ended up beating Ohio State 61-49. I scored a total of 37 points that game, 12 points in overtime alone. Risen fouled out in overtime. Ray later told me that as Risen walked past the DePaul bench, he was muttering to himself, "Nobody ever did that to me."

James S. Kearns of the *Chicago Sun* wrote about it this way:

"Even the last of the doubters must believe now that DePaul's Blue Demons have definitely arrived in basketball's biggest time ...

"Mikan, I thought, was superb. Never doubt that large boy had a bad ankle. He did, and it bespoke a helluva competitive spirit when he played all the way until the decision had been reached in overtime. A lot of good athletes would have wilted before that. Far from wilting, under pressure, under the discouragement of a bad slump in his marksmanship early in the second half, or under the pain of his injury, Mikan came through in the biggest clutch and broke up the ballgame with three baskets on three shots at the start of the overtime.

"That is championship class!"

With that win, DePaul had earned another trip to the NCAA Tournament. We were ecstatic, but the Buckeye players were feeling mighty blue, and for a good reason. At that time, Big Ten teams could only go to the NCAA, they couldn't go to the NIT. So those Ohio kids thought they'd just blown any chance for postseason play.

After the game, Ray was walking by the Ohio State locker room, and he could see that Harold "Ole" Oleson, their coach, and the kids were really down because they weren't going to a tournament.

"What's the matter?" Ray asked.

"Well, we can't go to any tournament," replied a player.

"Sure you can," Ray told them. "We'll take the NIT, and you can go to the NCAA." And that's what we did. They went to the NCAA Tournament.

It wasn't a difficult choice. The NIT was bigger back then because it was always held in New York. Everyone wanted to travel to New York and play in Madison Square Garden. I personally loved to play there — over the years, some of my better games took place in the Garden.

Back then, if you went to the NCAA, you were lucky to make

expenses. So when your team had a choice, you were going to make money and a better reputation in New York than in the NCAA tournament. It wasn't long after that, in the 1950s, I believe, that the NCAA grew in strength and made a rule that you had to accept an invitation to its tournament first.

C8

BOB KURLAND: *The NIT was the premier tournament [back then] because they had the arena to play it in [Madison Square Garden], in New York. The NCAA Tournament was played in different quadrants of the country. But you had a concentration of fans in New York City before the basketball scandals [of 1951] — you had 18-19,000 people in Madison Square Garden back in the forties. It wasn't any rinky-dink deal.*

But soon that changed. With the changes in travel, the promotion, the development of television and the tournament structure that was adopted by the NCAA, suddenly the NIT was overrun by the NCAA, and the NIT became the secondary tournament.

The thing that really blew it out of the tub was when Long Island and CCNY players were caught fixing games [in 1951].That's when New York City turned off to college basketball, and the NIT lost its base for existence because the fans wouldn't come anymore. The NCAA became the tournament of prestige and honor, so to speak. The other guys were just a bunch of damn crooks. And they've had all this time go by, trying to restore their respectability.

C8

The NIT was king back then, and here we were, headed to New York. We were pretty excited to be playing for the national title. And although we had kind of pieced our team together at the beginning of the season, we were feeling confident. We'd played in Madison Square Garden once earlier in the season, so we were starting to feel comfortable there.

We started the tournament by beating Muhlenberg, 68-45, in the first round, even though the Mules had flown in extra players to face us. I scored 27 points, playing against Bill Bunson. But that was only a warm-up for the war in the next game.

In the second round, we met the Oklahoma A&M Aggies, and I came face to face in my first battle with Bob Kurland, the 7-foot center from St. Louis. Kurland was an excellent basketball player, both for the Aggies and later for the Phillips Oilers in the Amateur Athletic Union, where he played after he graduated. We were two big men, goaltenders, the leaders of two tough teams, with nation-wide reputations on both ends of the courts. The newspapers hyped it as a "great duel between skyscraping centers," so the interest in this game was strong.

After the first ten minutes, we were in deep trouble, trailing 15-2. The Aggies had focused their whole defense on me, and at first that seemed pretty effective.

൦

RAY MEYER: Aggies coach Hank Iba was very sharp. His whole defense was to stop George Mikan. He figured if they stopped Mikan, they'd win. And Kurland was not interested in scoring. The whole team was interested in packing way back in, keeping the ball from George, and then running at him. So with doing that, they kind of held him down. But George was satisfied. When he got the ball, they double-teamed him right away, but he just threw it out. That's why the other players scored.

One of George's greatest assets was that he could pass the ball. He could see over his man, and he wasn't selfish. He didn't look to break records. There were many times when he could have broken records — he could have gone a lot higher than he did. But in checking the scores, it's amazing to see that when we won the close games, George got a lot of points. When we won big, he got very little.

൦

When the Aggies' defense sank in on me, I kicked the ball out to Gene Stump and Jack Dean, who did the bulk of the scoring that night. Personally, I didn't have a great game. My ankle had slowed me down, and Kurland clung to me so close that I couldn't do too much.

൦

BOB KURLAND: You couldn't let Mikan catch the ball. That was the hard part. Iba's forte was a sinking off-side defense. We fronted George with that, and he was still very effective in terms of the percentage of points that he got. We disrupted their offense to the point that we'd give George his fair share and try to limit it.

But the hard part about playing him in those days was you couldn't touch him. You had to be in position to prevent the ball from coming to him or have an off-side sinking defense, which gave you a hell of a lot of help. If he ever caught the ball, then you had to play the percentages, because he had a good hook shot.

൦

The battle of the titans never really materialized. Kurland was too busy defending me, and I was too busy trying to get the ball out from under him. I scored only nine points to Kurland's 14. Iba had been concerned with taking me out of the game, and he ended up being successful. Four minutes into the second half I fouled out and had to watch the rest of the game from the bench. Kurland fouled out soon after, and in a quirk of the rules, Oklahoma A&M had to finish the game only four men strong. DePaul won by a score of 41-38.

That victory put us in the title game against Joe Lapchick's St. John's club. Lapchick's boys were fast, and they had our number that night. They were so quick that I wasn't able to knock any shots out of the hoop, despite our team's height advantage. I scored 13 points, but fouled out in the second half. They beat us 47-39.

So St. John's took the 1944 NIT trophy home, and DePaul came in second. Still, we had reached the promised land. We'd come up short, but we were headed in the right direction. We were definitely looking forward to 1944-45: we hoped it had a lot of good things in store.

One thing that it wouldn't have is goaltending. Over the summer of '44, the NCAA made the ban on goaltending permanent. Ray had predicted that it would happen, so I wasn't too surprised. I wasn't too concerned about it either, even though some wags were predicting, "That's the end of Mikan." Both Ray and I knew that I had other abilities. We liked our chances either way.

CƷ5ꝏ
That Championship Season
1944-1945

Dick Triptow had been DePaul's team captain in 1943-44, but now, as we headed back to school in the fall of 1944, coach Ray Meyer made the decision to make Dick and me co-captains. Dick was a senior, and I was in my fourth year of college, but according to the rules back then I was only a junior in eligibility. Since I had one more year to go in my law degree, I would be a Blue Demon for another season.

CƷ

GENE STUMP: We never would have meshed as a team in 1943-44 without Dick Triptow — he was a great leader, and he worked well in conjunction with George. But in 1944-45, George just took over. He was awesome.

CƷ

As the 1944-45 season got underway, everyone was expecting DePaul — and especially me — to fall flat on our faces because of the recently enacted ban on goaltending. We were determined to show them how wrong they were. And we did. We had a great year. We jumped out of the gate to win our first six games. Then we lost to Illinois by three points before reeling off eleven more victories. All in all, during the regular season we played twenty games, but lost only two.

The *Chicago Daily News* summed up the feelings of all those folks who'd predicted my demise when they wrote: "The Rules Committee outsmarted itself. They figured out that Mikan wouldn't be worth a hoot if he couldn't use his 6-9 inches to bat 'em out of the hoop. Now, all they [really] did was make it possible for Big George to spend more time on his offense."

One of our victories that year included a close battle with our old friends Hank Iba, Bob Kurland and the Oklahoma A&M Aggies.

ℭ

BOB KURLAND: George was difficult, and when I say difficult I mean he was a guy who caused you to think about playing him.

What was different about playing guys like Mikan in those days is that the only time you saw your opponent is if you saw him in a tournament the night before. You didn't have the movies and television and the library of information that you have available now. It was a surprise to go play somebody [like George], even if you'd already played him, because in all probability, he had improved his skills and strengths. It would take eight or ten minutes before you realized how he had changed.

And George was constantly improving.

ℭ

We beat the Aggies by two points, 48-46, at Chicago Stadium. That game would come back to haunt us in postseason play.

In 1944-45, a lot of teams spent their time trying to find new ways to defend me in the middle. Some double-teamed me and tried to take me out of the game, while others decided to let me get my points and tried to win by shutting down the rest of our team. I don't remember too many games where there was only one guy defending me. Predominantly, our opponents double-teamed me. From that experience, I learned that if there was an extra guy guarding me, that meant one of my teammates was open. So I knew to get the ball to that open man.

Our offense developed around the pivot man, the position I played: the guards and forwards would feed the pivot and cut off of him. For instance, if a forward made a pass, he would be the first cutter by and he'd set a pick for the guard coming around. If the guard was the first cutter, he'd have the option to pick for his teammate, the guard or the forward. We had a cardinal rule that the passer must move to take his defensive man away from being in front of the pivot.

I think that some teams today should consider employing such a strategy. A lot of teams just stand around and pass the ball. The players don't move from their positions. That allows the defending players to drop back and foul up the pivot play, which makes it easier for them to two-time the big man. In our offense, it was important to have the guards and forwards move so that they'd take the defensive players with them, leaving an open lane in front of the pivot man. Once he had the ball, the pivot man could then pass or turn and shoot. I liked to do both.

The 1944-45 season was at the height of World War II, and our DePaul team got some strange looks whenever we traveled — a bunch of healthy young men running around without military uniforms on. Folks must have thought we were draft dodgers. I probably got the strangest looks of all because of my height. At 6 feet, 9 inches, I stood out wherever we went. "How's the weather up there?" — I must have heard that a million times. The skills Ray had taught me on the basketball court had given me new confidence about my size, but I still hated it when people pointed and stared. And I really didn't like being mistaken for Bob Kurland. No one knew that more than my friend and teammate Gene Stump, who loved trying to drive me crazy.

ଓ

GENE STUMP: George hated it when someone would walk up to him and ask, "How's the weather up there?"

I would send kids his way. I would bait them. I would tell a kid, "He's Bob Kurland. Go over and ask him for his autograph." One time, a kid asked him about the weather. George spit down on the ground nearby him and said, "It's raining," with a scowl that shut the kid up.

ଓ

Back then, there weren't too many folks my size, and a guy like me was expected to be ashamed of his height. I remember that before one game, the newspapers in Philadelphia called me a freak. Of course, after we played —and won — the papers the next day read, "My apologies to George Mikan."

ଓ

RAY MEYER: In 1944-45, I remember George starting to feel more comfortable with his height, and I saw a change in the way he carried himself. He would have been a good basketball player for a six-footer, but the height made him a great one. He had innate ability. I remember one time watching the All-Star game. George's team was down by one point, and I said to my wife, "The ball's going in to Mikan. He'll either make it or get fouled."

Well, George got fouled and had two free throws. "You can bet the house on this," I said. "He'll make both of them."

The thing that made George great is that he always wanted the ball in the clutch situations, and 99 out of 100 times he came through.

There have always been great basketball players who, in the clutch, didn't want the ball. I've seen George miss free throws all during a game, but if the game is on the line, I'd bet on him. That's the difference – he's a winner.

CR

DePaul finished the 1944-45 season with an 18-2 mark, and we were invited to our second consecutive NIT in Madison Square Garden in New York. By this time, co-captain Dick Triptow had left the team to sign a minor-league baseball contract with the Chicago Cubs, so I became sole captain of the team.

In the first round of the 1945 NIT, DePaul beat West Virginia 75-62, and I scored a tournament-record 33 points. That win set us up for a battle in the second round with Rhode Island State. That game took place on March 21, 1945. Rhode Island came into town with a good record and a good team. They played a different style from our slower, methodical, ball-control style of feeding the pivotman. Rhode Island was a fast-running club and had been known to score upwards of 100 points in a game, a rarity in those days. They felt pretty confident coming into the game.

CR

RAY MEYER: Before the game, Rhode Island coach Frank Keaney was standing in the wings, right off midcourt. I was a young guy, so he didn't know me from Adam, and he was telling some alumni friends, "We're going to take that big freak George Mikan and kill him. Mikan is a bum. We're going to show him how we score. We're going to run him right back to Chicago."

I knew how well George played when he was fired up, so I exaggerated everything Keaney said when I told him about it.

CR

Rhode Island added to the insult by having Ernie Calverley, a 6-foot, 2-inch All-American forward, take the jump against me. By not putting their center in against me, they made it look like a tilt.

The whole first half, Rhode Island was running like mad, but without the ball. And we were scoring — I got 27 points by the time the first half was over. We were even hotter in the second half. After the first couple minutes, I'd put in about 33 points.

CR

RAY MEYER: I was going to make a substitution when I got a note from the newspaper men saying, "Leave him in. The scoring record for the tournament is 33 points."

So I left George in, and he passed up 33 in a hurry, reaching 41 points. Again, I went to make a substitution, and they sent me another note: "45 points set by Harry Boykoff of St. John's. That's the Madison Square Garden record."

So I left George in again. When he passed 45 points, I called up his brother Ed and the second team. They all came up to me and said, "Coach, if it's all the same to you, we'll sit down. The only reason we're here is because of him. Let him set a record that will never be broken."

○8

In the last minute of the game, Rhode Island was coming down the floor with Keaney yelling, "Hold the ball! Hold the ball! Don't let them get 100." That was Madison Square Garden's team record at the time. We were ahead by more than 40 points, so Ray told us to stay back.

I didn't know it at the time, but if I would have taken one more shot, I would have beaten Rhode Island single-handed. I scored 53 points that game, and so did Rhode Island. Those 53 points set a Madison Square Garden record. It also set a DePaul record for single-game scoring that has never been broken, even now, fifty-some years later. And what people need to understand is that that record was set at a time when the game clock kept running even though the ball was out of bounds. The game was shorter, and there were fewer opportunities to score.

We trounced Rhode Island 97-53. As a team, DePaul set ten scoring records that night.

Next, we moved on to the championship game against Bowling Green and its own vaunted big man, 7-footer Don Otten. Otten was big and, therefore, so was the billing for the game, with one giant facing another.

○8

RAY MEYER: I went to the press conference before the championship game, where the press was telling me that Don Otten was too big and too strong for Mikan. I knew Mikan better than that, so I said, "Yeah, I guess he's too big." I helped build that Otten up to the skies. I made him [sound like] a great player.

In the game, we were down by about 14-8, and I called a timeout and jumped all over the players. George went right out and faked Otten so bad that if he had a cloth he could have dusted him off the lights. Otten went right up, and Mikan went around him and stuffed it in the basket. The game was over after that. Otten was a whipped dog.

The funny thing about the championship game of that particular NIT is that the newspapers didn't tell you that we won the tournament. All they did was tell how bad Otten was. So much in fact that after the game the headlines read "Otten is Rotten." It was unfortunate that the kid was built up that way.

୧୬

The final score was 71-54, and I was able to knock down 34 points to Otten's seven. Our team set fifteen records after everything was said and done, and I was awarded the tournament Most Valuable Player award. Winning the 1945 NIT was a very successful end to a great season for a ragtag bunch of kids from Chicago.

Our weekend in New York wasn't over, however. Someone had proposed holding a mythical national championship between NIT champion DePaul and Oklahoma A&M, who had captured the NCAA title. Proceeds from the game would benefit the Red Cross, a very worthy cause in this, the last spring of World War II. Well, the NIT had ended on a Saturday night. The Red Cross benefit game wasn't scheduled until the following Thursday. We wanted to return home to rest, but we didn't have the money to travel to Chicago and then turn around and go back again to New York. So we kicked around the city, virtually broke, until the game six days later.

We were staying at a hotel out near the airport, and we received a call there from a nearby army base, asking to play our team in a scrimmage game. Since we were waiting for the Aggies anyway, we said what the heck, why not? What's an unscheduled scrimmage going to hurt? Besides, it was patriotic, entertaining the troops and all.

What we didn't know was that that game would turn into an all-out war at the center position. Practically everyone from the army base was there, with generals and officers sitting in the front row. The army team was pretty good, but a lot older than we were. Their center, a guy named Fitzgerald from Seton Hall, was all over me. He was playing rough, and he wouldn't leave me alone.

୧୬

RAY MEYER: We tried to calm George down because we knew what was coming. George warned Fitzgerald, but he didn't stop. All of a sudden, Mikan let go with an elbow, and about six of the guy's teeth came right through his lip. He left George alone after that.

George was starting to build a reputation with his elbows. A year later, we were playing Western Kentucky. Before the game, a guy named Don Padgett was shooting off his mouth in the papers. "I been in the Marine Corps," he said. "I learned how to kill. That Mikan isn't going to push me around."

During the game, Padgett was going after him, and George was getting madder and madder. So I told George, "You can't hit him until we get 18 points ahead." So as soon as we got an 18-point lead, pow!

I went in their locker room after the game, and Padgett was laying on a table. I asked him how he felt. He said, "I've been kicked by a mule, but I've never gotten hit like that. What the hell did you do to him in college, sharpen his elbows?"

☙

In spite of scrimmaging with the army's finest, we were tired of sitting around New York by the time Oklahoma A&M and Bob Kurland finally showed up. We wanted the Aggies, but the six-day layover did not sit well with us. This game, featuring the two most dominant big men in college basketball, made for a great matchup in the eyes of the press — the whole country was watching us.

The newspapers blew that game up till it sounded like the game of the century. The New York media liked me and they liked DePaul, but they also liked the Aggies because they were colorful. A lot of people came to that game, which was played at Madison Square Garden. People liked to see the big guys play, and that was when college basketball was at its zenith.

☙

BOB KURLAND: We had the same game plan we always had. We didn't play Mikan any different than anybody else as far as the post was concerned. George and I were both pretty excited about the game. He had scored [a record 120] points winning the NIT and played a marvelous tournament. We had won the NCAA and were kind of underrated in terms of how good we really were.

☙

Aggies coach Hank Iba had apparently sent Kurland in with specific instructions to needle me, both physically and orally. Bob was a skillful basketball player, and he gauged every move to taunt me. He wasn't too bad with his tongue, either. He'd stick his elbow into my ribs on a pivot and then coo, "Oh, sorry, George." Or he'd say "No offense" as he knocked me slightly off balance when I was shooting. At the same time, the boys from his bench were calling out, "Hey, Mikan, you're up against a real basketball player now."

Iba's strategy worked. I lost my cool. We had gotten off to a quick 10-point lead, but I started jabbing back at Kurland and quickly picked up three fouls. In those days, four fouls disqualified you. I was screaming at the referee, "Look what he's doing to me!" but the referee just walked away.

ᘉ

RAY MEYER: We couldn't play without Mikan, so I called a timeout and told George not to commit any more fouls. "Just hold your arms up on defense," I said. "There's no way they can beat us if you just stay in the game."

ᘉ

Less than fourteen minutes into the game, Kurland turned and ran right into me on his way to the basket. In response, the referees called a fourth foul on me. And that was the end of the Red Cross game. I got benched, but I wasn't alone. John Allen, Gene Stump and Whitey Kachan were also called out on fouls. The team couldn't cope without its starting lineup. The only regular who wasn't disqualified was Ernie DeBenedetto.

ᘉ

BOB KURLAND: George fouled out in the first half because the referees wanted a situation where there was no rough play, so they called the fouls close. And George, being a little more aggressive offensively – and defensively, for that matter – got stung with a few fouls that he wasn't used to. It was kind of anticlimactic after George fouled out. The fans lost interest in the game because the two big guys weren't in there scrapping anymore. But it was a good game.

ᘉ

We lost the Red Cross benefit game 52-44, even though we'd beaten Oklahoma A&M 48-46 in Chicago Stadium a few weeks earlier. The only good thing about that game was that the crowd of 18,158 contributed more than $50,000 to the Red Cross. I didn't know it at the time, but there was a suspicion of foul play in that game.

ᘉ

RAY MEYER: Dave Blumenthal, a friend of mine who lived in New York, walked into my hotel room and asked, "Coach, how well do you know your players?"
    "Very well," I said.

"Well, I think one of them sold you out," he said. "Money is coming from all over the country on Oklahoma A&M."

This was before the point-shaving scandals that would darken the name of college basketball [in 1951], but a heavy flow of gambling money on one team just before a game was always a cause for concern.

When the game was done, twenty-five fouls had been called on DePaul to sixteen against the Aggies. I was so damn mad about the officiating that I wanted to go right to the press. I was going to blow the lid off college basketball.

Another friend, Ole Oleson, the coach at Ohio State, didn't want me to hurt basketball with unfounded allegations, so he wouldn't let me out of his hotel room. Later, I heard that a lieutenant from the New York Police Department had been looking for me all night, wanting a statement about my suspicions.

You know, I never had any evidence that anyone treated us unfairly. I cooled down and went back to Chicago.

଎

If I could play that Red Cross benefit game over, I wouldn't have lost my head. Kurland got to me with his strategy of verbal and physical abuse. It was designed to get me out of the game, and it worked. The following season, we would play them again in Stillwater, Oklahoma, and beat them, 46-42. This time, I didn't let their tactics get to me. I had learned my lesson in New York, to keep things cool upstairs, not to let my emotions get out of hand. But I never changed my aggressive style of basketball that was fueled by that emotion.

CB 6 BO
The Top College Player
1945-1946

L ife after World War II played out like a raft ride down a wild river: ups and downs, surprises and changes around every turn. The country was welcoming home its soldiers, and basketball would be impacted immediately, as all the players who had gone overseas were returning to play — or, at the very least, watch the game. The returning soldiers didn't have any effect at DePaul: we played the 1945-46 season with basically the same team as the year before. But in professional basketball, which I was about to be introduced to, the new crop of players who would come in after the war would have a profound impact. The pro game would never be the same.

CB

GENE STUMP: In 1945, we started getting back players from the war, coming out of the service. None of them really ever made it because the war just did something to them. They tried out, but some of them were so out of shape they never made it. So we went with what we had.

CB

For us DePaul Blue Demons, the 1945-46 season would be another success. I was team captain that year. We started out with a string of eight really strong wins, trouncing most teams by more than 20 points. In fact, in a game against Arkansas State we won by more than 50 points, with a final score of 82-26. Then, it was like we bottomed out — we lost the next three, and the newspapers started panning us. Well, Ray had an answer to them. "George Mikan isn't in shape," he explained. "He just can't hang in there in the last half. We need rest."

Ray was right. I had loafed during the summer and was tiring easily in the second half, when I was more prone to fouls. So we

61

tried one of Ray's favorite tricks: we relaxed for a whole week. No practice, no nothing. We started winning again.

Toward the end of the season, we played in a round-robin tournament at Chicago Stadium that included Bowling Green, Oklahoma A&M and Hamline University of St. Paul. The Aggies avenged their loss to us earlier in the season with a 46-38 win. We beat Hamline 62-51 to take a disappointing third place.

That game against Hamline was one of the brightest spots of that season because it was then that I met for the first time Vern Mikkelsen, my future friend and teammate with the Minneapolis Lakers.

○♂

VERN MIKKELSEN: My first meeting with George was as an opponent in the fall of 1945. I was a freshman and had just turned seventeen. Hamline played a national schedule in those years, and we were playing in a four-team tournament in Chicago Stadium. That tournament was awesome — absolutely awesome. Playing there were the three top college centers of 1945: George at DePaul, Bob Kurland at Oklahoma A&M, and Don Otten at Bowling Green. They were all 6 feet, 10 inches on up to 7 feet. It just so happened that Hamline played in that tournament with those three teams.

So I had an opportunity to play against the best. George was all-time everything at the time, and he was kind of my hero, my idol, the guy I wanted to emulate. Here I was a freshman center for Hamline, just barely out of high school, with the marvelous opportunity to play against the best.

I remember scoring a basket off of George, and then I apologized. He patted me on the shoulder and said, "Hey, kid, stay with it. Don't worry about it." He was a fierce competitor, but he was also a very gracious man.

○♂

I managed to score 25 points against Mik that night, but I don't remember doing that well against him ever again.

We finished the 1945-46 season with a 19-5 regular-season record and an average margin of victory of 23 points. In fact, only two of our wins that year came by less than 10 points. I was the nation's leading college scorer, with a 23.1-point average. We were undoubtedly one of the strongest college teams going that year, but for some reason we were not invited to either postseason tournament.

CB

RAY MEYER: Maybe I didn't shut my mouth soon enough [about my suspicion of cheating in the Red Cross benefit game]. In 1945-46, we had the same team, with a 19-5 record, but we didn't get invited to either tournament. Maybe my grumbling got back to the people who handled tournament selections. Or maybe we weren't invited so other coaches could take their pick between the NIT and NCAA without worrying about us. I never did get a good explanation.

CB

The last game I played at Chicago Stadium as a DePaul student was a 63-47 victory over Notre Dame. I put in 33 points that game. It felt great to put Notre Dame away so decisively.

I played my very last game for DePaul on March 9, 1946, a 65-40 win over Beloit. I never felt quite comfortable with the way my college career ended — it was kind of a slap in the face not to get invited to any postseason play.

But when I look back on my college career as a whole, I'm proud of our accomplishments. Ray Meyer had coached our DePaul team to an 81-17 record over four years, which included one NCAA Tournament appearance and two in the NIT: one runner-up and one championship. Personally, I scored 1,869 points (19.1 points per game) in 98 college games. For two seasons, I was the nation's leading college scorer, in 1945 with a 23.3 average and in 1946 with a 23.1 average. I was voted college player of the year in 1944 and 1945 and earned All-America honors for three seasons (1944, 1945, 1946).

Not too bad for an oversized, awkward kid with glasses. I felt pretty good about my achievements during my years at DePaul.

My awards were always a source of great pride for my family, and my grandfather loved showing them off at Mikan's Tavern. Unfortunately, a fire at my parents' home in 1949 destroyed all of their scrapbooks of clippings and photos from my DePaul basketball career — and Ed's, too. Some of our trophies were also lost in the fire. My memories are pretty much all I have left of that era in my career.

My parents were in Minneapolis at the time of the fire, to watch me play in a playoff game with the Lakers. My family remained close over the years and came to watch me play whenever they could, especially when we played in Chicago. Fortunately, my parents and my grandfather all lived long enough to see my entire pro career.

In my early years at DePaul, my height had sometimes made me feel awkward socially. No one likes to be called "monster," "goon" or "Frankenstein." I tended to steer clear of college dances and other social contacts, especially dates. I remember one blind date midway through my second year at college. I called at the girl's house and sat down in a light wicker chair in her parlor to wait for her. Unfortunately, the chair buckled and cracked under my weight. The girl's mother looked at me askance. "Do you always break the furniture?" she demanded.

So the real highlight of my 1945-46 season was meeting Patricia Lu Daveny, the beautiful young lady who would later become my wife. In 1946, we met at team trainer Eddie Kolker's campus restaurant, a hangout for college kids where all the basketball players worked from time to time. I was behind the register when she walked in, and I knew I wanted to get to know her.

CR

PAT MIKAN: Kolker's was a hangout, all the kids went there — just a little place near DePaul. You'd go there with a bunch of different kids and eat lunch or wait for your classes to start. Our meeting was very casual, no formal introduction.

I had just spent four years at an all-girls Catholic boarding school in Iowa, so I didn't know anything about basketball. I didn't know anything about the game or the players or how good a team DePaul was.

Later on, George wrote a postcard to me when he was on the road and said that when he got back, he'd like to invite me to a game. So when that finally came around, I told my parents that I had met somebody at school and I was going to go to a game and probably bring him home eventually to meet them.

"He's kind of tall," I said. "He plays basketball."

And they just said, "Oh, good."

When George finally did come to meet my parents, they were amazed. "What do you mean 'kind of tall'?" they said. "He's quite, quite tall."

George invited my family all to come to a game down at Chicago Stadium, and we just went on from there. George was very easy to like, he has a wonderful smile, a wonderful personality. He was just fun to be with. My whole family — aunts and uncles and cousins included — took to him right away. They all became basketball fans after that.

CR

All smiles on George and Pat Mikan's wedding day in spring, 1947.

(Courtesy of George Mikan)

I fell in love with Pat, and we were married the next spring, in May of 1947. We took a month-long honeymoon trip to Florida, Cuba and Nassau. It's been a great marriage that's lasted our whole lives long. Over the years, we would have six children — four boys and two girls: Larry, Terry, Pat, Mike, Tricia Ann and Maureen. Now, we are the proud grandparents of thirteen grandchildren, and one great-granddaughter, Rorry O'Connor.

Before Pat and I got married, however, I had to move on to the next stage in my life: playing professional basketball for the Chicago American Gears in the National Basketball League. Of course, I wasn't the only one of my DePaul teammates to head off to the pros. In 1948, my brother Ed signed with the Chicago Stags of the Basketball Association of America. Whitey Kachan, Gene Stump and Dick Triptow would also go on to pro careers. However, it was my turning professional that drew all the headlines. You see, my contract with the Gears made me the highest paid basketball player in the country.

ᘓ7ᘔ
American Gears
1946-1947

With one year left of law school, I turned pro in the spring of 1946. I had been determined to finish my law degree and had turned down several offers before this. But there was something different about this offer — it was for a hometown team, the Chicago American Gears of the National Basketball League. By staying in Chicago, Pat and I would be able to remain near our families, and I would be able to finish my law degree.

It was not long after the 1945-46 DePaul season finale when Gears owner Maurice White approached me with an offer to sign with his team. On March 16, 1946, after three days of negotiation, I signed a five-year contract worth a total of $60,000 — or $12,000 a year — for playing basketball and a future spot in the company's legal office. It made me the highest paid player in the league and a marked man, to boot.

While the rest of the league took a deep breath at the sound of such a salary ($350 per game), I simply took my first check, my signing bonus, and signed it over to my parents to help them pay their debts. I had no problem accepting the money, which came in awful handy for my hardworking family.

Basketball contracts, like a lot of things with the game, were quite different back then. My contract doesn't compare to the huge salaries paid today, but it was still large for the time, and I think it indicated the way in which the professional game was headed. In fact, White so wanted a championship that he was willing to pay his players bonuses to perform on the court, actually installing a policy in which he'd pay $5 for every field goal made and $2 for every free throw. In an attempt to thwart an "every-man-for-himself" mentality, he paid $2 for each assist, as well.

Needless to say, I was eager to cash in on these bonuses, despite my relatively large salary. To be paid to play the game I loved was an incredible feeling for a child of the Great Depression. Of course, professional basketball was quite different than the college game I had just left, and the higher level of competition was only the beginning of the differences.

I joined the Gears right away for the remainder of the 1945-46 season. The team set up a special scrimmage to help me get accustomed to its style of play, and then it was off to our first game, a practice game against the Anderson (Indiana) Chiefs. In my first outing as a member of the Gears, I scored 17 points on the way to a 68-60 win for the team, but I landed on the bench by the third quarter, called out on fouls. I had encountered the same kind of vocal and physical barrage I used to deal with when playing against Oklahoma A&M's Bob Kurland, except on a pro level, and unfortunately it had the same result.

Back then, joining the pro ranks was not as prestigious as it is today. I was a college boy with a substantial reputation, but I was coming into a professional game that had always been populated by a bunch of tough, road-weary, street-wise working stiffs who were anything but All-American boys. Since I'd reached the pinnacle in college, I naively figured that I would have my way in the pros, also. I found out, however, that I may have graduated, but my education was not complete.

During the few weeks of the 1945-46 season that I played with the Gears, Ray Meyer was hired as a consultant to help ease my transition into the pro game. (This maneuver was actually a thinly veiled, and failed, attempt to hire him as coach.) Ray would come to the games, help coach, and help me analyze the other teams and figure out how I was going to play the opponents. In one of my first games, we were playing the Oshkosh (Wisconsin) All-Stars, who had Leroy (Cowboy) Edwards out of Kentucky, the league's top center at the time. Edwards was 6 feet, 9 inches, 280 pounds, and strong as a bull with a temperament to match. Ray said to me, "George, whatever you do to him, stay away from him. Give him a lot of room."

"Geez," I thought, "I'm just coming out of college. I'm in the best shape of my life. I weigh a strapping 190 pounds. Bullshit, I can handle him."

The first play of the game I was going to guard Edwards close, so I was up against him, determined to hold him out of the lane. He

Family and friends at Mikan's Tavern: (From l to r) Pat and Ernie DeBenedetto, George's sister Marie and her husband Al Spiers, Ed and Mary Ann Mikan, Pat and George Mikan and Joe Mikan. *(Courtesy of George Mikan)*

reached down with his left arm and grabbed me above my knee and squeezed it. It just petrified me, and I couldn't move. He turned around and hit a hook shot.

On our second trip down to the Gears' defensive end, I still hadn't learned my lesson. I was on Edwards, and I tried to hold him out — you could hear my gym shoes squeaking as I strained to hold my position. Cowboy threw a nice little elbow and hit me right in my midsection. He knocked me over and made another hook shot.

I looked at the bench. Ray looked at me and threw his hands up, saying, "Well, I told you so."

From that point on, I gave Cowboy a clearance of about three feet. He would try to reach back to grab me because he had to touch you in order to have his coordination to hit the shot. And from then on, he didn't make another point. He was throwing it over the basket and up against the backboard and everywhere but in the hoop. The laughable part about it was that the next day in the paper it read: "The greatest guard in the game, George Mikan." Hell, I was dancing like Fred Astaire back there, trying to guard him and not get hurt.

Edwards must have read that story, however, because the next time we played, he reminded me of what I learned. I got too close to him again, and he hit me with an elbow in the mouth that knocked four teeth out. I learned my lesson the hard way. I darn near swallowed my teeth.

With little time left in the 1945-46 season, I contributed what I could. The Gears had been invited to the World Professional Basketball Tournament, an annual invitational tournament sponsored by the *Chicago Herald-American* newspaper to decide a national champion out of the numerous leagues and independent teams in existence at the time. The tournament took place over two weekends starting March 25, 1946. Fourteen teams took part, but as the top collegiate player of the year, I was the drawing card. Ads for the tournament trumpeted "Mikan — And the Rest!"

The Gears knocked off our first two opponents, Pittsburgh and Sheboygan (Wisconsin), easily. But in our third game, against Oshkosh, I got riled up and got a little too free with my elbows. I fouled out in the third quarter, and the Gears lost. We went on to beat Baltimore in the consolations and finished third in the tournament. I put in a total of 100 points over four games, which broke existing tournament records, and was given the tournament Most Valuable Player award.

Our finish wasn't bad, but Maurice White was intent on a title. With a maturing Mikan, now 6 feet, 10 inches and gaining weight, he felt that he would soon have one, maybe even as soon as next season.

Even with the World Professional Basketball Tournament, it was still difficult to tell who was the top team back in those days. In the years since basketball began, there had been more professional leagues than scuff marks on a court floor. At the time I was playing with the Gears, our league, the National Basketball League or NBL, was considered the top league. It had been in existence since 1937, but it was hardly the only game in town. There also existed the American Basketball League (ABL), which was an eastern basketball league started in 1925, as well as other smaller pro leagues and various independent teams like the Harlem Globetrotters and New York Renaissance, who were not associated with any leagues. On top of that, a very strong amateur league was in operation: the Amateur Athletic Union (AAU). Teams in the AAU were affiliated with industries and offered the promise of a regular job with decent pay as well as the opportunity to play ball. For a collegian like myself, stepping into the precipice of post-college basketball, the choice of what to do had been wide-open. I chose the pros, while my college counterpart Bob Kurland went to the AAU.

൦ൈ

BOB KURLAND: George and I made two different decisions as to what careers were about in those days. I think that in terms of notoriety, we had been about equal. The Aggies were out here in Oklahoma and probably didn't get all the ink that DePaul got out of the Midwestern papers and Chicago. But on the basis of professional offers, our choices were more or less equal.

In those days, 1946, the NBA wasn't even established, there were no arenas, no TV, or anything else. Playing for any pro team was risky business in terms of stability, security and opportunity. George and some kids that came home after the war decided to try the pro deal, and there was some vision on their part as to what was going to come. It took about ten years or more to get established, but eventually the pro leagues did well.

൦ൈ

While I continued my schooling and played with the Gears, Kurland went to work for Phillips Petroleum company and played for its company team, the Phillips Oilers, in the AAU league. Kurland had seen years of different leagues in his time and was unsure of pro ball's stability. Working with Phillips gave him a good job and ultimately a career, plus the chance to play AAU ball — and the chance to play in the Olympics, as well.

ଓ

BOB KURLAND: Guys like Bob Cousy, who was a freshman when I got out of school, never made over $35,000. I thought with my background, I wanted to do something that was more stable and had the promise of opportunity. Phillips was a relatively young company, just getting into the petrochemical field. Since my background included some studies along those lines, that's where I went. I never regretted it.

The AAU league was the equivalent of the NBA in those days, because the NBA was just getting structured. But that changed after a while. [The AAU got its start because] industries such as Goodyear, Phillips, Caterpillar and other companies on the East Coast and in the Midwest figured that basketball teams could get their organizations publicity in the papers. In this country, getting your name in the sports page is like getting in the Bible. People are nuts [about sports]. Companies thought that if you could get your name in the paper in a good light as a sports team, then your products would be well accepted. And they capitalized on that.

But when the pros started [getting established], the newspaper editors and publishers started saying, "Wait a minute. If industrial firms want space in our paper, let 'em buy it."

The next thing that happened was that arenas started getting built and there became some stability in the pro leagues. As soon as players had some promise of getting paid [decently], the good kids coming out of college decided that instead of coming to an industrial firm and having some promise of a job and a program of development, they were going to get the money. When that happened, the attraction for sportswriters to write about industrial teams diminished, because the good players were going into pro ball. Soon after that, the industrial league and AAU basketball at the higher level disappeared. I think the last Phillips team played in 1967.

ଓ

Apparently, the many leagues that existed in 1946 weren't enough because the 1946-47 season brought the birth of another one: the Basketball Association of America. The BAA was a conglomeration of teams owned by arena owners in the Northeast. Many BAA owners owned or had ties to the American and National Hockey Leagues and were trying to fill the open dates in their arenas with basketball. The BAA teams were located in big-time cities like New York, Philadelphia, Washington and Chicago. This was in sharp contrast to the NBL, which played in smaller auditoriums and high schools in burgs such as Sheboygan and Oshkosh, Fort Wayne (Indiana), and Syracuse and Rochester (New York).

Definite battle lines were drawn between the BAA, which had the arenas and bigger potential crowds, and the NBL, which had all the big-name players and an established following. And nowhere was that league war fought harder than in Chicago, where the NBL's American Gears were forced to battle a new BAA franchise, the Chicago Stags, without ever meeting them on the court.

It looked like the Gears would be the first casualty of the league wars when the schedule for the 1946-47 season came out. The Gears were to play in the International Amphitheater, a smaller stadium outside of Chicago, while the Stags played at Chicago Stadium, a more prestigious venue. Even worse for the Gears, the Amphitheater was holding a livestock show for the first few weeks of the season, so the Gears had to start the season on the road.

Maurice White feared that the Stags would have nearly a month to establish themselves before the Gears got back to town. He publicly declared that Chicago couldn't afford to support two pro basketball teams. But he "had Mikan," and he figured that I'd draw the crowds no matter where our games were played. With me playing at center, White rationalized, coupled with a winning record when the Gears came home, "everything will be all right." He needed us to get out of the gate with a fast start.

An early indication of how we might do came in the *Chicago Herald-American* College All-Star game played on November 29, 1946. Fort Wayne, the NBL champion for three years running, represented the pros and took on a group of college players, the cream of the previous season. Although under contract with the Gears, I played for the college all-stars. We beat Fort Wayne 57-54 in front of a capacity crowd of 23,000 at Chicago Stadium, and I scored 16 points. After that night, White was convinced that the fans were all there to see me play and that they would do so when I played with the American Gears, no matter where we played. The Stags would give us no trouble, he assured me. I wasn't so sure.

The 1946-47 season started inauspiciously: we dropped our first two games before winning one on the road against Rochester. By the time we got back to Chicago with only a marginal record, the Stags had already been drawing crowds for weeks. On the night of our home opener, the Stags were set to play Cleveland at Chicago Stadium. It was the worst possible scenario for the Gears.

On the afternoon of the game, Maurice called me into his office to talk. He was having money trouble. Earlier in the week he'd cut four ballplayers, one of them my brother Joe, without any warning. The players had been at the railroad station, boarding the train with the team, when they were told that they were no longer wanted. Moves like that make people upset, and I was in a belligerent mood.

"George," White said, "basketball is a business and when a business is not doing so well, you start to cut corners. The biggest corner I can see right now is you."

Maurice wanted me to settle for $6,500 rather than the $12,000 I had coming to me for the season. That request, coupled with the way he treated my brother, sent me over the edge. I told White that I was not going to accept any cut in pay.

I was still upset that night and couldn't have played worse in our first home game of the season — and the place was packed. We lost to Oshkosh, 44-41.

I was so angry, I quit the Gears after the game. The next morning, the headlines in the *Chicago Tribune* read: "Mikan Retires After Gears Lose."

Upon consulting with a friend of mine, attorney Stacy Osgood, we determined that we had a case against the Gears for the way my contract was structured and the team's neglect to fulfill it, and so we sued them. The NBL had a limit on player salaries of $7,000 a year, but Maurice had made a verbal agreement to make up the difference by paying me to stop in his law office once a week. The Gears counter-sued for $100,000 and sent me fine notices, $150 per game, for the next six weeks in which I did not play.

Finally, the case was presented before a friendly judge who urged both sides to settle their differences, which we did. The suits were withdrawn. It had not been a very good introduction to the pro game, and it convinced me to work all the harder to get my law degree.

When I returned after missing nineteen games, the Gears had been struggling but were starting to come out of it thanks to the addition of player-coach Bobby McDermott, the great-shooting, hard-living guard from Fort Wayne. When I walked back into the locker room after my little legal hiatus, McDermott said, "Hello, George, you're starting tonight." That's all there was to it.

McDermott was a breath of fresh air who added a little life to the Gears' locker room. His favorite saying was, "When you take the court, you have no friends. Whack 'em, knock 'em down, do whatever it takes to win. But when the game is over, buy 'em a beer." And that's just about the attitude that you had to have.

Maurice White had first noticed McDermott at the World Professional Basketball Tournament, and that's where he decided that Bobby would be just what our squad needed.

ი3

GENE STUMP: The World Professional Basketball Tournament that year had the NBL's best teams, the Eastern League's [best], and two black clubs from New York, the Renaissance and another. Well, one player from the Rens undercut a Sheboygan player in a semifinal game, and he broke his leg. Bobby McDermott and Fort Wayne were playing the Rens in the finals the next day. So McDermott and some Fort Wayne players go up to this Sheboygan player's hospital room and ask the guy if he has any money to bet on the championship. The guy says a little, and McDermott tells him to have his wife wire it down so they could bet it for him.

So they bet the money for [this Sheboygan player] on Fort Wayne. The next day, on the opening tip-off, McDermott hits this Rens player in the jaw and knocks him cold. The 10,000 people watching this game see this guy laying on the floor out cold. Needless to say, Fort Wayne ran away with the game.

Another time, I went on an exhibition trip with the Gears, before I signed with the Celtics. It was a three-game swing out to Rochester, Syracuse and somewhere else. I was getting paid $50 per game, and Bobby McDermott says to me, "Gene, I want to make sure, whenever we stop for a game and then get back on the train, there's two or three cases of Schlitz on the train. That's your job, make sure it's there and it's iced."

I was on the road with the Gears for five days, but I never played a minute. All I had to do was make sure I got those cases of beer on that train.

McDermott would stay up three-quarters of the night, drinking beer and smoking cigars. We'd pull into town two hours before game

time, but he'd walk into the auditorium with his hair slicked down,
throw in about 30 points, and walk off. He was an amazing athlete.

cʒ

McDermott wasn't the only tough character in pro basketball. There were so many teams and leagues struggling for respectability and legitimacy — not to mention some hard-earned cash — that it translated down onto the court. Rough treatment and fights were common, and as soon as a couple of players started swinging, everyone joined in. My old buddy Cowboy Edwards was one of the roughest guys I ever played against. During one game, he got angry at me and grabbed me by my shirt, my skin, and all, and lifted me up in the air. "Well," I thought as I hung up there, "that's good enough for me." As soon as he let me down, I got the hell away. I knew enough not to tangle with Cowboy Edwards.

Some teams liked to send players out to get me. Sheboygan, for example, had a football player playing for them, a fullback from Green Bay named Ted Fritsch. During one game there, I was coming down court with the ball, and I heard this thump, thump, thump, behind me. I took a look over my shoulder and saw this fullback, about two feet off the ground, trying to hit me with a nice tackle. I just threw the ball up at the basket and raced ahead of his grasp. The next thing I heard was him going through the end zone doors right out into a snowbank.

I went back to the bench and told the coach, "I think I'm getting a little tired. The game's almost over — no use getting hurt, right?" The coached laughed and took me out.

The Gears won the first game I played after I came back from my "retirement" — I got 22 points in that 62-60 game over Syracuse. We won plenty more from then on. After I came back, we were undefeated at home and very tough on the road. Winning was very important, and McDermott, who was coaching us from the floor, settled for little else. As he used to say, "You've got to score because you have to go in to negotiate your next year's contract."

McDermott was quite a character. His pregame pep talks were short and sweet, doled out in his strong Eastern accent. "All right, guys," he'd say, "the most important thing is to get the 'pernts.' Let's go get the pernts. I'll start out by shooting four or five baskets, ten pernts." Then he'd turn to Billy Hassett, who played the other guard at the time, and say, "Next, you take your shots."

To Bob Callahan, a big left-hander, McDermott would say, "You go to the right side of the court because you come across and shoot left-handed." And to Bruce Hale, "You go to the left side because you're right-handed." Then he'd add to Hassett, "When you get out there, you throw the ball over your shoulder, and I'll be there and you can block for me."

And I said, "What about me?"

"You play the pivot," Mac said, "and we'll get to you, eventually."

McDermott liked to have a distribution of points, so everybody could score. No player-coach could do it any other way.

The Gears' momentum carried us to the playoffs, where we met Oshkosh, a team that had beaten us seven straight that season. But with Mac's shooting and some strong play underneath by our frontcourt, we were able to best them, 61-60, for a chance at the title. I scored 22 that game.

In the championship round, we met the Rochester Royals in a best-of-five series. Rochester took the first game, 71-65. I put in 14 points that game, but fouled out in the third quarter. We went on to beat Rochester in all three of the next games. With our 79-68 victory in the final game on April 9, 1946, we were champions of the National Basketball League. The season ended exactly as Maurice White had hoped.

In the twenty-five games I played that season, I averaged 16.5 points per game. With that average, I won the NBL's scoring title. In the playoffs, however, I upped my average to 19.7 points.

Such a successful season's conclusion was more than could be said for our hometown "rivals," the Chicago Stags, who finished runner-up to the first BAA champion Philadelphia Warriors. Talk of a charity game between the Gears and the Stags never amounted to anything, so we settled for the NBL title. We considered it to be a national title, since before the BAA arrived, the NBL was considered the number one league.

Still, the BAA had done considerably well in its premier season just by establishing itself as a viable entity — despite the fact that the NBL had lured most of the top college ballplayers to its teams. The BAA had done so well, in fact, that it was sharing billing with the NBL as the top professional basketball leagues.

Oddly enough, one person who was buoyed by the BAA's performance was our own Chicago American Gears owner, Maurice White. Flush with the glow of his first title and confident with the likes of Mikan and McDermott on his squad, Maurice figured there were plenty more championships to come. And he had come up with a plan to capitalize on our success.

After the season, Maurice called me into his office to lay out his new idea.

"I've been looking at the attendance figures around the league," he said, "and I find that we outdrew everybody else in the outfit. Rochester, Syracuse, Indianapolis, Oshkosh — they all had good years. But no matter how well they were going, they always drew more people against us."

So, his point was that our opponents had their biggest night at the gate when they played us. I waited to find out where he was going with this.

"George, that proves one thing," he said. "You're the biggest drawing card in basketball today."

While I didn't necessarily agree with him, I certainly didn't like the conclusion he drew from the figures. His idea was to start a whole new league in which the Gears would travel all over the country playing other teams and selling out arenas. He wanted this new league to be centered around the Gears, and more specifically, one player, me.

I told him that I thought this was a ridiculous idea and that I didn't think it would work. But I was under contract to play ball and not make league decisions, so my thoughts only carried so much weight. White chased me out of his office and went ahead despite my concerns.

Pat and I were married shortly after that, and when we returned from our honeymoon, I read the announcement in the papers that the Professional Basketball League of America had been formed.

That fall, with a new wife and a new basketball league, I went back to work. Maurice had set up PBLA teams in places stretching from St. Paul, Minnesota, to Birmingham, Alabama. He sank $600,000 of his own money into the various teams as seed money and actually got a league of sixteen teams off the ground. Maurice was handling everything for his far-flung league, from salaries and transportation to scheduling. After less than a month, the league hit the skids. The official reason was poor attendance, particularly in the South. Maurice had a nervous breakdown and went to the hospital.

In the few weeks that the PBLA existed, the Gears played eight games, all victories. We were leading the PBLA Northern Division when the league folded. Our last PBLA game was in Louisville, a 65-56 win. We returned to Chicago on November 13, 1947, to read in the newspapers that Maurice's dream had died.

The expatriated American Gears tried to re-enter the NBL, but the NBL owners soundly rejected their application. In a matter of weeks, we had gone from champions of one league, to the center-piece of another, to a team without a league, and then finally no team. The Gears were dismantled and the players split up and drafted by other NBL teams.

Once again, my pro basketball career came to a screeching halt. I had been drafted first in the league dispersal draft by the newly formed Minneapolis Lakers. Minneapolis officials had purchased the Detroit Gems, the previous season's last place team in the NBL. I also received offers from Fort Wayne and from Les Harrison, the owner of the Rochester Royals, but my rights belonged to Minne-apolis.

I had no desire to leave the friendly confines of my hometown Chicago for the cold and unknown of Minnesota. Besides, I still had some law school to complete. But the instability of professional basketball had hit home. The actions of one man could topple a whole league and derail a career. I could only hope I could get mine back on track.

Part III

A Giant in the Land
of Lakes

George Mikan, the Minneapolis Laker. *(Courtesy of the Minnesota Historical Society)*

∝8∂
Worst to First
1947-1948

I never really wanted to play basketball in Minneapolis. When I was with DePaul, we had played the University of Minnesota in a game on New Year's Eve, 1945, and Minneapolis was as cold a place as ever I'd imagined. It didn't help that we got beat, but the city was a frozen tundra compared to Chicago, where the breezes blowing in off of Lake Michigan kept the winters mild. I wanted to stay in Chicago, play basketball near my family, finish my law degree at DePaul and generally stay warm. I thought Minnesota was Siberia.

I was soon to change my mind.

There was no question that Ben Berger and Maurice Chalfen, the owners of the brand-new Minneapolis Lakers franchise, wanted me to play in Minnesota — they were one of the teams that had voted against the Chicago Gears re-entering the NBL after the PBLA collapsed on November 13, 1947. The way Berger and Chalfen figured it, the Detroit Gems, the franchise they'd purchased and moved to Minneapolis, had the worst record in 1946-47, and that record would entitle the Lakers to pick first in the dispersal draft of the PBLA. If the Gears had been allowed to re-enter the NBL, I would have stayed with Chicago, plain and simple. Berger and Chalfen were smarter than that. They lobbied hard to disallow the Gears back into the league and ensure their new team the rights to me.

After the PBLA died, I thought I was a free agent. That's what the newspapers were saying. So I just kept on with the three classes I was taking at the DePaul law school and waited to see what would happen. The Rochester Royals and Fort Wayne Pistons were only two of the teams who expressed interest in me. But I was looking to stay as close to Chicago as possible.

So I guess I was mildly surprised when Max Winter, who was

running the Lakers franchise, called and told me, "George, you belong to the Minneapolis Lakers."

"Hah," I thought, "The Gears folded, the league folded. There wasn't any semblance of a contract left. I don't belong to anybody but myself."

Still, I had to talk to the Lakers. With my lawyer Stacey Osgood in tow, I flew to Minneapolis two days after that phone call to meet with Winter and *Minneapolis Tribune* sportswriter Sid Hartman. Hartman was heavily involved with running the team, albeit unofficially, since he still kept his job at the *Tribune*.

Winter, Hartman, Osgood and I met for three hours in the Lakers' office in downtown Minneapolis, and I wasn't sold. I was asking for $12,000 a year, which was what I had been getting with the Gears, so I didn't see any reason to take less.

Rather than reject Winter and Hartman's offer outright, Osgood and I decided to head back to Chicago after the meeting. This would give the Lakers time to reconsider my price — and me time to consider other offers. After all, I had an NBL championship under my belt, and this franchise had been the worst team in the league the previous season — I knew they needed me.

Before we left the office, Winter, speaking in Hebrew, covertly told Hartman to get lost along the way while driving Osgood and me to the airport to catch our plane. I realize now that he wanted to buy some more negotiating time.

Well, Hartman took us on the longest, slowest tour of Minneapolis and St. Paul I've ever experienced. He drove us leisurely around the cities, trying to keep us going in the opposite direction of the airport. All the while he drove, Sid talked about the many virtues of the Twin Cities, pointing out the parks, the lakes, the golf courses. He must have known that I like to play golf during the off-season.

By the time we got to the airport, our plane had departed, and Stacey and I were stranded in Minneapolis for the night. I was glad that November was still fall in Minnesota. Of course, Stacey and I saw through the whole charade, and we got a good laugh out of it. Since Sid had gone to all that extra trouble, we figured that something was up.

The next morning, Hartman and Winter met with us again. I got the money I was looking for — $12,500, even though rumors said I had held out for $15,000 — and I signed the contract. I figured that any franchise who wanted me as much as the Lakers seemed to was going to appreciate my services. It was less than a week since the PBLA had folded, and here I was, a Minneapolis Laker.

The people in Minneapolis were excited to have their first major professional sports franchise. For the record books, it was a second for Minnesota, however: St. Paul had previously landed the St. Paul Saints, a basketball team in the PBLA. But that team had gone the way of the Gears — the Lakers had actually signed Jack Dwan from the Saints in the dispersal draft. Now the Lakers, only four games into their first season, were the professional sports king in town.

When I joined the team, it was starting to establish itself, having won three of those first four games. Winter and Hartman had done a good job in putting together a basketball team despite the fact that Berger and Chalfen had received only the franchise rights and some worthless old uniforms when they purchased the Gems for $15,000 from Detroit — the NBL had already assigned the Gems players to other teams.

The biggest name the Lakers had signed was Jim Pollard, a forward out of Stanford who had been playing some AAU ball for the Oakland Bittners. Pollard was a highly skilled basketball player who could jump like a gazelle. They called him the "Kangaroo Kid" for his leaping ability. Throughout his Hall of Fame career, Pollard demonstrated why his talents could easily transfer to today's game. Jim was the first player to really play the game "above the rim," where much of modern basketball is played.

Along with Pollard, my new Laker teammates included Tony Jaros and Don Carlson, who both formerly played with the Chicago Stags. Jaros was a solid, hard-nosed ballplayer, originally from Minneapolis, who always played good defense and gave his all every night. He was always there to back me in case anyone wanted to mess with the Lakers' lanky, bespectacled center. He told me he knew what made the team run and he wanted me around to get them that playoff money.

Don Carlson played forward, and he was a real fireball on the court. He loved to hit the pivot, and I'd pass off to him as he went by me to the basket for a lot of easy layups. Don used to tell me that he enjoyed that play because as he cut past he could always hear his defender running into the brick wall of a pick I'd set for him. "When I heard the 'Oooohhhhh,'" Don would say, "I knew I was home free." Don was a real team player who had a lot of fight and a lot of spirit.

Behind the bench was first-time professional coach John Kundla, who was only thirty-one. Kundla had left his coaching position at St. Thomas College in St. Paul to join the Lakers. It almost didn't happen, however; the instability of the pro ranks in the late 1940s did nothing to entice talented coaches to leave their stable jobs.

CS

SID HARTMAN: Our first choice was Joe Hutton, who was coaching at Hamline University, but he had his son, Joe Hutton, Jr. coming up through school. In those days, pro basketball wasn't any big thing, and Joe Hutton, Sr. wasn't going to quit a secure job at Hamline and take a chance on us being in business a year or two and then folding. Kundla was at St. Thomas at the time, and he didn't want to take the chance, either. He lived in a little apartment with his wife, Marie, over on Broadway Avenue in north Minneapolis, and I talked him into taking the job.

CS

JOHN KUNDLA: I turned the job down three times — there was the question of whether pro ball would [be successful] here in Minneapolis. Nobody would take the job. They wanted Joe Hutton, Sr., but he turned it down, and they couldn't get anyone else. I think [Laker player] Don Smith recommended me. He knew Sid Hartman, and Sid talked to me about it. I turned him down, until they finally gave me a three-year contract [worth] twice as much as I was making at St. Thomas. So, I figured I couldn't lose. As I say, nobody wanted the job. But I took the job and got fortunate enough to pick up Mikan in the draft when the Gears folded.

CS

My first night in a Lakers uniform was actually not. The first game I played as a Laker was an away game against the Sheboygan Redskins on November 20, 1947, and Minneapolis didn't have a uniform to fit me yet. Pete Mikulak, the Lakers' clubhouse handyman, told me that my number 99 jersey and uniform shorts were still being made and that nothing they had in stock would work. The biggest jersey he had was number 21, and so for this one night, I stretched that jersey over my 6-foot, 10-inch frame.

For trunks, Mikulak and I had to improvise, and it became our little secret. I wore my old Gears shorts, only days old at this time, when I took the floor that night to score 16 points. The mixed uniform was not something you'd get away with these days, but it worked at the time.

I was photographed quite a bit that first game, but no one really said much about the shorts. More of a fuss has been made, through the years, about my jersey. In perhaps the most-often reproduced photograph taken of me in those days, I'm wearing the garb I just described. I became known as "Big Number 99," and yet I've seen the photo of me driving down court in my Gears shorts with a 21 on my chest more often than most others. It happens to be one of my favorite photos, just the same. I like it for the intensity and drive that comes through in my expression, not to mention that I'm not yet looking like the senior citizen I am today.

When people ask me about that photo, they always bring up the number 99, wondering why I chose that number. I always tell them that 99 cents isn't quite a dollar and that the number inspired me because it reminded me that there's always a higher level to play up to. It became my trademark — the biggest guy wearing the highest number — but I saw it as a subconscious incentive to reach for higher goals.

But something more important than the uniform was amiss that first night. I was penciled in to start, and in most of the team's mind I was going to be the missing piece that their brand-new franchise needed. Pollard, a natural forward at 6 feet, 5 inches, had been playing center for the team's first four games, and my arrival for their fifth game allowed him to move back to forward.

But that wasn't the problem. The problem arose out of how we were working together. Given all the press I'd been getting, my new teammates naturally figured they'd better take advantage of this big guy with a championship under his belt. But coach Kundla and the other Lakers weren't used to playing with a big pivot player, so their idea was to feed me the ball every single time they got it. It didn't take long for our opponents to figure out this game plan, and they sank in on me so tight that it was hard to raise my hand to catch a pass, even if I wanted another one. We lost to Sheboygan, 56-41.

ও

JOHN KUNDLA: Mikan didn't join us until the fifth game of the year. We put him in and then lost four out of five games because all we'd do was lob it in to him and he was getting killed. Finally, we got a pattern up and got some plays going. We had better balanced scoring after that.

CR

One thing that really helped us start pulling together was when we acquired a new ballplayer, guard Herm Schaefer, who signed shortly after me. Herm, who played college ball for Indiana University, had been playing for Fort Wayne before coming to the Lakers. Well, the Pistons were having trouble and when Fort Wayne hired its third coach in a very short period, Herm quit the team. Winter then signed him to a contract with the Lakers, which was a very good move for us. I guess Herm was acting out an early form of free agency.

Herm became our playmaker. He was a stabilizing factor for the team, deliberately and methodically dribbling down the court to start all the plays. I guess you'd call him a point guard today, but back then he was just a guard who brought the ball up and called the plays. Herm had a pretty good outside shot to keep the defenders honest. But mainly he fed me and worked off the pivot. Herm would hit me, and the rest of the team would do their cutting past the post. I would acknowledge the open man and pass off. Herm wasn't fast, but he was a steady ballplayer. He had moderate speed; he was no Slater Martin, who came along later and was lightning quick.

Herm played with his head — he was a very smart player, and he showed it shortly after joining the team. After watching us struggle on the court in my early going, he cornered me in the locker room.

"Mikan," he said, "you're a fool."

I'm not usually one to take that sort of talk kindly, but he was new. So rather than tell him what I really thought, I just said, "What are you talking about?" and started to walk away.

"The Lakers have got a great thing going," Herm explained, "what with you and Pollard both on the same front line, and we're wasting it. By both trying to right the ship's wrongs, you're playing against each other. Jim Pollard is a great basketball player. He can do anything with that ball, including pass it to you. But you've got to pass it to him, too. You can't win all the games by yourself. If you and Jim work together, we can finish ten games ahead of everybody."

It made sense. Herm was describing basketball fundamentals that I had followed all my life, but wasn't playing now. We were forcing the ball in to me, which is where it stayed because of our opponents' sagging defenses. I needed to get the ball back out where my open teammates had a better shot. We had to stop reading press clippings, and I had to stop worrying about justifying my huge contract.

Jim and I talked it over and worked out a signal for a return pass, which made all the difference in the world. Jim was so quick that all he needed was a step and the ball, and he was in for an easy layup. If he missed, I would slide open after the pass and be set for the rebound and easy putback. It worked like a charm.

The next night, we beat the Flint (Michigan) Dow Chemicals by 25 points and cruised on to win twenty-seven of the remaining thirty-three regular-season games. Along the way, I was able to improve my game, as well.

On January 18, 1948, I set a new NBL single-game scoring record of 41 points against our soon-to-be archrivals, the Rochester Royals, who were owned and coached by Les Harrison. The game had come down to the last minute, tied at 73, and we held onto the ball for most of the final forty seconds, content to play overtime if our final shot failed. George Beahon of the *Rochester Democrat and Chronicle* described the final play this way:

"Jack Dwan flipped the cowhide into Mikan in the pivot with five seconds showing on the clock. He missed the attempt, and the ball was frantically batted into the air by the Royals defenders. But Mikan provided the Frank Merriwell finish by grabbing the loose leather and pitching in a short set shot that was the killer."

That shot put us past the Royals on the scoreboard and me past Bob Carpenter of the Oshkosh All-Stars in the record books. (Carpenter had a 40-point game in 1946). I played all forty minutes of the game that night in Rochester, and the entire second half with four fouls. (Five fouls were needed at that time to be disqualified.) There was a strong effort from everyone on the team that night, and we were able to grab a big win.

Another highlight that season was a small detour from the regular schedule that team management had set up for us. Max Winter and Abe Saperstein, owner of the Harlem Globetrotters, the best black professional basketball team in the country, had agreed that the Lakers and Trotters would play an exhibition game on February 19, 1948, before a BAA game in Chicago. Now, while I didn't think the Lakers of the NBL were mere pregame fodder for any BAA teams, I was happy to play an exhibition against the Globetrotters in my old hometown. The Trotters had a lot of great talent; they were the most popular team in the country and a great challenge to play.

The hoopla surrounding our exhibition proved that it was a bigger attraction than the main contest. The Trotters, with their road show of basketball antics and a current 102-game winning streak, were a huge draw. And of course, Chicago still remembered who I was. The papers were predicting that the crowds would double what Chicago Stadium usually held for a regular-season game. (Which is precisely what happened.)

At the time, black players had only just begun to be integrated into the white professional ranks. (The first two black players, Pop Gates and Dolly King, had been signed by Les Harrison and the Rochester Royals in 1946; the first black drafted in the NBA would be Chuck Cooper, picked by the New York Knicks in 1950.) This game, which would turn into a series of six Lakers and Globetrotters games over the next three seasons, was a huge step forward in the integration of black and white basketball. At the same time, having the popular Globetrotters, a team that had been around for decades, pitted against our young franchise brought a lot of interest to the rollercoaster of leagues that eventually formed the NBA.

So on February 19, we took a side trip to Chicago Stadium to battle the 'Trotters. The game certainly helped our team coffers, but it was more a point of pride for the players. We weren't paid for the game because it was unscheduled, but every one of us wanted to show who the better team was.

A total of 17,823 spectators jammed Chicago Stadium to witness a barnburner. Goose Tatum was the reigning clown of the Trotters' show — as a center, he'd be facing me in the game. He had been a very good player in his heyday, but now he was on the downside of his career, more of a showman than a scorer. The Trotters played the game straight, only once passing the ball between a Laker player's legs for a basket. Tatum did a bit of his post-up routine, flailing his arms and playing to the crowd, but he always knew what he was doing. He was so funny that once I forgot I was guarding him and began to enjoy watching him. But the moment I dropped my arms, he flew right around me for an easy basket. I guess that stuff really worked.

Goose nailed nine points to my 24, but his team still came out on top. The game was tied at 59 with seconds to go when a shot by Big Presley of the Trotters bounced off the side of the backboard and landed in the arms of one of his teammates. That player was clearly standing out of bounds, but the whistle did not blow, so he quickly threw the ball to Ermer Robinson. Robinson shot before the last second ticked off the clock, and the ball went in — 61-59 final.

Winter was not happy with the game officials, both of whom were supplied by Saperstein. When we lost to the Trotters the next season in another close exhibition game, Winter had had enough. He told Saperstein that any subsequent games would have one referee supplied by the Trotters and one by the Lakers. The Lakers never lost another game to the Globetrotters.

The Lakers finished the 1947-48 season with a 43-17 record and the Western Division title. Thanks to my teammates, I was able to set a new single-season scoring record for the NBL. I finished the fifty-six games I played as a Laker that season with 1,195 points — my total had nearly doubled the existing record set by the Royals' Al Cervi, who had tallied 632 points the previous season. My 21.3 points-per-game average was also a league high, beating the previous record of 20.2 points per game. All in all, I set six league records that season, was picked in an almost unanimous vote as the league's Most Valuable Player, and made All-NBL First Team for the second consecutive season (the first was with the Gears).

Our friends the Rochester Royals had won the NBL's Eastern Division with a 44-16 record, and we had the feeling that we would probably end up facing them and coach Les Harrison for the championship.

CB

LES HARRISON: George was the best center in our day. And when they voted on the best center in the country [in later years], I put him over Bill Russell and all the other centers. He was averaging 25 points a game in those days, and back then the rules were tougher.

In the first round of the NBL playoffs, we met the Oshkosh All-Stars, defeating them three games to one in the best-of-five series. That was followed by a sweep of the Tri-Cities Blackhawks in the semifinals. Before we could play the Rochester Royals in the championship round, however, there was the little matter of the World Professional Basketball Tournament in Chicago to attend to.

Back in those days, there were so many professional basketball leagues and independent basketball teams that it was hard to know who was the best. The World Professional Basketball Tournament was an invitational tournament sponsored by the *Chicago Herald-American* newspaper that allowed the best teams from various leagues to compete. The results were unofficial, but it was still an honor to be asked.

In 1948, the tournament took place at Chicago Stadium over the course of four days, April 8-11, and eight teams had been invited. This was the tournament's tenth year, and it would be its last, although we didn't know it at the time. It was a detour from the playoffs at hand, but a worthwhile pursuit nonetheless.

On the first day of the World Professional Basketball Tournament, the Lakers played the Wilkes-Barre (Pennsylvania) Barons, champions of the Eastern League (which would eventually become the Continental Basketball League of today). We beat them by 50 points, 98-48. Not everyone was pleased with this showing, calling us "disgusting" for beating someone by so many points.

It should have made those critics happier when we beat the Anderson Packers by only three points the next day. After a one-day rest, we advanced to the tournament championship against the New York Renaissance, popularly known as the Rens, a black team out of New York City.

The Rens played superbly, especially Sweetwater Clifton, and it was a battle for the lead throughout the fourth quarter. But in the end, we beat the Rens, 75-71. I knocked down 40 points, which set a tournament record and helped earn me the tournament Most Valuable Player award. In the last World Professional Basketball Tournament ever held, I became the only two-time winner of the MVP award in the tournament's ten-year history. It was the perfect momentum to send the Lakers on to the NBL finals.

With one day off, we quickly prepared for the NBL champion-

George Mikan and his Minneapolis Lakers teammates celebrate their first title (NBL, 1948) in the locker room after the game. The players congratulating George are (from l to r) Tony Jaros, Arnie Ferrin, John Jorgenson and Jack Dwan. *(Courtesy of UPI/Corbis-Bettmann)*

ship series. Such a rigorous schedule was the norm for pro basketball in those days. It wasn't rare to play back-to-back games in different cities: playing in New York one night and travelling by train all night to play in Minneapolis the next. We played a lot of games in succession — that's why I did a lot of sleeping on trains.

Meeting Rochester in the finals was a challenge we looked forward to, but it would never happen again. After this season, the Lakers and Royals were placed in the same division and never met again for the championship. But we played many times in the semifinals, and they were always tough battles. I always told Les Harrison that the Royals were in the wrong division. "Les," I said, "we would have played some great championships series." And since they won only one title to our six in those years, he had to agree.

The 1948 NBL finals were supposed to be a battle of the big men, me against Arnie Risen, my former foe from Ohio State. Risen had come to Rochester in a very suspect manner, at least according to Max Winter. Early in the season, Risen was playing for the NBL's Indianapolis Kautskys, and Harrison bought his rights from them. Winter claimed that the lowly Indianapolis team needed Risen much more than the powerful Rochester Royals and that the transaction violated league bylaws because it was made after the player trading deadline. Max vowed not to recognize any games that Risen played for the Royals as legitimate games.

Some people claimed that Max was making complaints like this about the NBL because he was positioning the Lakers to jump to a new league the following season. They may have been right — Winter was even calling for the resignation of the NBL's commissioner, Piggy Lambert. But in the end, all of Max's posturing about Risen didn't matter. Arnie had broken his jaw in an earlier round and missed the championship series. Some critics said that we wouldn't have won if Risen had played, but there's no way to know that.

We beat the Royals three games to one in the best-of-five series, to win the 1948 NBL championship. It was the Lakers' first year in existence, and here we were with the NBL title. The Lakers franchise had gone from worst to first in one season, which did plenty to put Minneapolis on the professional basketball map. Ironically enough, however, as the 1948-49 season neared, we were preparing to change leagues, making that ever-changing map quickly out of date again.

ൠ**9**൧
Barnstorming
1948-1949

I'm not sure where the term "barnstorming" came from, but when I think back to places that the Lakers visited on our early cross-country tours, I'm convinced that it could have originated then. Compared to today's plush, finely appointed arenas with gourmet concessions, video monitors for instant replays, and carpeted, sound-proofed luxury boxes, the places we played were one step up from barns. They were small, smoky, aging auditoriums, sometimes high school gyms, with broken-down locker rooms and the occasional rat nearby. Of course, when I give thought to some of the denizens of those old 'barns' — the fans waiting to see us play — well, the metaphor rings even truer.

Professional basketball was a different game back in the late 1940s. The league would lay out the schedule of games for a season, but depending upon what league you were in, you might not even play the same number of games as your opponents because some leagues had an odd number of teams. But those were just the scheduled games. In order to pad their profits (or break even, for that matter), team owners took their teams on barnstorming tours to smaller arenas for exhibition games. Our games against the Globetrotters were a prestigious example, but most exhibition games were played in much humbler places against less-heralded opponents.

For the Lakers, barnstorming helped owners Berger and Chalfen pay our salaries and then some. As a very tall player, I was a bit of an anomaly back then and a big drawing card. People who knew basketball as a sport of small, quick players would flock to see how this "gentle giant" could excel at the game.

Pro basketball's reputation had been less than stellar in the 1930s and early '40s, back before I played. Professional cagers were mercenaries looking for some quick money but with little regard for the integrity of the game. The more physical the game, the better, seemed to be the thought of players and team owners alike. Games often became bloodbaths, especially under the basket. The frontcourt was no place for the squeamish, and the front row, where fans sat who were just as rough and raucous (and who often participated in the action), was no place for women or children. Basketball was a very hard game.

But around about the mid-1940s, the college grads, like myself, and returning war veterans who began joining the professional ranks started to change all that. We took people's perception of the game out of the rougher, dark side of town and started to bring it into the light of the mainstream. The game could still be just as rough, and it was still played in small, loud, smoky arenas, but the public's perception of it was beginning to change. And in those pre-TV days, the barnstorming Lakers were a popular show who helped bring that about.

CS

JOHN KUNDLA: Guys [like Mikan] brought the game into its popu-larity. The pros before this time were just a bunch of bums and tramps. In our era, college graduates started to come in. Mikan and Pollard were from college. The old pros from Sheboygan and Oshkosh, for in-stance, were a bunch of pickups, you know, they never went to college or anything. They were called sandlotters. Pro basketball became real popular because of the new breed of men coming in and their character.

CS

The transition didn't happen overnight. But we Lakers did our best to bring quality professional basketball to the rest of the coun-try. We rode the bus all through the Dakotas, Wisconsin, Iowa and the Tri-Cities area — I swear, we stopped at every American Le-gion Club in the country as part of the tour. (In later years, as our popularity grew so did our exhibition tour, taking us all the way to Hawaii.) The Lakers played a lot of exhibition games, often smack dab in the middle of the season between regularly scheduled games, whenever we could get a date.

It was a wonderful experience because we met so many differ-ent people. The fans would drive for miles and miles to see us play. We would play the local team and then pack up and leave for the next town. I can still remember bouncing into those small towns, my lanky frame folded to fit on the board-hard seats of the bus. At

6 feet, 10 inches and 245 pounds, I could have done without all the bus travel. But we were young — I was only twenty-four — and we enjoyed the opportunity to play. We didn't know enough to complain about all the extra games, which we usually weren't paid for.

In the NBL, the teams played in small towns like Sheboygan, Oshkosh, Syracuse, and, of course, Fort Wayne. The Fort Wayne Zollner Pistons played their games in a small enclosed gym at the North Side High School. It was known affectionately as "The Snake Pit." The court was enclosed on all sides by seven-foot walls that were only a couple feet from the endlines and sidelines. A fast-break layup was a dangerous proposition there — you could easily break a bone crashing with a defender into the wall.

ᑕᏰ

BOB PETTIT: I remember playing in Fort Wayne, Indiana, in that small gymnasium, where the fans would reach out to a guy like Mikan and grab at him or throw things. In Syracuse, they had a guy they called "The Strangler." He'd reach over and grab an opposing player by the throat. I caught the end of that type of thing, where they were playing in high school gyms.

I think that George, more than any other player, brought basketball from the small town, high school arenas to the metropolitan cities. He also ushered in the era of the big man. Up until that time, he was the biggest man in the game.

ᑕᏰ

Fort Wayne was a tough place to play. Worse than the walls were 5,500 screaming Indiana fans hanging just above you over the top of the walls. You felt like you were playing basketball in the old gladiator days. Instead of throwing you to the lions, Fort Wayne fans would throw things at you.

The Lakers were playing in the Snake Pit one time in 1949 after Slater Martin had joined the team from the University of Texas. As we warmed up before the game, he listened to the fans yelling and hollering at us. Now, Slater was only 5 feet, 10 inches tall and fresh out of college. He came over to where I was shooting and said to me, "Well, I'm going to stand next to you in case they get violent."

About that time, somebody had unscrewed the regulator cap off a radiator, which heated the place, and threw it down on the court. It bounced in front of Slater and me and then over our heads. Martin says, "I'm getting away from here — they're aiming for you."

The starting five members of the 1948-49 BAA championship team: (from l to r)
Don Carlson, Jim Pollard, George Mikan, Arnie Ferrin and Herm Schaefer with
coach John Kundla. *(Courtesy of George Mikan)*

He went over to warm up with the rest of the team, who knew better and had already abandoned me.

Sometimes it was tough just getting onto the court in Fort Wayne. One particular Pistons fan was an older woman by the name of Ma Collins, and she had a big saddlebag purse that she always carried. As we would come into the arena, she'd be sitting up by the player entrance, and she would wield that saddlebag and whack us over the head with it before the game even started. I used to go after her and growl at her to move her back to her seat so she wouldn't hit us.

Ironically, Ma Collins and I got to be great friends. Later on, when she was dying of cancer, Fort Wayne officials asked me to go visit her in the hospital. When I went up to see her, she said, "George, we always liked you guys, but we liked our team better."

I just asked her where she learned to swing her bag like that — she was pretty good at it.

Fort Wayne was a place where anything could happen. I recall one mid-February game when we were battling it out with the Pistons. The fans were particularly raucous that night, giving me the usual bad time but with a little more intensity. We held the lead for most of the game. In the fourth quarter, I was fouled and went to the line for my shot. (At the time, the rules allowed only one free throw after a foul.) I used an underhand style for shooting free throws throughout my career, and just as I dipped down to make the shot, I felt what appeared to be a bee-sting on the back of my left leg.

I rubbed my leg and wondered what a bee was doing inside the building in the middle of the winter. Then again, it was the Snake Pit — who knew what could be in that place. Just then, I was stung again, this time in the rear-end. I complained to the referee, even showing him the red spot on my leg where I had been bitten, but he merely laughed it off.

I quickly dipped and made the free throw and forgot about it until a few minutes later, when I went to the line again. There were only seconds left, and the game was tied at 79, so the shot was important. I lined up the shot, dipped and then straightened out as if to shoot and was stung again. I whirled quickly and saw a small orange BB pellet rolling on the floor.

I picked it up and told the ref, "Hey, they're shooting at me!"

I made the free throw, but I still have the shot in my leg today. I used to be able to feel the BB in my leg, but it has moved.

At the time, I thought the authorities were derelict in their duty for not jailing the culprits. As I said then, "I'm studying to become a lawyer, and I know there are laws against hunting inside the city limits."

Raucous fans were not limited to Fort Wayne. In many of the small arenas, like Syracuse and Oshkosh, the fans were rabid for their team. Unfortunately, they were also situated very close to the court. Since the players were known less for their table manners than for their rough brand of ball, their aggressiveness seemed to transfer to the intensely loyal fans in these smaller towns. When an on-court brawl broke out, it was not uncommon for fans to join in. And when a visiting player was knocked into the first couple of rows by an opponent, he often didn't get out of the seats without first picking up a few more bruises.

Just taking the ball out of bounds was hazardous. Fans would pinch us, hit us, pull the hair on our legs, try to burn us with lit cigarettes, or throw things at us, like bolts, paper clips or packs of gum. It was a bit distracting, but you generally laughed it off — if you didn't get hurt — and ultimately you got used to it.

In fact, back in the early 1920s, basketball courts had been enclosed with rope netting, like cages (hence the name "cagers" for players). When the cage was later outlawed, places such as Davenport and Moline kept the netting behind each basket because fans would often throw bottles or cans at players and even shake the basket when visiting teams were shooting at it.

That kind of stuff from the fans wasn't so bad, though. It just made me want to beat their team all the more.

CS

VERN MIKKELSEN: The fans were pretty rough on George. They always cried the old refrain that he was coming in there and beating up on their players. And George thrived on it. The more they hollered, the more they screamed and the more they booed, the more George said, "Give me that ball. Let's get this game going."

He would thrive on that kind of atmosphere. That was his determination, an absolute in-born desire to win the game against all odds. He could be 10 points down with two minutes to go and on a timeout, and he would be after us to get with it, saying "We can win this game.

Let's not give up. Let's do it." With leadership like that, the rest of it comes easy.

☙

As a team, we wondered if all the rowdiness might change in the 1948-49 season because the Lakers moved to a new league. After just one season in the National Basketball League — and a championship season to boot — the Lakers pulled up stakes and joined the rival Basketball Association of America. The BAA played in big arenas in major cities, so hostile crowds and claustrophobic courts were a thing of the past, right? Well, not exactly. Rochester, Fort Wayne and the Indianapolis Kautskys (who would rename themselves the Jets), three of the NBL's top teams, had defected with us. We still had to play in the Snake Pit.

There were bigger concerns, though. The NBL threatened lawsuits because they claimed the BAA had raided its league, forcing it to struggle along for the 1948-49 season. And that's precisely what the NBL did, try to put together a season out of the remaining teams and a few odds and ends of players. But looking back on it now, what would happen almost seemed inevitable: The BAA, a new league formed mainly by hockey team owners looking to fill empty dates in their arenas, had the big money, the big cities and the big arenas. But the NBL, a more established league, had the stars, and the powerful BAA team owners wanted the stars in their big arenas — particularly me. They saw the crowds the Lakers drew barnstorming around the country or playing the Globetrotters in Chicago Stadium. The places were always packed to see us play.

Sid Hartman was at the meeting of BAA owners with Max Winter when the move happened.

☙

SID HARTMAN: The BAA tried to steal two teams. They didn't really want Minneapolis and Rochester initially — they just wanted Fort Wayne and Indianapolis for their Eastern division. Max and I knew that if Fort Wayne and Indianapolis left the NBL, eventually the league would fold. The BAA officials had a meeting at the Morris Hotel in Chicago, and Max and I prevailed. We met with the BAA, and then they took us in. Later that same day, they took Rochester in. You could jump in those days.

The BAA didn't want Minneapolis originally, because they didn't want Mikan playing with Minneapolis. They thought by taking Fort

*Wayne and Indianapolis, they could break up the NBL. I suppose they
thought if the [NBL] folded that one of their clubs would get Mikan.
Mikan in one of the bigger cities — that would help their league.*

*We had to get voted in. At the meeting, Max Winter made a
wonderful plea and they decided to take four teams rather than two.*

cs

There were also rumors of my going to play for the Chicago
Stags that summer of 1948, but I was happy playing for Minneapolis, no matter what league we were in. The BAA was my third league
in three seasons, so I set out to conquer that as well.

We improved our team in the 1948-49 season by adding three
players who would make an impact with our squad: guard Don
Forman, from New York University, guard Whitey Kachan, an old
teammate of mine from DePaul, and 6-foot, 4-inch forward Arnie
Ferrin. Ferrin joined the Lakers from the University of Utah, where
he had just helped his school win the NCAA title. We figured that
the new competition in the BAA would just make us stronger.

The biggest difference I found in the new league was two more
minutes attached to each quarter of the game. Games in the BAA
were forty-eight minutes long rather than the forty minutes we'd
been used to in the NBL. Many people thought it might take its toll
on the big men, such as myself. "You'll probably knock a couple of
years off Mikan's basketball career," Max Winter was told.

But I looked at the longer game as giving us more chances to
score. And in our first game in the new league, against the defending BAA champion Baltimore Bullets, we did just that. Herm
Schaefer scored 23 points as we knocked off the Bullets, 84-72. It
was a great way to start the season, going into a battle of two league
champions and coming away with a win.

We actually struggled a bit out of the gate, though, losing four
of our first seven games in 1948-49. But probably the biggest game
of the early season for me came on November 19, 1948, against the
Chicago Stags in Chicago. Not only was it a homecoming for me in
my new league, but it was the first time I would face my brother Ed
in the pro ranks.

The Chicago media made a big deal of Mikan vs. Mikan, calling
it a family feud between two brothers on the court. Ed was 6 feet, 8
inches at the time and playing center for the Stags, who were rolling along without a defeat that season. It would be a tough road

game for the Lakers because Chicago, once again, had a Mikan on a home team.

Ed was quoted as saying that once we got on the court, the fact that we were brothers was irrelevant. The papers made a big deal out of that. But Ed was right. We had played hard against each other at college practices for DePaul — we were certainly going to give it our all now as opponents for the first time.

When Ed and I met for dinner at Mikan's Tavern before the game, we kidded back and forth, each asking the other to take it easy. Mom wanted us both to score the same number of points in the game so everyone would be happy. But both Ed and I knew that when we took the court, the only blood to be worried about was the blood spilling out of yourself.

My future teammate Slater Martin remembers another dinner at the Tavern that illustrates how, in the Mikan family, basketball was thicker than blood:

కు

SLATER MARTIN: George is from Joliet, and every time after we played in Chicago, we'd go over to his family's place and eat with his mother and father and all. George's brother Ed was playing with Chicago, and we were playing them one time and his mother and father came to the game with his other brother, Joe. George just beat up on Ed something terrible. He hit him on the eye, kind of put a little gash over it, scratched him all up.

After the game was over, we were sitting around talking, and his mother says to him, "Georgie, how come you hit your brother Eddie?"

"Momma," he says, "we were playing a game. If you had been in there, I'd have to hit you, too." That's the kind of competitor he was.

కు

That Lakers-Stags game was every bit the battle it was touted to be. The Lakers won 85-81, led by 28 points from Herm Schaefer. In the battle of the Mikans, I scored 20 points and held Ed to 0. I was berated by some DePaul students after the game for giving my brother such a beating. But winning was the point, and if I had allowed Ed to score just 5 points, the Stags would have beaten us. That's not what the Lakers paid me to do.

The Lakers faced Ed Mikan in the annual College All-Stars game a couple weeks later. As winners of the World Professional Basketball Tournament the year before, we were invited to represent the

George, surrounded by most of the New York Rens, goes up for two of his 40 points in a 1948 game. *(Courtesy AP/Wide World Photos)*

pros. As one of the top college players the previous season, Ed was playing the pivot for the collegians. But Ed and I didn't spend much time on the court together that night — he didn't get into the game until late, and I fouled out shortly after. But let it be said that I never shut out Ed again. He made sure of that.

Sizing up the rest of our new league, the Washington Capitals appeared to be the cream of the BAA crop. They started out the 1948-49 season by winning their first thirteen games and looked to be the new team that would give us the most trouble.

Of course, we still had Fort Wayne and our old nemesis, the Rochester Royals, to contend with. And with those teams, things stayed pretty much the same. In other words, we'd get harassed in Fort Wayne and would battle Rochester in close, tough games.

Throughout the 1948-49 season, I engaged in a battle for the BAA scoring lead with the jump-shooting Joe Fulks from the Philadelphia Warriors. The media had a lot of fun with it, but Joe and I were just playing our game, trying to help our teams win. Fulks held the BAA scoring record from 1946-47, and I guess I fired the first salvo on January 30, 1949, by setting a new BAA single-game mark at 48 points. (The old record was 47 from the previous season, held by Carl Braun of the New York Knicks.) Fulks scored 63 a few weeks later, and the press ran with it, talking about a Mikan-Fulks feud, even to the point of fueling trade rumors that had me or Pollard going to the Warriors for Fulks. After Fulks got on a roll, Philly coach Eddie Gottlieb reported that he "wouldn't trade Fulks for Mikan and $10,000 to boot."

Coach Kundla just called the trade talk ridiculous. He pointed out that Pollard and I both had an ability to rebound and pass the ball that Fulks didn't. (I had 140 assists to 53 for Fulks at one point in the season.) John noted that we were in first place, compared to fourth for the Warriors. He didn't need to say any more.

I ended up having a decent season, scoring 1,698 points for a 28.3 points-per-game average. That number was a league-leader and quickly put the Fulks-Mikan scoring feud to rest. In the papers, I was starting to hear people refer to me as "unstoppable." With my passing and Pollard's quickness, I could get out of the double team, and there weren't enough big men to stop me consistently one-on-one. Many of our opponents were at a loss on how to defend the Lakers because Pollard and I caused such problems underneath. Later on, Gottlieb was heard to recant his statement and say he would trade his whole team (except for Paul Arizin) for Mikan.

As players, we tried to remain above the media hype. After the season, Joe Fulks sent me a Western Union telegraph that read:

> *"George Mikan: Congratulations on new record. Better start taking it easy. You're making the rest of us look like amateurs.*
> *— "Joe Fulks Phila Warriors."*

The Lakers finished the regular 1948-49 season with a 44-16 record, one game behind the Royals in the Western Division, but good enough to be in the BAA playoffs. But first we had to play the Globetrotters in Minneapolis in another pre-postseason tune-up. We had played them earlier that year (February 28, 1949) at Chicago Stadium, and now we had a loss to avenge. In Chicago, we had played without the services of Jim Pollard and Swede Carlson, who were sitting out with injuries, and the Trotters had cleaned up on us. They had even felt comfortable enough with their lead to have some fun, putting on quite a show for the fans and topping it off with a 49-45 win.

When the Globetrotters trotted to Minneapolis on March 14, 1949, we made sure that wasn't going to happen again. The Globetrotters were a big attraction, but we were a championship team and we had some pride of our own. So I met with Pollard before the game, and we decided to take it to them. When the dust settled, we beat them 68-53 in front of 10,122 fans, the largest crowd ever at the Minneapolis Auditorium. It was kind of fun to watch Don Forman do a little entertaining of his own by performing a dribbling act to rival the best of the Trotters' ball handlers.

As soon as this fun was over, it was back to the serious games at hand. In the first round of the BAA playoffs, on March 23, we played the Stags and young Ed Mikan. The Stags also had the previous season's leading scorer in Max Zaslofsky, but we were still too much for them. In the first game of the series, Ed played like he can and scored 10, while Zaslofsky put in 22. I scored 37 on our way to an 84-77 win at the Minneapolis Auditorium. The next night in Chicago, we beat them 101-85 and I scored 38. It was a fast series and a good one to get out of the way, because the Stags had a good club.

We were rewarded with Rochester in the second round of the playoffs. Arnie Risen was well and whole this time, so there would be no complaining about unfair matchups by Royals fans.

The first game, played in Rochester, was one to remember. We actually had a 17-point lead well into the second half, thanks to a strong defense that held the Royals down. But Rochester made a surge and came back to take the lead with less than two minutes remaining in the game. Tony Jaros tied it with only eighteen seconds to go, and then Arnie Ferrin was fouled with six seconds remaining. Our team had missed only one free throw all night (23-for-24) when Ferrin came to the line — and he was the guy who had missed it. But this time Ferrin connected and knocked down the winning shot for an 80-79 victory on the road.

Heading back to Minneapolis, we encountered a problem that would plague the Lakers throughout my career. The Minneapolis Auditorium was booked with a trade show, so we had to find other accommodations for the second-round BAA playoffs. Unfortunately, our second home, the Minneapolis Armory, where we played many of our games, was also taken, so we headed to St. Paul to play the game.

Such a move bolstered the confidence of the Royals. We had a very good home record at the Minneapolis Auditorium, and Royals coach Les Harrison felt that the chosen site, the St. Paul Auditorium, would be like a neutral-site game. He was right.

It probably had much to do with the name of our team, the Minneapolis Lakers, but St. Paul never supported us as strongly as her sister city across the Mississippi River. Thankfully, many Minneapolis fans crossed the river to give us some hometown support. But it would not be the last time the Lakers went in search of a building to play their playoff games.

Fortunately, the new site didn't affect the outcome of the game. The Royals squad boasted several future Hall of Famers in Bob Davies, Red Holzman and Bobby Wanzer, yet they could not hold their third-quarter lead. We kept the high-powered Royals offense from scoring a field goal in the final quarter of the second game and beat them 67-55. That loss meant the end of the series. Afterward, Harrison said he'd never seen his team held without a field goal for an entire quarter, and he predicted an easy victory for the Lakers in the finals.

On April 4, 1949, we met the Washington Capitals for the first game of the BAA championship. The Capitals had finished the regular season with a 38-22 record and had outlasted the New York Knicks in the semifinals. The Caps were coached by a young fiery guy by the name of the Red Auerbach. Red, of course, went on to a nice coaching career in Boston, but he was skipper of the Capitals and then Tri-Cities before that.

I'll never forget the first time Auerbach came to the Minneapolis Auditorium. As he was watching his players warm up before the game, he seemed to be growing more and more agitated. Suddenly, he began complaining that the baskets were too tall. He demanded that the basket height be measured.

The refs thought he was crazy, holding up the game twenty minutes in front an increasingly hostile crowd for this grandstanding. After the game was over (which we won), Red stayed on the court and had a custodian measure the baskets with a ten-foot pole. No one wanted to go near Red with one after that.

Auerbach was wrong about the basket height, but he was right about another measurement in the Minneapolis Auditorium. He constantly complained that the court there was too narrow, and it was — at 48 feet across, it was 2 feet narrower than the normal 50-foot courts. Red liked to say that no one could get past our defense at the Minneapolis Auditorium because there was no room. When the 6-foot, 9-inch Vern Mikkelsen joined the Lakers in the summer of 1949, the rumor started flying that when Mikkelsen, Pollard and Mikan stretched their arms straight out from their sides, fingertip to fingertip across the court, they could reach from one wall in the Auditorium to the other.

While that was an exaggeration, our big line was pretty imposing at the Minneapolis Auditorium. On the other hand, the cramped quarters made it easier for opponents to sink in on me — and then we would turn around and do the same to them. The Auditorium was our home court, and we used it to our advantage. Unfortunately, it seemed as though we never got to play there when the championship was on the line. And the 1948-49 BAA was no different — the title game was played in St. Paul.

The first two games of the championship were played at the Minneapolis Auditorium, with the Lakers jumping out to a promising head start. In the opening game, we started real strong, but the Caps battled back twice to tie it. Ultimately, 42 points by me and late free throws by Don Carlson salted away an 88-84 victory.

The very feisty Auerbach told reporters the next day that, "George Mikan will not score 42 tonight." The Caps had had a little success clamping down on me late in the first game, and Red expected to use that strategy the entire second game.

True to their coach's word, the Caps held me to 10 points that game, a season low, thanks to double- and triple-teaming of the Laker offense. But John Kundla saw it coming, and we countered by having me pass the ball out to the perimeter for outside shots. That night, Schaefer had 16 points, Carlson had 13 and Pollard got the lion's share of rebounds, while I was tying up half the Capitals team. Kundla's plan worked to perfection, and the Lakers, accused of being a one-man team, showed how effective we could be when that one man passes rather than scores. With a commanding 76-62 victory, we took a 2-0 lead in the series.

When the best-of-seven series moved on to Washington, we grabbed a 94-74 win and Harrison's prediction of an easy championship for the Lakers was starting to look pretty accurate. The Caps had their backs to the wall, and I was back scoring 35 points. Pollard and I were unbeatable on the boards, nearly shutting Washington out of rebounds, and Jim knocked down 18 points to boot.

Things looked real good for the Lakers to grab another title in another league, when in game four, the unexpected happened. It was four minutes into the game, and I had already scored 12 points to give us a 16-7 lead. I went up for a rebound with the Caps' center, Kleggie Hermsen. The collision knocked me into the first row of seats and I hit my right arm on the back of one chair, breaking a bone in it near my wrist.

I remember laying near the end line. I didn't know my arm was broken — all I knew was that it hurt like heck. My old friend Red Auerbach came up to check on my condition. He said, "Drag him off the court, and let's get the game going." Red doesn't remember it that way, though.

&

RED AUERBACH: No, [I never said that]. He's full of shit. George didn't need any help. He was so damn good that he didn't need any more help.

&

Senator Hubert Humphrey signs George's cast on his broken arm while he is in Washington for the 1948 BBA championship series against the Capitals. *(Courtesy of UPI/Corbis-Bettmann)*

Well, we got the game going again, and I managed to score 15 more points left-handed. But I wasn't myself, and my teammates seemed more concerned about my arm than playing. We lost 83-71, which gave the Capitals new life. They ran with it, too, winning the next game by a score of 74-65. I played with a wrap on my arm because the officials wouldn't let me play with a cast. But I still managed to score 22 points, mostly by shooting left hooks. We still led the series, three games to two, but we would have to return home to finish the Capitals off.

We played the sixth game at the St. Paul Auditorium because of scheduling conflicts at both the Minneapolis Auditorium and the Armory — at least Red Auerbach could be happy with that news. But by the final reckoning, we won by 21 points, 77-56. Auerbach said, "Mikan was Mikan, but Schaefer did it." I scored 29 points, but Herm's 17 points plus dominance on the boards by Pollard and Ferrin gave the Lakers our second consecutive title in the same number of years.

The Lakers had now been the champions of two leagues, and I personally had played on three title teams in a row. I was beginning to feel comfortable in my new home of Minnesota and really excited to be in a basketball league that was on the verge of making the game grow. We weren't about to stop barnstorming the small arenas around the country, but at least the Lakers had made a name for themselves in the biggest ones, as well. It was an exciting time to be in professional basketball. You could sense that the game was changing and there were good things ahead.

Taking barnstorming to the next level: George is greeted in style when the Lakers visit Hawaii. *(Courtesy of George Mikan)*

⚞10⚟
Another Season, Another League, Another Title
1949-1950

Travel is a given in professional basketball. It's just that in those days of all-night train rides, buses on back roads and making connections at four in the morning, it was a lot harder than it is now. But we expected the travel. What we never expected was to be moving from one league to the next quite so often. Now, as the Lakers prepared for the 1949-50 season, we were also readying ourselves for yet another new league — our third in three years.

For me, jumping leagues was becoming old hat. In the spring of 1946, I'd gone from the NCAA to the NBL and the Chicago Gears; in 1947, I moved with the Gears to the PBLA and then three weeks later, when the PBLA folded, to the Lakers in the NBL. In 1948, the Lakers and I went to the BAA. Now, in the fall of 1949, we were heading to the newly formed National Basketball Association, the NBA, created by a merger of the NBL and BAA.

In a span of three-and-a-half years, I had competed for two different professional teams under the auspices of four different governing bodies and won three championships. It was enough to make a guy's head start spinning.

Perhaps because of my experience in jumping leagues, I was keenly aware of the instability of pro basketball. I'd seen leagues start up and I'd seen them fail, so I made sure to have backup plans for me and my growing family. Pat and I had had our first child, a son named George Lawrence Mikan III but called Larry, on April 8, 1948. The spring of 1949 brought Pat and me our second child, a son named Edward Terrence and called Terry. On June 8, 1949, I received my law degree from DePaul. I figured practicing law to be a good alternative if basketball went down the tubes.

But even though this new league seemed another herald of instability, in reality the prospects for professional basketball had just taken a turn for the better. There was something different about the NBA. It had been created by the merger of two existing leagues, rather than cropping up as a new league to siphon strength from the others, as had happened in the past. The NBA was based on the promise of joining the best of those two leagues together, and with that came a sense of hope.

And while I didn't know it at the time, the Lakers and I would play a big role in helping this new league to thrive and grow.

CB

BOB PETTIT: I never played much against George in his heyday — I came into the league with Milwaukee in 1954 — but he was one of the real super players that ever played in the NBA. I thought the NBA owes George Mikan a great debt of gratitude, because he brought the league almost single-handedly out of very small humble beginnings that it had into making it a household name around the country. I think of George Mikan, and I think the NBA and all of us ought to be extremely proud that he played and was able to give us a lot of the opportunities that we had coming after him.

CB

The NBA was formed out of a tough battle between two feisty rivals. After the BAA had "raided" the NBL of four teams in 1948, the NBL had been left in a shambles. No one expected it to survive the 1948-49 season, much less be a player when the 1949-50 season came around.

But after the 1949 college basketball season ended, NBL officials got together and signed en masse the graduating seniors of Kentucky, a team that had just won back-to-back NCAA titles. This group of Kentucky players had also made up a good portion of the 1948 Olympic team. The new NBL franchise called itself the Olympians and located in Indianapolis, where the BAA had just acquired a team. It was a brilliant move, and probably came about because the players were given stock in the team. With big names like Alex Groza and Frank Beard, the NBL had once again kept the star players out of the BAA's big arenas.

The formation of the Olympians hastened the inevitable. For the 1949-50 season, the six remaining NBL teams joined the eleven BAA franchises, and the NBA was off and running. While the league has today played its fiftieth season, it went through some pretty spectacular growing pains in its infancy. (Groza and Beard, for example, were banned from basketball for life when their part in the 1950 college basketball scandals came to light.) Over the next few seasons, teams folded and new ones joined until in 1955-56 the NBA was whittled down to an eight-team league of solid teams. Boston, Fort Wayne, Minneapolis, New York, Philadelphia, Rochester, St. Louis and Syracuse became the basic league structure that has evolved into today's 29-team league. Those core teams have changed and moved over the years — the search for greener pastures has always been part of professional sports — but the Celtics, Pistons, Lakers, Knicks, Warriors, Royals (now Kings), Hawks and Nationals (now 76ers) are franchises that still exist today.

Back in 1949, however, we had the whole future still to create. It was exciting being in a new league, especially because no matter how you looked at it, the Lakers had to be considered the reigning champs. In the past two seasons, we had won crowns in both the BAA and the NBL. This meant that the sixteen other teams in the new league would be gunning for us. So what did we do about it? We drafted three new rookie starters for our team.

Joining Pollard and me in the starting lineup for 1949-50 were Slater Martin, a former All-American from the University of Texas, Bob Harrison, a 6-foot, 1-inch guard from the University of Michigan, and Vern Mikkelsen, the powerful center from Hamline University in Minnesota. A month into the season, we picked up another Minnesota player, forward Harry 'Bud' Grant from the University of Minnesota. Bud would later switch sports and go on to become a successful football player in Philadelphia and an award-winning football coach in Canada and Minnesota. He led the Minnesota Vikings to four Super Bowls on his way to the National Football League's Hall of Fame. But before that, Bud played basketball with the Lakers and earned himself a championship title. Long before anyone heard of Deion Sanders or Bo Jackson, there was another two-sport professional athlete in Bud, one who reached some of the highest honors in both.

Bud played reserve forward for the Lakers for two years, and he was a great defensive player — often assigned to cover the opponents' best offensive player. But it was tough for him to crack a lineup that included such heavyweights as future Hall of Famers Pollard and Mikkelsen. Once Mik started playing forward, the size of our front line became the biggest and most dominant in the league.

Grant was only going to get so much time with such a lineup.

Slater Martin would become our point guard, bringing the ball up court and calling the plays. When he was first drafted, though, coach Kundla hadn't known exactly what to do with him. The 5-foot, 10-inch Martin was fleet-footed and used to a less deliberate style of play than we followed. However, his quickness soon became a powerful weapon in our offense. Slater was a great playmaker, outstanding on the defense, and had a great outside shot when we needed him to score.

The Lakers always had a theory on the court, one that every team in history has probably had as well: feed the hot hand. One night in Fort Wayne, Slater was playing the point and he was hotter than heck. He scored 42 points on our way to a victory, which was a fantastic total for a guard back then. After the game, a few of us were outside signing autographs, and a member of the crowd yells out: "Hey, Slater, you sure were lucky tonight."

Without looking up from the autograph, Slater tells the guy, "Yeah, it seems the harder I work, the luckier I get."

Mikkelsen was not a starting forward right away. As a college center weighing in at 6 feet, 7 inches and 230 pounds, he was brought in to understudy me at the post. I was only twenty-five at the time, and Mik was twenty-one. For a time, he wasn't sure what he was doing joining the Minneapolis Lakers, who already had the best center in the game.

ଔ

VERN MIKKELSEN: I was a center in college, and to come over and play with the Lakers didn't seem to offer many opportunities. George was all-everything by that time. Here I am, an All-American, I've got credentials, but I'm certainly not going to move him out of there. Anybody could figure that out. Therefore, I was reluctant to sign with the Lakers, simply because there wasn't going to be an opportunity to play.

At the time, Max Winter convinced me that George was going to retire soon, so I figured it would be OK. Of course, Mikan played for five more years.

But come draft time, a team takes the best player available and then figures out what to do with them afterwards. Which the Lakers did. I know they didn't have a blueprint that would move me over to the right forward spot and make me into a power forward. That wasn't even contemplated, but that's what happened. So it worked out very well.

Two Hall of Famers: Lakers' coach John Kundla and George Mikan. The pair won six professional basketball championships together. *(Courtesy of George Mikan)*

cs

It was around Christmas-time in 1949 when that happened. Coach Kundla wanted to figure out some way to get me and Mik both on the court at the same time. Mik was a tough ballplayer and a good rebounder who was trained in the classic back-to-the-basket manner of a post player. Kundla wanted both of our talents (not to mention our size) on the court at the same time.

Kundla started with the idea of a double-pivot offense, which had both of us playing the center position, Mik playing a high post and me playing the low post, underneath the basket. But with both centers' defenders crashing the middle, it became too crowded for me under the basket. It simply didn't work.

So Kundla went back to the drawing board. This time, he pulled Vern out of the lane and turned him around to face the basket, thus creating the NBA's first power forward. In doing so, Kundla moved Mik out to the perimeter, where Vern worked hard to develop a set shot from which he could shoot or pass underneath to me.

For Mik, it was a huge adjustment. He had played with his back to the basket his entire career, and now he was shooting the ball head on. But Kundla was determined to keep Mik on the court for rebounding, and the result was a very powerful defensive and offensive rebounding front line. Mik scored plenty, primarily off offensive rebounds. Over time, his unique style of play developed into the modern-day power forward position, which serves as a big body to clear out defenders for the shooters (in our case, me and Pollard) and crashes the boards in a big way for rebounds. And Mik could clear the boards with the best of them.

cs

The 1949-50 season was a bit of a rollercoaster ride. We started out strong by beating Philadelphia and Joe Fulks, who had battled it out with me the previous season for the scoring title. Fulks held the only BAA scoring record that I didn't own — the most points in a game with 63. This particular night, he bested me, 20 to 17, but Pollard topped us all, scoring 30 to lead us to victory in our NBA season opener. We went on to win the next three games.

I was a little out of shape early in the season, and we lost five of our first fourteen ballgames, mostly on the road. I needed to put in a little outside work, so I started heading down to the YMCA instead of going to a movie on road trips. My teammates picked up the slack while I got myself into playing shape. It took me about three weeks. But sometime after the Christmas holidays, what with my being in shape and our innovative starting lineup of Mikan, Pollard and Mikkelsen, we started to get back on track.

With our new, huge front line, the Lakers went to town. We were particularly tough on our home court, the Minneapolis Auditorium, because it was two feet narrower than most courts, which made us even more formidable. We lost only one game there all season.

Our tough lineup didn't make us any friends on the road, of course. The Rochester Royals had moved to the NBA along with us, and they were getting tired of being beaten by the Lakers — as were their fans. One game in Rochester, Jim Pollard was driving to the basket, wide open, and a Royals player tackled him on his way to the basket. And the referees called it a jump ball.

I went crazy and ran down the court to complain. I was the captain, and it was my job to try to talk to the officials — which was occasionally very difficult. We were standing there jawing about this football play on the basketball court, and suddenly some fan throws a knife at me. It stuck right in the wooden court at my feet. I just stood there watching it wobble back and forth.

"Oh, man," I said, stopping in midsentence. I was a little shaken up. I just turned and walked away — I didn't wait around to give the person who threw it another shot.

The next day, the reporters mentioned the incident in the papers. A few days later, I received a package in the mail from some Royals fan. He had carved my name into a knife handle and sent it to me with a little note that read: "Here, go ahead and finish the job." Shortly after that, another letter arrived for the Lakers from Rochester. It contained a series of razor blades, and on each razor blade was a little epitaph for each player. Mine instructed me to cut my wrists. The fans were sort of volatile toward us in those days.

But we were also the NBA's biggest drawing card, making headlines and bringing in fans wherever we played. On December 14, 1949, we were to play the Knickerbockers in New York, and when we got to town, the marquee outside Madison Square Garden alerted the city to that fact. Only the sign read slightly different than you'd expect, and it got me a in a lot of trouble with my teammates. The marquee, in big, bold letters, read "GEO MIKAN VS. KNICKS."

"Oh, man," I thought to myself, "they shouldn't have done that." And I was right. My teammates never let me forget it.

CB

VERN MIKKELSEN: There's a very famous photograph of George up on a stepladder wiping off the letters on the marquee outside Madison Square Garden, which read Mikan vs. the Knicks. Well, way back when, we figured to have a little fun with it.

Now, each player has their ritual that they go through before each game — you sit in the same place and take your clothes off in the same manner, the whole bit. So we come into the locker room, and with George's eyes, if he takes off his glasses, he can't see his hand in front of him. When George would get ready for a game, the first thing he'd do was take off his glasses and put them on top of a locker so nobody would step on them. Then he would very leisurely go about getting his clothes off and putting on his playing gear. And the last thing he would do was put on these playing glasses with a plastic band around the back of them.

We knew this ritual, so before the [December 14] game, Slater Martin says, "When George takes off his glasses, let's pretend like we're all getting dressed for the game. But we'll just sit there in our street clothes and act like we're going through the whole routine."

So we did that. We started talking about what we did that after-noon, talking about the pregame meal, saying "How you doing, George?" and joshing around. Finally, George gets all his gear just right. He stands up and puts on his playing glasses, and he turns around and we're all sitting there in our street clothes.

He says, "Hey, what are you guys doing?"

Slater says, "Didn't you see the marquee out front? It says you're playing the Knicks — go on out and play 'em."

George had a few choice words for us and told us to get our uni-forms on. We had a good laugh as we dressed for the game. And George enjoyed the joke as much as the rest of us.

CB

I guess you could have called me the original marquee player after something like that, but I knew full well I had a real good team behind me. And nowhere did I know that better than playing in the NBA. All the teams from both the old NBL and BAA had taken their lumps from the Lakers the previous two seasons, so they were constantly trying to figure different ways to beat us. Many of our old foes from the NBL were happy to have another crack at us.

A lot of our opponents' game strategy revolved around how to defend against me. So when they doubled- or triple-teamed me, or even sank down a couple of front men inside, it was essential that I had great ballplayers around me that I could pass to. My teammates had to be able to finish the play, and we had that kind of team.

One defensive strategy was to foul the heck out of me. In those days, the rules called for only one free throw after a foul, so some coaches preferred that I take a foul shot for one point rather than shooting the easier two points from under the basket. Eddie Gottlieb, coach of the Philadelphia Warriors, for example, had his players constantly foul me before I could shoot. Much to his chagrin, I was a pretty good free-throw shooter (sinking nearly 80 percent in 1949-50), and his strategy didn't always pay off. I used an underhand free-throw style that was popular in my day, but has since gone out of fashion. It wouldn't be bad for a player like Shaquille O'Neal, who struggles mightily at the free-throw line today, to try this underhand shot. What it lacks in style points, it more than makes up for in points on the board. A high percentage of players who used it were above-average free-throw shooters. I myself posted a career average of .767 from the line.

I encountered another defense when we played the Globetrotters on February 21, 1950. Trotters' coach Abe Saperstein appeared to have told his team to gang up on me. I remember that by the end of the game they had two men guarding me tight on both sides, and then floated two more in front of me. But that left Vern and Jim open for double-figure scoring, and we beat them by 76-60. I was still able to chip in 36. An unprecedented crowd of 21,666 fans, incredible for that day, watched the game at Chicago Stadium. It was also our first televised game, shown on WCCO-TV in Minneapolis.

But our slow start at the beginning of the season hampered us in the end, because we finished with a 51-17 record. Rochester, on the other hand, had gone on a big winning streak and ended the season tied with us, which forced a one-game playoff on March 21 for the Central Division championship (and $2,500 bonus money for the title). We flipped a coin to decide where to play, and the Royals won the flip. Winning in Rochester was always tough, and this game would be no different.

In the past, the Royals had tried everything to stop me: they'd doubled me, tripled me. This time, they covered me one-on-one.

Their game plan was to give me my points, but not let the rest of our team have theirs. They figured I was going to score, so if they kept the other players off the boards, they could win. It worked to a certain extent. We played a wild, see-saw game that was tied at 76 with only seconds remaining.

In the last seconds, coach Kundla called a play for Tony Jaros to bring the ball up court and work it in to me for the final shot. But the Royals must have anticipated that because they covered me tight under the hoop. Jaros threw the ball in to Pollard, who was supposed to get it in to me, as the clocked ticked down. But I was blanketed by several players, so Pollard threw the ball back to Jaros, who was not known as a prolific scorer. Jaros desperately moved around the perimeter, trying to find an opening to get me the ball. It didn't happen.

The time was nearly gone. Tony had back-pedaled to about 40 feet from the basket, and I was still covered. The only thing to do was shoot, and that's what I yelled: "Shoot, Tony, shoot!" With only four seconds to go, Tony let one fly from 40, a beautiful shot that went right through the hoop. It was an exciting win, and another tribute to the fine team we had.

The win over Rochester is especially amazing when you consider that only the night before we'd been at home in the Twin Cites playing another exhibition game against the Globetrotters. On March 20, 1950, we posted yet another victory over the Trotters, 69-54, at the St. Paul Auditorium. It was our third straight win against them. I got 21 points, Mikkelsen put in 18 and Pollard tallied another 16. Playing the Trotters exhausted us, but we were still able to pull together in Rochester and win.

After beating the Royals for the Central Division title, it was on to the playoffs themselves. That first year of the NBA's existence, there were three divisions, which made playoffs complicated. We won seven straight playoff games, beating the Chicago Stags, Fort Wayne Pistons and Anderson Packers in succession. That led to the finals against our friends from the NBL, the Syracuse Nationals with their player-coach Al Cervi. The Nationals had finished with a 51-13 record, the only team in the NBA with a better winning percentage than ours. And while the New York fans in Syracuse were not as vicious as those in Rochester, they felt the same about me and they relished a chance to renew their hatred now.

For the first game of the finals, the fans packed the State Fair Coliseum, where the Nationals had been 34-1 that season. The Nats' fans did plenty of yelling to get me off my game. But I loved the attention and scored 36 points in the opener to give it back to them in the only way I could. The first game against the Nats was back-and-forth, a lot like the Rochester game. As the game wound down, with only a minute remaining, we were behind by two, 66-64.

This time, we called a play for Pollard. The plan was for Bud Grant to dribble the ball up court and pass to Pollard for the tying shot. The appropriate picks were set for Pollard. He got the ball, but he was still covered and quickly threw it back to the rookie Grant. Grant says he was surprised as anyone to have the ball, but he took a long shot that went in to tie the game.

Syracuse then drove the ball back down court. Al Cervi took a shot, but I blocked his game-winning attempt. Grant rebounded the ball and threw it up court to Bob Harrison, who launched a forty-footer for the win as the time ticked away. Harrison, another rookie, just about jumped through the rafters in joy. We were lucky to come away with that 68-66 victory in the Nats' home stadium — lucky and pretty happy to boot.

Despite my teammate's last-minute heroics, it was still me that had inspired the Syracuse fans' ire — they would do anything they could to help their home team. After the first game, Kundla was being interviewed in the locker room, and he happened to mention that I was allergic to smoke and didn't really appreciate playing in smoky arenas. When that gem hit the papers the next morning, the Nats fans had their edge.

Before the second game that night, every single Nats' fan must have bought a cigar and brought it to the game to smoke it. Men, women and even some children, I suspect, were smoking cigars that night. The arena was so choked with cigar smoke, you couldn't see from our bench to the basket at the end of the floor. A wall of smoke hung like fog over the court the entire game.

ೞ

VERN MIKKELSEN: We were always the bad guys. But that always happens. When you win, everyone is after you. Every game is a championship game for every other team. We had to win just to prove that we were good enough. The fans would get all over us, and George was, of course, the perfect foil. He didn't take any back talk from anybody.

Deep in his heart, I think he enjoyed it. He was of the mind, "They're giving me a bad time, and here's looking at you," and then he put the ball in the hoop.

CR

Despite the smoke screen, I still managed to score 32 points, but the Nats pulled out the game, 91-85.

The series shifted back to Minnesota for the third and fourth games. We had to play at the St. Paul Auditorium again because of a trade show booked at our home court. We won both games anyway, taking a commanding lead in the series. The Nats clamped down on Pollard, so Mik and I were free to shoot. In the third game, I scored 28 and Mik scored 27 for a 91-77 victory — Mik played a whale of a game. The next night, we won 77-69 to go up three games to one.

When we returned to Syracuse, the fans got out their cigars again and the Nats beat us 83-76 in the fifth game. But we ended it in on our home floor, the Minneapolis Auditorium, in game six with a decisive 110-95 victory. I was able to score 40 points, and we won the admiration of the Nats' shooting star Al Cervi, who said we had a great ballclub.

He was right. In our first NBA season, we won the Central Division title and the NBA championship and took two games from the Globetrotters in exhibition play. We had also won our second consecutive College All-Star game earlier in the season, winning 94-86 and beating Alex Groza of Kentucky. The 1949-50 season had been a huge success for our team, including our three young starters. The future was looking bright for the Lakers.

Personally, this season was also one to remember. I was voted to several all-star teams, including the inaugural All-NBA First Team. I captured the league's scoring title, totaling 1,865 points over 68 games for a 27.4 average, my fourth scoring title in a row. I was also voted best player of my third consecutive league. All that, and I had golf to look forward to that summer.

But no award in basketball has made me happier than the one that I was given in the spring of 1950 when I was named Mr. Basketball of the first half of the twentieth century. That title was awarded by the Associated Press sportswriters and broadcasters of the United States. It put me in a group with Bobby Jones (golf), Jack Dempsey (boxing), Bill Tilden (tennis), Jim Thorpe (football) and

Man O' War (horse racing), who had won the honor for their respective sports. It also aligned me with my boyhood hero, Babe
Ruth, who was named Mr. Baseball of the first half-century. I never
cherished an honor more than being named Mr. Basketball alongside the great Babe Ruth. The Babe was long gone from baseball by
then, but my career was just beginning, so I felt determined to live
up to that honor in the time I had left. I never had to look any fur-
ther than that award for inspiration.

George battled Philadelphia's Joe Fulks for the scoring title in 1948-49, winning the first of three consecutive NBA titles for Big George. *(Courtesy of George Mikan)*

ೞ11ೞ
Playing with Pain
1950-1951

Pro basketball in the 1940s and '50s was a rough game — in some ways, I believe, rougher than it is today. Today's game is still physical, of course, and the players are certainly bigger and stronger than when I played. And with all the money tied up in professional basketball, well, bigger stakes always mean physical intensity. I just think that back in my day players generally accepted the pain associated with the game more. Let me cite an example:

During the 1995-96 season, forward A.C. Greene of the Phoenix Suns (formerly of the Los Angeles Lakers) received an angry elbow to the teeth from New York Knicks forward J.R. Reid. Reid knocked out Greene's two front teeth, and to Greene's credit, he did not retaliate. He simply walked over and collected his teeth. But the incident was hashed over in the media for weeks. Apparently, not much of this type of activity happens anymore, and the press had a field day castigating Reid.

Now, speaking as someone who had plenty of his own dental work rearranged on the court, back in the early days of the NBA that incident would have been just a blip on the screen. Greene, who was in the midst of a longest active consecutive game streak, played only one or two minutes each night following the incident until his mouth healed. While I applaud Greene for getting suited up and out on the court, such a maneuver to keep his streak intact would not have passed muster in our day. Someone would have probably hurt him worse. If we were able to still run and shoot, we would have kept right on playing. In those days, we kept playing out of fear for our jobs.

ೞ

BOB COUSY: [Back then,] the game was more difficult to control because there was so much less attention focused on it, certainly on a national level. Basketball was number four on the totem pole — we were last in line behind baseball, football and hockey. A lot of things would go on, fights and everything, that nobody knew about.

Nowadays, if Hakeem Olajuwon sneezes or throws an elbow you read about it in every paper in the country the next morning. In those days you could hurt somebody, draw blood, and nobody would know about it outside the city where it happened. The point is, I guess, that more outrageous things could go on without calling it to anyone's attention so it was more difficult for the officials to try to control the action.

ርጌ

VERN MIKKELSEN: A lot of people played with pain back then. I think I missed four games in ten years. At one time, I held the league record for most consecutive games [played]. People say you must have been pretty tough, but I say, "No, I was pretty stupid." We were afraid not to play. And we didn't let the coaches know when we were hurt. If you'd get out of the game, you didn't know if you were going to get back in again.

There was a huge amount of pride. I never heard of a guy not playing because of stomach cramps or saying "My back hurts" or whatever. Now we find that all the time. "I can't play because of back spasms." Well, you play through that stuff. You get the game going, the adrenaline starts flowing, and you don't even know that the pain is there.

I played one whole year with a terribly sprained ankle. Every game I literally made a cast out of tape for it myself. I wouldn't let the trainer do it because we had a different trainer in every place we played and they all tape differently. The ankle never healed, but I continued to play.

I had a shoulder with bursitis for two years [so bad that] I couldn't lift that arm over my head. But I didn't let anybody know about it — I did all my rebounding with my right hand. You were afraid of those things. There was no pension plan, no guarantees of any kind — it was pretty tenuous. We had to keep playing. "What do mean you're hurting? Get out there and play." That's what we were told.

ርጌ

Each team had a trainer but he never travelled with the team, so you had to learn to become your own trainer when you went on the road. Painkillers were nonexistent, and the injured reserve was an idea that was yet to come. If you were on the road and got cut, the opposing team might have someone on hand who could stitch you up or your coach might try to find a doctor in the audience. One game in Chicago Stadium, a guy put his finger in my nose and pulled it out, ripping my nose open like Jack Nicholson in the movie *Chinatown*. We just had the cut stitched up, and I got back in the ballgame.

Your coach didn't want you to miss any of the action, even if you didn't feel like playing yourself. And it wasn't only the Lakers with that kind of ethic. Just ask Ed Macauley, center for the Boston Celtics.

CG

ED MACAULEY: Injuries were part of the game. I got hit one night when I was with Boston, and they didn't have trainers or doctors following along with us. I told Red Auerbach that I thought something was wrong with my ribs. He said, "Naw, just tape 'em up. They'll be all right."

Finally, I got an X-ray taken. But the doctors didn't tell us about the X-rays in those days. They just told the coach. We didn't know what was going on.

Later on, when I came to the St. Louis Hawks, I got hit again. I went out to the hospital, and Dr. Stan London looked at the X-rays and said, "Well, you broke your rib again."

"What the hell do you mean?" I said. "I never broke my rib!"

"Oh, yes, you did."

"That damn Auerbach," I said. "He didn't even tell me that it was broken."

CG

Although I was a target on the court, I wasn't always on the receiving end of the pain. Back at DePaul, Ray Meyer had taught me a shooting maneuver in which I would lead my hook shot with the elbow of my nonshooting arm. As I would turn toward the basket to throw my hook, I used my elbow like the business end of a tire iron and cleared out the path for an open shot.

Other times, I used my elbows more surreptitiously — I got away with a lot of fouls that could have been called. I made sure to keep two hands on the ball when going up toward the basket, thereby avoiding the offensive foul. If I would've taken a hand off the ball when muscling through my opponents, the whistle would have blown for a foul. My elbows were definitely a part of my game, but so was my brain.

Rough play was just the way it was played back then. A guy had to use whatever advantages he could to win. But since many of my opponents were about as tall as my raised elbow, it became a bit of a feared — and quite effective — weapon.

ଔ

ED MACAULEY: George knocked the filling out of my tooth one night in St. Louis. He came around with that elbow, and I was going up to block the shot with my right hand when he hit me on the right side of my face where my teeth are and really rattled me. I spit the filling out and went down the court and tried to score on him. His elbows should be in the Hall of Fame.

ଔ

I built myself a reputation with my elbows, one I richly deserved. In one game, I recall, I got Paul Seymour of Syracuse fouled out by using my elbows. In fact, two of the Nationals' centers fouled out that day. Seymour was guarding me with about five minutes to go in the game. The Lakers had a good lead, and we really had nothing to worry about. But every time I got the ball, Seymour would pinch me, trying to get to me.

"Don't do that, Paul," I said. But he didn't listen.

The next time I got the ball, he pinched me again, and I turned around and elbowed him right in the middle of the forehead. I made the basket, the whistle blew and they called a foul on Seymour. He had a big knob bulging out of his forehead, but they called the foul on him. He just went crazy. He was so mad at me, I thought he wanted to kill me. Instead, he turned on my teammate, Billy Hasset, who was trying to calm him down, and said, "I can handle *you.*" And then he whacked him.

ଔ

SLATER MARTIN: George had a short hook shot where he'd just turn around and then jab that elbow right in your jaw if you got in his way. If he went left, he'd just raise his left elbow and knock the hell out of you.

There wasn't much anyone could do. George was a big man, he was wide and big, strong as hell. If you started to go by him, he'd raise that elbow and hold you out. If they fronted him, we'd whip that ball around the other side and throw it back to him from the other side. They tried everything in the world to beat him, but they couldn't do it.

ଔ

But I got my just dues for all that elbowing. In my later playing years, I had to wear elbow pads to protect my battered elbows. And because I used my elbows so often on other players or just to break my fall on the court, they are not the same today. In each of my elbows, the radius was fractured so many times that when it healed the bone grew spurs. Now, the bones won't go back into the sockets. I have only half the rotation in each of my arms today.

Of course, administering pain was a two-way street back then. I got as well as I gave, believe me. I was the object of many an attack and came away from most games with my own battle scars. But not everyone believed that. A reporter once came into our locker room and said the other team was complaining about how rough I had been playing. Frustrated at hearing this complaint for the umpteenth time, I ripped off my jersey to show him the assortment of bruises, welts and abrasions peppered across my chest.

"What do you think these are?" I bellowed at him. "Birthmarks?"

I figure that I collected 166 stitches throughout my basketball ca-reer. When I was playing, I broke my leg twice, had broken bones in both feet and fractured bones in both elbows, and broke my arm, nose, thumb and three fingers. In later years, I had to have my right knee cap removed because of the pounding that it took. Couple that with the sprains, strains and stretched tendons that every athlete gets, and I become a fairly good candidate to promote a national health care plan. As Jim Pollard once said, "Nobody gave George anything, he earned his baskets."

CB

BUD GRANT: We had trainers, but we never had the sophisticated equipment that they have now for treating injuries. I remember George playing with broken wrists and things like that. In fact, I think a broken wrist hampered one of our championships. But you had to play through that. And the guys that achieved greatness were the guys like Mikan, Mikkelsen and Pollard, who played through all those injuries and yet could play week in and week out.

Nowadays, somebody might say they don't feel good and then don't play. They got the flu or something. Well, nobody in our day ever said they had the flu and couldn't play. Things are different. They have bigger squads now, and they play more games — maybe they can take a day off once in a while. I know that we didn't feel that we ever could.

CB

I never thought twice about the injuries. In my childhood, I'd severely broken my leg playing basketball and from that point on, playing with pain just seemed to be part of the game. While I'm a little slow getting around these days, I have no regrets. If I were young and you put me on the court today, I'm sure I would play the same way.

One thing I would do today, however, is dunk the basketball.

Dunking was legal in our day, but frowned upon by coaches and players alike. Kundla would only let us do it in practice. During a game, dunking was considered showboating — I don't remember anyone getting away with it. If you dunked the ball over someone, you had best come down quickly because if you spent anytime hanging in the air, someone was liable to knock you into the fifth row for being such a hotdogger.

Wilt Chamberlain was the first real dunker in the game, but he was so tall, he probably couldn't help it. Don't get me wrong, all of the Minneapolis Lakers could dunk (except the 5-foot, 10-inch Slater Martin) — despite what some people today might imagine from watching our old footage. We just felt that winning was a better way to show up your opponent.

CB

VERN MIKKELSEN: People today tell me we weren't dunking because we couldn't. That was stupid — I was dunking in high school. I was capable of getting up high enough to bring the ball down. We could jump back in those days, too.

Two reasons we didn't [dunk back then]: 1. There was a rule against it (for a time) and 2. They frowned on it. There was a certain amount of showboating that was frowned upon. There were also some negatives to dunking. You miss that dunk and the rebound can go to about midcourt, giving the other team an easy basket.

Today, dunking has taken some of the finesse out of the game. Without the dunk, a guy like George would get the rebound and go right back up to the hoop. He's struggling through half a dozen arms, people hanging on him, and he's got to use brute force and power to get up there. Then in order to put it in the basket, he's got to relax and have the touch of a piano player to lay it in softly.

With the dunk, you can use total power. Power up and power down. You don't have to worry about the finesse thing. It becomes a radical change where you lose something of the game. You lose the fine touch — you don't need to have it. You hear the commentators today talking about it. "He should have brought the ball on down through. He let up on it." Back in our day we weren't allowed to dunk so we had a better touch under the hoop. But that's history.

I see Hakeem, he plays the game a lot differently. He's developed that one-handed fade-away, semi-jump shot that's very effective. I shudder every time he takes it because I think it's a lousy shot. All he does is put it in the hoop.

CB

Back then, you didn't want to do anything inflammatory like dunking to raise the ire of any other player. It was easy enough to start a fight. With our raucous fans and intense competition, fists were always on the verge of flying. Dunking was a bad idea because it just gave someone a reason to belt you. And another reason was not needed back when we played.

I remember one game against the Baltimore Bullets, played in the close confines of the Minneapolis Auditorium. Blackie Towery was the Bullets' big forward at 6 feet, 5 inches. Towery was a tough, mean player, and he and Jim Pollard had a real battle royal going, banging and elbowing and knocking around the whole game. Finally, Jim had had about enough, and he took the ball from out of bounds and turned and threw it right into Blackie's face. From there, all hell broke loose. The benches cleared like it was baseball or hockey. I'm out there fighting with the best of them, and who do I see running out there to defend us but our own Max Winter.

Now, Max was only about 5 feet, 2 inches, but he was feisty for his size and he was out there swinging with the rest of us. Max ranged out onto the court and started chasing Baltimore's center, Walter Budko. Max caught up to Budko but got distracted by the melee and looked the other way just as Budko raised a fist to clobber him. Tony Jaros, tussling with someone nearby, grabbed Max and pulled him out of the line of fire just as Budko uncorks a right hook. I can still remember Max later saying that the wind of Budko's fist nearly knocked him out.

℘

JOHN KUNDLA: I've got a picture of one game against Syracuse where a fight broke out between Dolph Schayes and someone else. Everybody ended up fighting. Soon, everybody had picked a partner [and was fighting]. In the photo, there's Mikan out in the middle looking for somebody to fight. Nobody was around Mikan; he was all by himself without a partner. I got a big laugh — nobody wanted to fight with Mikan.

Once in Fort Wayne, the fans followed us out to the airport after we beat the Pistons. They wanted to boo George, or who knows what. George says from the plane, "Go out there and throw 'em a piece of meat."

℘

The fans liked to get into the action, and whenever a fight would break out it was an open invitation. One night in Syracuse we were all fighting on the court, and I was tangling with the Nats' Alex Hannum. We wrestled around on the floor. At one point, I was on top of him with my hands around his throat about to hit him when I looked up and there in front of me was a pair of black street shoes. I followed them up to a pair of black pants, a white shirt, a scarred face with an unpleasant demeanor, and then a fist cocked ready to smack me. The guy was an angry Nationals fan who'd jumped in to defend Hannum. Those fans in Syracuse, I felt, were always intense and a little overzealous.

I knew when I met my match, however. Cowboy Edwards was more than my match. At 6 feet, 9 inches and 280 pounds, he was strong as a bull, and he always saw red on the court, no matter what the other team's colors were. I was young when I played against Cowboy, but I learned quickly. Once, there was a brawl on the court, and he turned to me and said, "Do you want to fight?" I was a college graduate by then and had a few smarts, so I politely said, "No, we'd better sit this one out." Thankfully, Cowboy agreed.

We did play some basketball between all the fighting, and during the 1950-51 season we Lakers were hitting our prime. We started out the season by retiring the William Randolph Hearst trophy for winning the College All-Star game for the third consecutive year. I was triple-covered at times and held to 14 points, but I just kicked the ball out to my teammates, and Vern and Jim picked up the slack. We won the game 61-54 and retired that big silver trophy — it was the best way to start the season I could imagine.

The worst way was our loss to Baltimore a night or two later in the first game of the regular NBA season. My teammate Bobby Harrison reminded us that the 81-71 defeat was the first season-opening loss in Laker franchise history. It should have sounded like an omen, but didn't at the time — although I never forgot that fact all season.

The 1950-51 season was an up-and-down affair — sometimes we played like the Lakers of old, the winners of three straight championships, and other times we stumbled, tumbled and lost. The NBA had been whittled down to twelve teams, a more workable number than the seventeen of the year before. The weaker franchises had folded, and the experts felt that the redistribution of some of the league's stars just strengthened everyone else. "Just the kind of league that ought to beat Mikanopolis," crowed the Indianapolis

The famous George Mikan drop-step hook shot. He leads with the left elbow to protect the ball and then hooks it into the hoop. The shot was unstoppable.

(Courtesy of the Star Tribune/Minneapolis-St. Paul)

newspapers.

Our tough style of play took its toll that season, with players sitting out games due to injuries. Jim Pollard was out fourteen games because of a fractured cheekbone. Later, Mikkelsen sat out the only four games of his career with a sprained ankle. To win championships you usually need a little luck along the way, and that luck often comes in the way of good health. When you lose players of Pollard's and Mikkelsen's stature, it's hard to win ballgames. We lost all three games of an important three-game road trip early in the season, but after January we starting picking it up again, winning fifteen of the next seventeen games.

Also on the upside was our game against the Harlem Globetrotters in Chicago on February 23, 1951. It was the sixth meeting of the two teams, and the Lakers were up three games to two. Trotters owner Abe Saperstein wanted a win badly. He had just released a movie about the Trotters and was looking forward to a win over the Lakers for some additional publicity. We didn't oblige him, though. I put in 47 points for a Laker win, 72-68.

Abe Saperstein was so mad that he cancelled the return game scheduled for Minneapolis. He called Max Winter the next day and said, "The March 12 game in Minneapolis is off."

"What's the matter?" asked Max.

"Nothing. It's just off."

On the low side that season was one of the more memorable games of my career, and certainly one of the more interesting games in basketball history — unless, of course, you were a fan paying to watch it. On November 22, 1950, the Fort Wayne Pistons came to the Minneapolis Auditorium with a plan hatched by their coach, Murray Mendenhall. Tired of years of Laker domination, he figured that if Mikan and the boys didn't have the ball, they couldn't score. So he instructed his players to just hold onto it.

Without a shot clock or any other rule to prevent it, Mendenhall's players stalled, holding the ball in a stationary position for minutes at a time, rarely attacking the basket. It was the ultimate slowdown game, something every team in the league accused us of playing, but this time it wasn't us. It worked effectively to the point of a 19-18 victory for Fort Wayne — the lowest scoring game in NBA history.

Mendenhall had told his players to hang onto the ball until we came out to get it and not to take any shots that they didn't think they could make. But coach Kundla told us to hold back until they made some attempt to play the game. The Pistons took only thirteen shots the whole game, and we shot only eighteen. For 7,021 fans, that was a poor excuse for a ballgame.

&

JOHN KUNDLA: That was Fathers and Sons day at the Auditorium, and [the fans] weren't very happy. We talked about that game for twenty years — we never wanted to see a game like that again.

&

DICK ENROTH (BROADCASTER OF THE GAME): It wasn't a difficult game to call. I used to call games via the ticker, without seeing the game. So this one was not hard. The arena was very quiet, which was very unfortunate. In order to drum up attendance, the Lakers were giving away bicycles to the little kids, and that was a good draw. Here were all these kids seeing this very dull game.

&

At first, the fans booed loudly, and then they began to throw things to get us to stop. Soon, they resigned themselves to what they were seeing and started reading their newspapers. The thought of having to pay to watch ten men stand on the court and do nothing — it's terrible. Occasionally, we'd make an attempt to steal the ball, but Kundla told us to stay back until the Pistons attacked the basket. We went into halftime with a 13-11 lead, and Kundla was satisfied to sit on it until the Pistons made some effort to play the game.

&

JOHN KUNDLA: There was no shot clock. We played it careful. We weren't going to go out and foul them or anything. We played it normal — they just weren't going to play. I don't remember exactly how it happened, but Fort Wayne put in a last-second shot that was just a fluke. It shouldn't have happened. The last shot went up, and George touched it but it still went in. They won it by a big fluke. They were lucky to win.
*   A lot of fans went home [early]. It was an awful game to watch — 19-18. A lot of people thought it was a first-quarter score. But that game really changed the game of basketball.*

&

When you look at the box score of this infamous game, you can still see the travesty that it was. But at the same time, it was very interesting. A total of 31 field goals were made and 37 points scored. Fort Wayne scored 11 of its 19 points on free throws, while we scored 10 of our 18 from the line. I was the only player on our team to score a field goal (4-for-11), although Vern attempted two and Jim one. I ended up scoring 15 of our team's 18 points. Now, if you look at the percentage I scored of our team's points, it comes out to .833, which must be some kind of record. I never did that before, and the reason was because of the low score. Heck, even when Wilt Chamberlain later scored 100 points, the record for highest points in an NBA game, his Philadelphia Warriors team posted 169 points — his triple-figure score is a mere .591 by comparison. It was a strange game, indeed.

Pro basketball had been gaining some momentum in the public eye, and this game was single-handedly counteracting it. Maurice Podoloff, the NBA president, met with representatives from both teams to discuss it. "We don't want something like that to happen again," Max Winter said. "Our fans are mad. They won't come back."

The NBA, only in its second season, did not need this kind of slowdown boring the fans. Other teams would also try to stall, but none so spectacularly. Two weeks later, for example, Rochester and Indianapolis played a game with five overtimes, where nobody would shoot the ball. That season, several possible rules changes were discussed, but the 24-second shot clock did not come in until 1954, after I had retired from the game. The initial impetus for it, though, came from the Pistons' attempt to stop the Lakers' unstoppable offense.

Our opponents were always trying lots of different things to stop us, especially me. The first NBA All-Star game is a good example of that.

In January of 1951, the NBA held its very first All-Star game, in Boston Garden. Team owners were concerned whether the game would draw or if the NBA would be embarrassed. But it turned out the game drew more than 10,000 people, and everybody was happy.

I played for the West. Kundla was our coach, with Pollard and Mikkelsen also representing the Lakers. The East squad pooled its resources and tried to put the clamps on me. It worked — I scored a mere 12 points in a losing effort, 111-94. I was outscored by nearly everyone but the water boy.

क

ED MACAULEY: [On the East squad], we had guys such as Bob Cousy, Andy Phillip and myself. George was starting for the West team. I said to my teammates before the game, "I'm going to do one thing: when the West has the ball, I'm going to try to keep the ball away from George."

Now, that made me vulnerable if George's teammates lobbed the ball over the top of our heads — then he could get an easy shot. So I asked my guys to sag off of their defensive men, Dolph Schayes and Paul Arizin. I said, "The first five minutes of the ballgame, just try to keep that ball from coming over the top."

And they did a great job of it. I don't think George touched the ball for the first four or five minutes.

I also told [my teammates], the West has Ralph Beard, Bobbie Davies and others. They're all great ballplayers, and they'll work the ball around continually trying to get it to George. But when you're playing in an All-Star game, if a guy looks in and you're covered, they're not going to waste any time. They can score on their own, right? I said, I think they'll start shooting from the outside.

Which is exactly what happened. The West didn't get the ball to George as much as they should have, and they didn't work the ball long enough. It turned out great as far as I'm concerned, because I had a great night scoring and was voted the MVP in Boston. Turned out great because our strategy worked.

I think I may have made the comment after the game, the Big Guy will probably get forty the next time out. I think he got 44 two nights later in Boston.

We [Boston] would do the same thing. We tried to keep the ball away from George. But he was the greatest player in the game. He was the leading scorer in the league. You did everything you could to hold him to his average, and if you held him to 25, you were doing a good job.

क

I did get stopped, though, at the end of the season in a way that eventually stopped the Lakers, as well.

The Lakers finished the regular season in 1950-51 with the best record in the NBA, 44-24, three games ahead of Rochester in our new division, the Western Division. I totaled 1,932 points that season, for a 28.4 average, and captured my fourth consecutive scoring title as a Laker (fifth if you include the Gears).

But in the second-to-the-last game of the season, the wear-and-tear of this new, tougher NBA caught up with me. Playing at Tri-

Cities, I suffered a hairline fracture in my ankle, although at the time we didn't know it. Bob Polk, the Lakers' trainer, had the ankle X-rayed, but the X-rays didn't show anything. It hurt like hell, though.

For our first playoff game against the Indianapolis Olympians, I taped the ankle and took the court. I scored 41 points, and the ankle seemed fine. But two nights later, in our second game in Indianapolis, it was a different story.

"John," I said to Kundla, "this ankle is killing me."

"Well, then," he replied, "I don't think you'd better start."

"Oh, no," I said, "I'll play. But if I holler, get somebody in for me quick."

I hollered quick, too. I got only two points and played only a few minutes before sitting out the rest of that 108-88 loss. Back in Minneapolis two days later for the deciding game of the playoff, I tried again to the tune of 30 points. We beat Indianapolis 85-80 that night, with me battling their great center Alex Groza, whom I'd beaten for the regular-season scoring title. That win wrapped up the first round of the playoffs. Scoffers began to think I was kidding about the ankle.

That series, by the way, would be a sort of swan song for Olympians' stars Groza and Ralph Beard, who would be banned from basketball before the next season for their part in the point-shaving scandals in college basketball discovered in the early 1950s.

In the second round of the playoffs, the Lakers were going up against the Rochester Royals, the team we'd had a blood feud with since the beginning of our franchise. Kundla was still concerned about my ankle, though, and we managed to convince the league to postpone the first game for a day, allowing me a bit more rest. That extra day caused Les Harrison to blow a gasket. Smelling an opportunity to finally get past the hated Lakers, he was livid about what he thought was special treatment and he let the league hear about it.

It was to no avail, but it probably served to give the Royals even greater incentive, as if they needed any against us. After a four-day rest, I still wasn't quite right. Shortly before the game, coach Kundla came up to me. "George," he said, "you're not starting tonight."

Well, I nearly dropped my teeth. I couldn't believe it. It was the first time I had not started a game since I was told I couldn't play basketball back in high school, and it was definitely against my wishes.

Kundla started Mik at center instead of me. I helped out with 22 points and a few rebounds off the bench, and we won the first game of the series at home in the Minneapolis Auditorium.

My ankle took a beating, though. Two days later in our second playoff game, it was still throbbing as if Bob Cousy were dribbling a basketball on it. I scored 18 that night, but was useless on the boards. Rochester's Arnie Johnson, on the other hand, was great — he grabbed everything. We dropped that one on our home court, 70-66. When you lose a playoff game at home, you know you're in trouble. The series was tied heading to Rochester.

On the plane ride to New York, both teams flew together and we discussed my ankle. We were always friendly off the court. One of their players, Joe Coleman, told me about a numbing substance called ethyl chloride that freezes the injured area and numbs the pain. The Royals might have been our rivals, but they wanted to beat our best and didn't think twice about helping me get back on my feet.

For game three, I tried numbing my ankle with ethyl chloride, and it worked like a charm. But the Royals had smelled blood, and they went in for the kill. I wrestled with Arnie Risen and Arnie Johnson all night, and we even built several good leads early in the game.

ⵉ

ARNIE RISEN: The advantage I had on George [that night] was that I got up and down the court a little faster. Everybody thought George was slow up and down the court. [Ordinarily,] he wasn't as fast as some of us, but he was very quick. I don't think there was any [other big man] in the league that was quicker than George. His hands were quick, and he had quick movements in the pivot despite his size. Which I'm sure helped him a lot.

ⵉ

In the end, however, my 32 points were not enough, and the Royals finally got their long-hoped-for playoff series win over the Lakers, 80-75. By winning the series 2-1, they became the Western Division champs. Rochester went on to meet the New York Knicks in an all-New York finals that brought a lot of much-needed publicity to the NBA. It was a crazy finals that went back and forth, but the Royals won it four games to three, for their first and only NBA championship.

The Lakers and Royals had what I consider to be one of the all-time great NBA rivalries. Between 1949 and 1954, when the Lakers and Royals fought like a pair of hellhounds to beat each other, the Lakers won a total of 267 games to the Royals' 266 victories. Twice, they finished ahead of us in the regular-season standings. But when it came to head-to-head battles between the two teams, we usually came out on top. The Lakers beat Rochester 38 times, compared to the 28 matchups they won.

It was great for Rochester to finally get the recognition they deserved, but I've always felt they stole one of our titles.

CB

ARNIE RISEN: We were opposite types of teams. George's team was the old school of the big men being dominant, and using your size and power — outpowering the other team. Rochester's team was basically dominated by smaller players, the outside guards, as evidenced by the Hall of Fame. We've got four guards that I played with in the Hall of Fame: [Bobby] Wanzer, [Red] Holzman, [Bob] Davies and [Al]Cervi. For the Lakers, George, Jim Pollard and Vern Mikkelsen made it (also Slater Martin) — those guys made a very formidable front line.

Playing with Rochester against the Lakers, we played pretty even over the years. If we had a few days off in between games, we could usually give them a better game. But back then, you played just about every night. You played a lot of back-to-back games, and we just weren't a match for them in back-to-back games. They were just too big. They'd poop us out.

I guess we liked each other, though. I'm not sure that today the players do. We'd fight like heck to win and then laugh and joke together. Sure, I had quite a few broken bones playing back then. The first year I was with Rochester, I broke my jaw. We might have beaten them that year [except for that] — that might have been the first one we would have beaten them. Unfortunately, the year we did beat them, George was hurt. We might not have gotten away with it except for George's injury. He played, but he wasn't up to par. Then again, it could have happened the other way, too.

CB

I guess a broken ankle stopped me from winning in 1950-51, but it didn't stop me from playing. I missed only two games during my entire Lakers career, mostly because I loved playing. I never wanted to sit out. And when I played, I played to win and tried not to let a little pain stop me. Nothing was going to stop me from doing my best.

ᘓ12ᘔ
Changing the Game
1951-1952

When someone talks about how he changed the game of basketball by the way he played, well, that might seem kind of presumptuous. And I don't feel entirely comfortable giving myself so much credit. But the fact of the matter is professional basketball was so young when I played that it was bound to change. And I was a record-setter, a popular player and the focal point of a championship team, which is where a lot of changes originate. I guess I was a pioneer. The way the Minneapolis Lakers and I played basketball did have a significant effect on the game.

In the late 1940s and early '50s, professional basketball was struggling to establish itself, and sometimes it had to change to survive. As players, we were not only experiencing those changes but shaping them at the same time. To compete, you either play like a winner, find a way to beat a winner's style or find an even better way yourself — change the game. The Lakers were the team to beat. The other teams wanted to stop us, and we wanted to be constantly improving.

From Cousy to Jordan, from the Celtics to the Bulls, all the great players and teams have brought something new to the game, simply by trying to be better than their competitors and win championships. They were all pioneers of the game. Now, you can see players like Shaquille O'Neal having an effect on the game. He plays a total power game, thanks to his 7-foot, 1-inch, 301-pound frame, which may soon require players of similar size to compete against him. And when you watch someone like the Minnesota Timberwolves' Kevin Garnett play, a 6-foot, 11-inch forward with the agility and skills of a guard, you wait in anticipation of the changes he has in store for basketball.

C**3**

RED AUERBACH: George was a pioneer. There are few pioneers in this game. Hank Louisatti was the pioneer of the one-handed jump shot. Bill Russell was the pioneer of making shot blocking an art. Wilt Chamberlain was the pioneer of the dunk and use of power. Sam Jones [was the pioneer of] the bank shot from the sides. Kareem Abdul-Jabbar popularized the jump hook: it was impossible to block. Dr. J [Julius Erving] popularized hang time in the air. And Bob Cousy popularized ballhandling skills and behind-the-back dribbling. Those were your major pioneers, and Mikan was one of them. He popularized the hook shot, getting position underneath [the basket] and utilizing the body.

C**3**

To trace my effect on basketball, you have to start with the ban on goaltending, enacted in 1944 while I was in college, and look at several things that happened up to the advent of the shot clock in 1954, shortly after I retired. I've talked about a lot of these things in more detail in other places, but here's a quick rundown:

Goaltending. In college, I was one of a very small number of players who could block shots seemingly at will by simply jumping up and grabbing them before they hit the rim. The practice infuriated a lot of people on the basketball scene and was quickly outlawed.

Mikan Drill. The great DePaul coach Ray Meyer created this figure-eight layup/rebound drill to help develop my shooting touch and rebounding abilities. I spent hours and hours on that drill, until I could shoot equally well with either hand. Thanks to Ray and me, potential centers from grammar school to college would be introduced to what became known as the Mikan Drill. Hard work does pay off, I guess.

C**3**

KEVIN McHALE: Yeah, I did the Mikan drill, but I didn't like it because it was tough − swinging hooks left and right, left and right, left and right. I thought this Mikan guy must be a real mean guy, [because] this drill is hard.

C**3**

Role of the Big Man. Before my time, the center was primarily a stationary position. By becoming an offensive force in the post, I changed the perception that the big man was just a huge body, good only for rebounding, blocking the lane and providing some shade. My ability to excel in what was then considered a small man's game of speed and agility also helped with people's perceptions off the court — we big men weren't all clumsy oafs, good only for high-altitude weather forecasting.

Power Forward. I had an indirect effect on this because Minneapolis Lakers coach John Kundla had the good fortune to have two great centers in me and Vern Mikkelsen, and of course, he wanted to use us both in the same lineup. By putting us both on the court at the same time and turning the wide-bodied Mik around to face the basket, Kundla created the game's first power forward.

Modern-Day Lineup. With the talented Jim Pollard at the other forward position, Kundla and the Lakers created the blueprint for the modern-day frontcourt: center, power forward and small forward. We used one guard to bring the ball up as point guard and another to shoot (shooting or off-guard). Before us, the two forwards had been basically interchangeable; the same with the two guard positions. Modern-day lineups have followed our pattern.

Shot Clock. Our opponents tried all kinds of different schemes to slow the Lakers' powerful offense, but perhaps the most blatant was the stall attempted by Fort Wayne in the lowest-scoring game in NBA history (19-18) on November 22, 1950. It took the league a while to figure out the best response, but the 24-second shot clock was finally installed in the 1954-55 season. It put an end to slow-downs for good.

Widening the Free-Throw Lane. The most obvious and transparent attempt to thwart my effectiveness under the hoop greeted me at the start of the 1951-52 season. There was no attempt to hide just who the change was aimed at, since it became known as "The Mikan Rule." The Lakers weren't even coming off a championship season that summer, but someone felt it was time to clamp down on us anyway. Here's what they did.

Since the beginning of basketball, the area underneath the basket — known forever as the lane, but now called "the paint" — was 6 feet wide. Since 1932, the lane was (and still is) governed by a rule that doesn't allow offensive players to remain in it for longer than three seconds at a time. Defensive players can roam at will under the basket, but offensive players must take position outside the lane and move in and out, generally when they are receiving a pass to take a shot or have a chance at a rebound.

If you've ever looked at a picture of the old 6-foot-wide lane, you can tell how the entire free-throw area — lanes, free-throw circle and all — got its nickname of "the key." Back when the lane was narrow, the area looked just like a key, with the lanes extending from the circle toward the basket. Nowadays, when you hear a broadcaster say a player is "shooting from the top of a key," it's a little less clear than it used to be where the player is shooting from.

What the Mikan Rule did was widen the lane from 6 feet to 12 feet. (It remained at that width until 1964 when it was expanded again to 16 feet.) At first, experimentally, the lane was widened to 10 feet, but finally it went to 12 feet.

When the lane was 6 feet, I could use my drop step and hook shot quite effectively because I was playing so close to the basket. In fact, it was easy to get in and out of the lane since it was so narrow. By widening the lane, all players were forced to run their offenses a little farther away from the basket, opening up the lane for more defensive rebounding — and basically, keeping George Mikan out of there.

ଠ

VERN MIKKELSEN: I don't know of any other sport where a rule was changed to legislate against a player. But that's what happened when they widened the free-throw lane. It was done solely because of Mikan's dominance. From 6 feet to 10 feet to 12 feet. That is where they changed the game considerably. George is responsible for widening the lane, which to me is the biggest change that has happened in the last fifty years. It's opened the middle up to allow us to see all this fantastic stuff that we see today.

ଠ

The strongest proponent of widening the lane was New York Knickerbockers coach Joe Lapchick. The Knicks were without a dominating center at the time, and Lapchick was frustrated at getting beat by the Lakers so often. During my career, the Knicks never won a game on our home court of the Minneapolis Auditorium, which was 2 feet narrower than other arenas to begin with — but I'm sure Joe hated playing there no matter what the size of the lane.

Old Joe lobbied hard for the rule change, and at first it seemed to work. My scoring average, which had been 28.4 the previous season (and tops in the league), dropped to 23.8 in 1951-52. The

Mikan Rule might have slowed my scoring, but it didn't prevent me from helping my team win. The wider lane just opened up our game. It forced me outside and opened up the middle for my quicker teammates to cut to the basket and receive assists from me. And I wasn't half-bad as a passer — just listen to Joe Lapchick himself, who was quoted in this 1952 New York *Times* article:

> *"George Mikan dominates every game he plays in because he is the most prolific scorer the sport has ever produced. Coaches have been wracking their brains for years to slow him down or clamp the lid on his scoring effectiveness. The solution still is eluding them. Finally, they enlisted the rules makers into the plot by having them widen the verboten territory under the basket from six feet to 12. That would stifle Mikan the Mighty, they felt. No longer could he get those tap-ins and fingertip flicks from underneath.*
>
> *'See these grey hairs?' Joe Lapchick [asks the reporter]. 'Mikan put most of them there. We've tried every known defense on him and nothing works. Sure we can stop him by covering him with three men but then Pollard and Mikkelsen and the rest of the Lakers score like crazy. What have you gained? Nothing. In fact, you've lost more than you've gained.*
>
> *'Big George reminds me of Babe Ruth. When Babe Ruth was hitting home runs, everyone forgot that he'd once been an exceptional pitcher and that he was a fine outfielder. Everyone also forgets that Mikan is the best feeder from out of the pivot that the game ever had. He whips in a bounce pass to cutting teammates that can't be stopped. He creates all situations. Cover him normally and he kills you with his scoring. Cover him abnormally and he murders you with his passes.*
>
> *'I'd thought the new rule might help. Minneapolis screamed the loudest when it went in, but I'd insisted from the start that the widening of the foul lane would have no effect on the genuine stars. It would only hinder the clowns. It's my opinion that it's made Mikan an even better basketball player. No longer can he plank himself under the basket and use his size, weight and elbows to advantage. He has to maneuver more and he maneuvers beautifully.'"*

∞

It's true that Max Winter had declared that the Lakers would never widen our lanes (although we did), but I never complained about the rule. I knew it was legislated against me, but I knew it was also good for the game. That season, I was a guest columnist for the *Minneapolis Star* newspaper, and I wrote as much:

> *"They tell me the new 12-foot free-throw lane was written into pro basketball rules just to make it tougher for a guy named Mikan.*

If that's true, the rules makers did themselves a double favor.

They not only made things tougher for me, but they also made the game better than it has been since Doc Naismith hung up the first peach basket.

The 12-foot free-throw lane is the greatest thing that has happened to basketball since the elimination of the center jump [after every basket].

Simply, the new rule provides a bigger area under the basket in which the offensive team cannot stand around and wait for something to happen.

The rule forces action. It forces wide open play and more outside shots. It's faster and demands better defense.

Me? Well, I'm down from 28.4 points per game last year to 24.8 [at that point in the season]. But it's still a better game this way."

cs

By forcing me to make changes in my own game, the wider lane helped me to be a better playmaker. Rather than concentrating on throwing in hooks from the post, I spent more time passing off to any number of great Lakers players. As a team, we had more balanced scoring than ever before. In fact, 1951-52 was the first season that both Vern Mikkelsen and Jim Pollard averaged more than 15 points per game. All three of us in the front line hit the 1,000-point mark for the first time that season.

Another new Laker benefited from the new rule: Frank "Pep" Saul, a new shooting guard we acquired that season. Since the larger lane meant that more of an emphasis would be placed on outside shooting, Sid Hartman figured we needed to bolster our guard position. And how he came about picking up Pep is quite an interesting story.

Pep Saul had spent the previous two seasons languishing on the Rochester Royals bench behind future Hall of Famer Bob Davies. He was Davies' protégé but was not about to crack the lineup with Davies in front of him, so he asked for a trade. Hartman knew that the 6-foot, 2-inch Saul had the shooting skills the Lakers would need in the backcourt.

Because the Lakers and Royals were embroiled in their ongoing rivalry, Hartman was certain that Rochester owner Les Harrison would never trade Saul to the Lakers. Hartman was still burning over an attempt by Harrison a couple of seasons earlier to convince Laker Herm Schaefer that he was underpaid. Sid saw this as an opportunity to get Harrison back while helping the Lakers at the same time.

Sid called Clair Bee, head coach of the financially struggling Baltimore Bullets, and told him that he would give $5,000 for the rights to Saul. When Bee asked Hartman if he thought he could get Saul from the Royals, Hartman told Bee that Saul would cost all of $1,500 and Baltimore could keep the change from the $5,000.

Bee promptly bought Saul's rights from the Royals for the $1,500 and within a few days sold those rights to the Lakers. Les Harrison went through the roof. He complained to the league, but to no avail. What would probably be considered collusion today was perfectly legal in 1952. Hartman had exacted his revenge, and the Lakers had picked up a great young shooter and passer.

Saul joined a Lakers squad that had earlier added three Minnesotans to its roster. Joe Hutton, Jr. and Howie Schultz came to the Lakers after playing college ball at Hamline University. Hutton was the son of the Hamline coach who had turned down the Lakers' first coaching offer. Schultz had been a two-sport man, playing first base for the Brooklyn Dodgers and basketball for the Anderson Packers. The third player was Myer "Whitey" Skoog, a jump-shooting guard who came to the Lakers directly from the University of Minnesota. As a Gopher, Skoog had introduced the Midwest to the jump shot, producing countless high-school carbon copies of his style throughout the state.

For all the scoring done by my teammates that season, I wasn't exactly shut out, either. My season average may have narrowed just as the lane was widened, but I still made my mark when it came to shooting baskets. Ironically enough, in the season I was supposed to be shut down, I posted the highest point total for a single game in my basketball career. On January 20, 1952, I scored 61 points against those old Rochester Royals in a 91-81 victory. Les Harrison didn't like it.

"He's just a monster," said Harrison at the time. "Just a basketball monstrosity."

The game was our third win in four against the Royals, and Harrison claimed that everyone from the referees to the official scorers were conspiring to help me. "It's a miracle the way a monster like that can bull his way around like he does," he said, "and not have any fouls called on him."

Actually, I did have some help — my teammates were throwing the ball to me all night long. Les did his share, as well. In the first half, he tried his usual strategy of giving me my points and hoping that his team could outscore the rest of the Lakers. But by halftime, I had scored 36 points, and he had to change his strategy. For the first half, Harrison had had Arnie Risen guarding me alone, but in the second half Les sent a triple-team of Arnie Johnson, Alex Hannum and Odie Spears at me. I played the entire game, including two overtimes, without a rest, but I'm proud of the total, which surpassed my previous professional (and collegiate) high of 53. I guess I exacted a little revenge for the past season's playoff ouster, myself.

My 61 points were just two points shy of Joe Fulks' NBA single-game record of 63 points, set back in 1949, so I didn't set a league-wide record with it. Neither did I win the scoring title for 1951-52, the first time in my professional career that I didn't win it. With all the league changes, it's hard to keep track today, but for the record I had the highest scoring average in the NBL in 1946-47 (Gears) and 1947-48 (Lakers), in the BAA in 1948-49, and in the NBA in 1949-50 and 1950-51.

Of course, a major reason I didn't win the title in 1951-52 is the Mikan Rule widening the lane — it was meant to slow down my scoring, after all. Still, the entire season I battled for the title with Paul Arizin of Philadelphia. Back and forth we went, giving the sportswriters plenty to speculate about — a "basket battle," they called it. I would put in a respectable 1,523 points (23.8 ppg) for second place, but Arizin won with 1,674 (25.4 ppg).

What I lacked in scoring in 1951-52, I made up on the boards. With the wider lane changing my scoring ability, I threw myself into improving other aspects of my game. After all, it was important to do anything I could to help my team win. I finished the season in third place for rebounds, with an average of 13.5 per game. On March 4, 1952, I pulled down 36 rebounds against Philadelphia, which bettered Dolph Schayes' NBA record by one.

As I continued to work on my rebounding technique the following season, I would improve to the point of leading the league in rebounds for 1952-53. That year, I grabbed 1,007 rebounds, for an average of 14.4 per game.

Another highlight of the 1951-52 Lakers season was meeting the Trotters again in exhibition play, even though owner Abe Saperstein had unceremoniously cancelled our second game the previous season. This season's game took place on January 2, 1952, in Chicago Stadium and ended in an 84-60 win for the Lakers. It was the final blow. Saperstein was so upset after the game that he took a walk and was gone for hours. When he came back, it was the end of the exhibition games between the Lakers and Trotters.

Abe wanted nothing to do with us after that. He must have seen the writing on the wall. We had won the last five games in the series (5-2 overall). Twice, the Lakers had stopped the Trotters in the midst of incredible 100-plus game winning streaks. Even worse for Saperstein, the Trotters were starting to lose players to the NBA. Chief among them was Sweetwater Clifton, who had joined the New York Knicks in 1950 as one of the first black players in the league.

The Globetrotters had been the greatest basketball team of their day, but the times were changing. Looking back, the end of the Lakers-Trotters series seems to herald the end of the barnstorming era itself. As the NBA was growing in popularity, basketball fans were turning to the established league. The days of playing 50 to 60 exhibition games a season would soon be a thing of the past.

After I had retired, the Lakers would face the Trotters one more time, on January 3, 1958, in Chicago. The Lakers would post a 111-100 win, but it was already like an asterisk to history.

Pollard, Mikkelsen, Kundla and I again got to represent the Lakers on the West team at the second NBA All-Star game, held February 11, 1952 in Boston Garden. Paul Arizin of the East and I both scored 26 that game, a new record, but Paul got the Most Valuable Player honors. It was a close game right up to the middle of the final period, but the East won again, 108-91. It wasn't hard to see who the Eastern Division crowds were rooting for that night. Walking onto the court, Ed Macauley and Bob Cousy were greeted with wild clapping and hurrahs; I got boos and Bronx cheers.

Anyway, the Lakers finished the regular season in 1951-52 with a record of 40-26, which put us one game behind Rochester in the Western Division. We beat the Indianapolis Olympians in two close games in the opening round of the playoffs. In the second round, we again met our rivals, the Rochester Royals, who were the de-

The toughest front court of its day and the blueprint for the modern-day lineup:
(from l to r) Small forward Jim Pollard, center George Mikan and Vern Mikkelsen,
the game's first power forward. *(Courtesy of George Mikan)*

fending NBA champions from the previous season. There was enough bad blood between these two teams that the stage was set for a battle royale.

The series started out in Rochester on March 29, 1952. The Royals took the first game, beating us 88-78, despite a 47-point effort from me. We desperately wanted to win one of the first two games in Rochester, so on the second night we changed things up a little and I became a passer.

In game two, I knocked in 17 points, but so did Jim Pollard and Pep Saul, while Vern Mikkelsen bettered us all with 19. For Saul, the former Royal, it was great revenge as he bottled up his former teammate Bobby Wanzer, holding him to only three field goals. The Lakers beat Pep's former team on its home court by an 83-78 count in overtime.

That momentum carried us back to Minneapolis, where we would play two more games in the best-of-five series. On April 5, we won game three, 77-67, avenging the Royals' 10-point margin of victory from game one.

In the deciding fourth game, the order of the day was balanced scoring, as both Pep and Mik had 18 points and I put in 16. (I was more proud of my seven assists, though.) The game was tied with two seconds to go when Jim Pollard tapped in my errant shot for the lead. That 82-80 victory meant we were heading back to the championship series after a season away. I was happy to have done that by going through Rochester.

In the finals, we met the New York Knickerbockers, who were returning for their second consecutive year after losing to the Royals in 1951. The series started out on April 12, 1952. We had the home court advantage because of our superior regular-season record, but unfortunately we didn't get to play on our home court. A scheduling conflict at the Minneapolis Auditorium forced us back across the river into St. Paul. We won the first game anyway, 83-79 in overtime.

The Knicks took the second game, 80-72, in St. Paul. From there, we went to New York, where we beat them 82-77. It was a seesaw series like that the whole way though seven hard-fought games. In the fourth game, not only did we lose, but Jim Pollard hurt his back, which kept him out for the next two games.

Game five was played back in the St. Paul Auditorium. Having Pollard out inspired me and Mik to redouble our efforts — we each scored 32 as the Lakers trounced the Knicks, 102-89, to take the lead in the series, three games to two. Everyone expected that the Lakers were a sure thing after that. In fact, the 69th Regiment Armory, the Knicks' home court, was only half-filled for game six. But the Knicks surprised everyone by winning 76-68.

That brought the championship game back to Minneapolis — and for the first time to our real home court, the Minneapolis Auditorium. New York didn't stand a chance. Pollard was back, and once again, our forte was strong team scoring and tough defense. We won handily by a score of 82-65.

Personally, I got to show Knicks coach Joe Lapchick just what his Mikan Rule had wrought. I blocked several Knicks' shots and scored 17 points in the final tilt, but four of them came on two end-to-end romps. Twice, I dribbled the length of the floor to score baskets, finding a way to score other than "planking myself" under the basket. I was even jokingly called "George 'Fast Break' Mikan" in the press, despite my reputation for lack of speed and slowing the game down.

I guess old Joe's rule might have changed the "monster" that Les Harrison liked to complain about, but it created another one in its wake. The Lakers were back on top in 1952, and we planned on staying there for a while. Legendary Kentucky coach Adolph Rupp was a believer after watching us play and told a *Minneapolis Morning Tribune* columnist as much:

"They did everything to Mikan but tie his shoelaces together," said Rupp, "but he got out of every straight-jacket they put him in and rolled in the baskets. What a beating that fellow takes. Yet, after trying everything, including some rule changes, they still can't stop him. Those Lakers, I don't know how anybody ever beats them."

The Mikan Rule's wider lane didn't beat me, even though that was its intention. Only one thing did that season: late in the year I was out with a viral infection for two games, the only two games I ever missed as a Laker. It was quite the infection — my whole family caught it. My wife was nine months pregnant at the time and ended up bedridden. My mother-in-law had come to Minneapolis to help out; the virus landed her in the hospital, along with one of my sons.

Two weeks later, my third child, a son, was born. We named him Patrick. With three children, I had to prepare for my post-basketball future. Such planning was important in those early days of pro ball — after all, for winning the 1952 championships, the entire Laker team got to split just $14,750. I was planning to practice law, so I spent the off-seasons studying for the Minnesota bar exam. Pat and I had pretty much decided to settle in Minnesota — in 1951, we'd built a new home that we helped design in a suburb of Minneapolis. The 17-room, two-level rambler was custom-built to accommodate my size, with seven-foot doorways. I also had a seven-foot bed and a nine-foot couch custom-made — a guy likes to feel comfortable at home.

The year 1951 also marked the publication of my first autobiography, *Mr. Basketball*, written with *Minneapolis Star* columnist Bill Carlson. It was the story of my first 27 years and ended ironically with the Lakers' loss of the championship in 1951. At the time that autobiography was published, we didn't know that the Lakers would regain the title in 1952. There was plenty about the future that I didn't know.

The 1952-53 NBA championship team. Many on the squad considered this title to be their favorite. *(Courtesy of UPI/Corbis-Bettmann)*

⚝13⚝
My Favorite Title
1952-1953

Each year, Max Winter and Sid Hartman would make changes to the Minneapolis Lakers to maintain our championship play and keep building on our winning tradition. But for the 1952-53 season, they decided to stand pat. The only addition was rookie Jim Holstein, a 6-foot, 3-inch guard from Cincinnati. Our starting lineup remained intact with Slater Martin and Pep Saul in the backcourt and Vern Mikkelsen, Jim Pollard and myself on the front line. This fact alone sent coaches back to the drawing board to devise new ways to stop us — because we were planning to defend our championship trophy.

The previous season's rule change that widened the lane had altered my game and changed the dynamics of the Lakers' scoring, but not our successful results. The Lakers were evolving as a team, depending less on my big scoring numbers underneath and more on a balanced attack. The plays that coach John Kundla had developed for us were always the blueprint for our success, and as we kept on winning, the other teams took notice and tried to emulate us.

⚝

JOHN KUNDLA: We changed the game because we had plays — plays for each player. We had a play called the JG play for Jim and George, the Askov play for Mik [named after his hometown], and for Martin we had a play called Pensacola.

We played as a team and played pattern basketball. Everybody laughed at us because when we first started playing, the other teams were free-lancing, using a lot of weaves and figure-eight drills. They didn't play a half-court situation game.

We had patterns set up to get the ball to Mikan (most of the time). When we got the ball to Mikan, we made sure to never follow through. You didn't want to bring your man into him. You threw the pass to

George and then went away from him, so your guy wouldn't sag in on
him. People laughed at us at first, and the league said that we played
too slow. [But] the Boston Celtics eventually went to plays — they had
more plays than we did after a while. Most good teams did go to plays
after that, away from the free-lance.

cs

The other teams were mostly using inside weaves. They'd throw
the ball underneath, go inside and set a pick, one after another until
a man broke open for a shot. They called it a five-man weave. Some
teams had a few little set patterns; for example, they'd throw the
ball into the center and then crisscross. They called it high post and
crisscross — just a few little simple plays like that.

But we had regular pattern plays for everyone. I think that helped
change the game. For Jim and me, we had the JG play, which was a
pick-and-roll routine. It was incredibly effective.

In the 1952-53 season, we began to see an earlier trend mush-
room into standard practice. Intentional fouling — that is, fouling
an opponent as a deliberate defensive tactic rather than a mistake
— grew to the point of epidemic that season. During that one year,
the league experienced more called fouls then any other season.
Officials called an average of 58 fouls per game, which resulted in
teams shooting upwards of 2,400 foul shots that season, rather than
the 1,500-1,600 that had been the norm.

Basketball has always been a tough game to officiate. Back then,
we had only two referees (instead of three in today's game), and
they couldn't possibly see everything going on under the basket.
Players took advantage of that and tried to get away with whatever
they could to score or play defense. It probably led to more fouling
just out of the nature of the tactic: when you foul someone, it often
hurt, which would mean retaliation. The refs knew you were going
to retaliate, as well, and watched you closely after you got hit — so
you had to choose your spots.

We used the foul as an intimidating factor. I always said that
when you foul an opponent the first time, foul him real good and
make sure he feels it so he doesn't want to play you so close the
next time around.

A lot of teams employed a designated hacker, or hatchet man,
whose job it was to foul opposing players, trying to slow down the
opponent's best player or get him to retaliate and foul out of the

game. You see, the penalties for fouls were not stiff enough back then — a team could send out a player not needed for scoring and have him slow the opponents down. Unfortunately, the strategy was beginning to slow the game down as well. For years, league officials had noticed an increase in fouls, and the time taken to set up for the free throw, shoot it and then restart the game was starting to drain the game of its exciting pace.

All that excessive fouling came to a head in a playoff game between Boston and Syracuse on March 21, 1953. In that game, which was a four-overtime affair, 107 fouls were called and 130 free throws were taken. Bob Cousy scored 50 points in the game, but 30 of them came from the line. The final score was 111-105, with Boston winning, but the foul fest did little to capture the imagination of basketball fans.

Since the beginning of basketball, the rulemakers have tinkered with the rules on fouls, trying to figure out the best way to deal with them. At one time, back before I was born, there was a designated free-throw shooter, a player who took all the free throws for a team. Later, in 1954, the NBA would experiment with saving all the fouls until the end of the half. Five fouls disqualified you back at the beginning of the century, and then it was four. In 1944, the number of personal fouls needed for disqualification went back up to five again — years later, it would become six, which is where it is today.

It seemed the rulemakers were going to change the foul rules until they got them right, and the fouling frenzy in 1952-53 pretty well ensured that some new legislation would be coming. We just didn't know what. Of course, the shot clock in 1954 served to speed things up and take away some fouling. Then in 1957, a bonus free throw was awarded to a team after its opponent commits seven fouls in a half — today, that team foul limit is five in each quarter before the bonus.

I was the object of a lot of fouling through the years, which is one reason that I set quite a few league records for the number of foul shots taken and made: for four seasons, from 1947-51, I led the league in both categories. Since many teams were at a loss for another way to stop me, they figured fouling was the best method. They'd either foul me and give me the chance to make only one point from the free-throw line rather than two, or they'd try to get me riled enough to commit my own fouls and spend some time cooling down on the bench. Changing the rules didn't always matter to that kind of strategy.

℃3

ED MACAULEY: I'll never forget the [1954] All-Star Game in New York City. We had just gone through all the intentional fouling, which had slowed down the game so badly that it was just a free-throw contest. So a resolution was passed in a meeting of the owners before the All-Star Game — a gentlemen's agreement — that there would be no intentional fouling [in the All-Star Game]. Now, if you've ever had much experience in professional sports with gentlemen's agreements, well . . .

Anyway, I'm on the East team and George is on the West team. With about ten seconds to go, we've got a two-point lead. We go into the huddle. Joe Lapchick is the coach that night. He gets all the All-Stars huddled around him and says, "What do you want to do?" And to a man, everyone says, "Foul him, right now."

So the ball went in to George, and Ray Felix, the guy guarding him didn't foul him right away. If Felix had fouled him right away, George would have gotten one shot (there was no one-and-one) and we would have gotten the ball back. But Felix fouled George just as he was going into his shot, making his move toward the basket. So George got two free throws.

I think the buzzer had gone off. But George stood up there, no problem, and sank both free throws and tied the game. Now, we won it in overtime. But there were 18,000 fans screaming against him and it didn't bother George, he just knocked them in.

℃3

Well, that was 1954. The 1953 All-Star game had gone a little better for the West team. John Kundla was the coach for the third year in a row, and he really wanted to win. Joining me on the West squad were Lakers Vern Mikkelsen and Dugie (Slater) Martin. Both were instrumental in the game's outcome, hitting clutch shots down the stretch, and the West won its first All-Star game (79-75).

Kundla used me for forty of the game's forty-eight minutes, which helped me pile up some decent numbers. I scored 22 points and grabbed 16 rebounds to corral the game's Most Valuable Player honors. Altogether, I played in four All-Star games (the tradition didn't start until 1951), and this was the only one that my team won. Perhaps the league should have let the Lakers play the East team rather than the West All-Stars — we might have done better.

The Lakers finished the 1952-53 regular season with the best record in basketball at 48-22, one game ahead of the Eastern champion New York Knicks. Our scoring was nicely balanced, thanks to the wider lane. My average was down slightly to 20.6, second in the league behind Philadelphia center Neil Johnston, but the rest of the Lakers' points showed how evenly our offense was being distributed. Mik's scoring average was 15.0, Pollard's was 13.0, and Slater Martin, who never took a shot unless it was absolutely necessary, averaged 10.6. Reflecting my new role of playmaker, I captured my only NBA rebounding crown that season, pulling down 1,007.

Some of our critics thought the Lakers came by our league-best record that season with some help from the referees. Now, while I can't deny that the home team occasionally got the benefit of the doubt from officials' calls, the practice was universal (and ongoing). That's why every team has the same number of home games. Fans referred to the practice as "home cookin'," but the refs are human, after all. It's difficult to ignore thousands of screaming fans to concentrate on a play underneath the crowded hoop that occurs in a flash of an instant — especially when the fans throw things. I can't blame a referee for being influenced by a rabid crowd, even though at the time I occasionally did. And I guess I wasn't alone.

ᘓ

RED AUERBACH: The Lakers stole one from us. I'll never forget that as long as I live. We were playing in Minneapolis, with twelve seconds to go, and we're three points ahead and we've got the ball. So they call a timeout. All of sudden the whistle blows, "Technical foul against Boston. Too much time in the huddle." That's the only time in all my years in basketball that that one was called.

The Lakers shot the technical and kept the ball. They threw it in to Mikan. He tied it up, and we lost it in overtime. The referee quit after that game and never worked again. He's a former player, and to this day he can't tell you why he made that call. The crowd was so noisy that you couldn't hear the ref's whistle when the timeout was over. Usually, they come over and tell you, "Hey, c'mon guys, the time is up." But never, ever was that thing called.

ᘓ

I guess Red would have agreed that there were too many fouls being called.

The Lakers' regular-season finish was four games better than the Rochester Royals in the Western Division, which was the largest margin between us in the four seasons we'd played in the NBA. And we avoided them in the playoffs, as well. They got knocked out by Fort Wayne in the first round.

We beat Indianapolis and Fort Wayne handily to meet the Knicks in a finals rematch, their third straight year playing in the championship series. Joe Lapchick and his boys were hungry for a title and were determined to steal one of the first two games in Minneapolis. Our better regular-season record gave us the series edge in home games. Due to a change in the playoff format, however, the series would be played two games in Minneapolis, three in New York and then two in Minneapolis, if the series went the full seven games.

Luckily for the Knicks, the first two games were played in the Minneapolis Armory due to a scheduling conflict at the Minneapolis Auditorium — New York had never won a game in the Auditorium. The Knicks were able to pull out the opener, 96-88, thanks to a strong performance in the fourth quarter when they scored 30 points. Lapchick double-teamed me with Sweetwater Clifton and Connie Simmons, and I only scored 15 points that night.

We came back in the second game with a 73-71 victory, narrowly escaping being down 2-0. We were ahead at halftime 47-30, but the Knicks caught up in the third. And then in the fourth quarter, the Knicks changed their strategy, trying to slow down the game by fouling me. In fact, the game became sort of a free-throw shooting contest after that. But their idea backfired, since I shot nearly 75 percent from the free-throw line that night.

Both games were well-played, pitting the Knicks' speed against our sure-fire control game, but the Knicks had stolen one on our home court. So they were brimming with confidence as they headed home to the 69th Regiment Armory. (Madison Square Garden was booked with a circus.)

The Knicks came into New York as five-point favorites, and everyone was talking about how they had the edge with three games at home. In fact, the Knicks started talking quite confidently — the newspapers all carried players' bold predictions that the series would not return to Minneapolis. And as Mik said after it was all over, "They were right. It didn't." The Lakers won all three games in New York for the franchise's fifth title in six years.

Game three, the first game in New York, was close in the early going, perhaps primarily because I was doing a little free-lancing.

The jump shot was becoming more and more popular around the league, and I didn't want to be left behind, especially in New York, where I always had good luck. So I started experimenting with one in the first half. Unfortunately, the NBA finals was not a place to experiment.

Sid Hartman had asked Ray Meyer along on the trip as a sort of consultant. Ray sat on the bench the entire first half, not saying a word as I misfired on several jump shots. When we got to the locker room at halftime, he let me have it. "Stick that jump shot up your ass, George," he bluntly said.

I always listened to coach Meyer. We turned the tight game into a blowout in the second half, winning 90-75. Ray always knew how I should play.

Game four was a little closer than the previous night's finale. I fouled out with the score tied and less than two minutes left, but Whitey Skoog put in a couple of field goals that saved the day and let us eke out a 71-69 victory.

Coach Kundla gave us the next day off, so after the game — this was late Wednesday night – we proceeded to enjoy New York City as it's meant to be. Several of my teammates were fans of Billy Eckstine, a popular musician in the early 1950s, and we caught his act at a Broadway club – until about four-thirty Thursday morning.

Thankfully, Kundla left us alone on Thursday, but he worked it out of us on Friday during a one-hour practice. Our adventure probably contributed to the close contest that game five ended up being that night.

Game five took place on April 10, 1953, before a capacity crowd of 5,200. We took the lead early on; by halftime we were ahead 44-35, and by the third quarter we'd increased our margin to 20 points. In the fourth quarter, though, the Knicks pared our lead back to two points with less than two minutes left. The only weapon left in the New York arsenal was fouling. At that time, fouls committed late in a game were followed by a jump ball, and to the Knicks' chagrin, that put the Lakers back in command — I was able to control all the jumps. This fact, of course, was not lost on the rulemakers, who were undoubtedly in attendance in New York, because that rule was later changed.

I fouled out late in the fourth quarter, but Whitey Skoog came off the bench, as he'd done in the two previous contests, to keep us in the game. Pollard was the game's high scorer, putting in 17.

Winning game five by the score of 91-84 put the Lakers back on the back-to-back title track after a year off. In our six years of existence as a franchise, we'd won five league championships. After the game, a reporter asked me if I thought we'd win again the next season.

"Damn right," I told him, "we're going to win again next year. We'll keep the title as long as this bunch keeps playing. And nobody here is ready to quit."

I certainly wasn't.

With that win under our belt, I also had an answer for those critics who'd been saying I was losing my edge and getting too old to play. "I get a kick out of you guys," I said. "I'm only 28 years and you say I'm old. Sure I limped out there. But who wouldn't if he took as much of a battering?"

As a team, we still look back on the 1953 NBA title as our favorite. We had our best regular-season record ever and surprised the critics in the playoffs by beating the Knicks three-straight on their home floor — a feat that wouldn't be repeated for almost forty years, until the Detroit Pistons beat the Portland TrailBlazers at home in 1990. Come fouls, come rule changes, come home-cookin', come-what-may, we were champions once again — which meant there was only one thing left to do . . . head back to Broadway!

⚝14⚝
The Transition Game
1953-1954

After the excitement of the Lakers' fifth championship died down, we all went back to real life. I'd passed the Minnesota bar in October of 1952, and in the spring of 1953, I started practicing law. Mikkelsen was working on his masters degree in education, and Whitey Skoog was selling insurance. The players were always working on jobs outside of basketball in those days, because what we got paid was not enough to retire on. In fact, with as rough as the game was back in the 1950s, you never knew when an injury could end your career. It was always good to be prepared.

As the 1953-54 season rolled around, however, the Lakers all prepared to defend our title again. Our two previous consecutive titles had put us back on top after a one-year hiatus, and we all felt like we had plenty of basketball left in us. The rest of the league must have been afraid that we did. The Lakers' incredible success seemed to breed a certain amount of contempt from the basketball establishment — like any dynasty, everyone was always trying to take us down. That's what the rule changes were meant to do, to minimize the effectiveness of the big man and lessen our dominance in the NBA. The other teams, trying to find new ways to beat us, were changing their style of play, and we started to see the NBA change around it.

I believe many people welcomed the change, especially in retrospect. Some of today's basketball minds dismiss the Minneapolis Lakers' style of play far too easily. For example, in explaining how I functioned throughout the playoffs after I broke my ankle at the end of the 1950-51 season, John Kundla said at the time that I played, but it was at half-speed. Modern basketball writer Roland Lazenby responded to that in his 1993 Lakers' biography, *The Lakers: A Basketball Journey*. He wrote, "Half-speed of slow must have meant that the Lakers were almost motionless." I don't think Lazenby liked our style.

Well, call us slow, but the year I broke my ankle was the only year the rest of the league could beat the Minneapolis Lakers. Between 1947 and 1954, no one could really figure us out at any speed. Lazenby can look back in hindsight, comparing us to the supercharged athletes of today, and call us slow, but he's only seeing part of it. We did usually play a slower, controlled, methodical, powerful game — one that conformed to my style — but we did it because it worked. Believe me, the Lakers could run the floor with the best of them.

We also played a transition game. As soon as Mik or I would get the rebound, our first move was the outlet pass upcourt. Slater wanted to run and Pollard was a gazelle, so we'd hit Martin and he'd run the fast break, or transition game, as it is called today. Racing up the floor, he'd pass the ball in to Jim, already heading in for the uncontested layup. The ball rarely touched the hardwood floor.

If the break wasn't open, we'd take the ball up the floor and get set in our half-court offense. And why not? We dominated the league with that offense. It was effective. I was the centerpiece of our pattern offense, and it worked better with me in position. The plays were called, the ball passed all over the court — once again rarely finding the floor — until the open man put it in. Our offense worked quite well, and it became the prototype of the modern game.

In 1951, when the NBA widened the lane, the game started to change right along with it — pro basketball began to pick up speed. By tinkering with the foul/free-throw process, the league officials were trying to streamline the game, which, of course, is what happened when they put in the shot clock. All these rules were designed not only to quicken the pace of professional basketball, but to shorten the games, as well. And it worked — a faster game was beginning to evolve.

Many players coming into the NBA in the early 1950s were suited to the quicker pace of the evolving game. Players like Boston's Bob Cousy and Ed Macauley were built for speed and the coming game. The Celtics played a different style than the Lakers — faster but less powerful — because their personnel dictated as such. But it wasn't until I retired from the Lakers that they had their huge success with it. The game evolved because of their success, much as it had with ours.

ଔ

BOB COUSY: Minneapolis slowed the pace of the game down; they would wait for George to get down the floor. So they didn't play a transitional game. [However,] they pretty much controlled the tempo of the game because they were such a strong rebounding team.

Kundla's basic strategy was to control the defensive boards, in other words, keep you to one offensive shot. You very rarely got much offensive rebounding done against that front line. They'd hold you to one shot offensively, slow the pace of the game down, and just walk the ball up the floor until George and the other two got into position. Then they'd get the ball inside to him. Simple as that, really.

Given the fact that they were the strongest rebounding team in the league, you really couldn't do much to try to accelerate the game. If you did extend your defense — like they do today — and go out and trap, then they had little Slater Martin, who would penetrate and get through the trap. When one of the defenders would come over and pick him up, Martin would lay the ball down to one of the big guys, anyway. So it was literally impossible, as I recall, to interrupt or change their basic control of the game.

It really didn't serve your interest to try and shove it down their throats. You tried to beat 'em at their own game. And that simply wasn't done too often. I don't remember that we even beat them in those days.

ଔ

Whenever we played Boston, Ed Macauley had to guard me, but at 6 feet, 8 inches and 190 pounds, he wasn't near my size. And that physical difference dictated our different styles. Cousy tells the story of when the Celtics traveled by train, "Easy" Ed, who had quite a sense of humor, would have a little fun with me. In the train station, he'd purposely bump into a pillar or a telephone pole and say, "Oh, excuse me, George." I guess that's how Macauley used to feel about guarding me.

Still, he did all right. Ed used his speed and quickness against my size and power to try and beat our team. On some nights he was successful, but Boston usually wasn't. Over the six seasons that my Lakers team met the Celtics, we won twenty-four games to their thirteen. Until I left the game for good, their game plan was still to get me out of it.

෫

ED MACAULEY: George was the meanest man around. He used to beat my brains out. I played when George was 6 feet, 10 inches and 240 pounds. I was 6 feet, 8 inches and 190 pounds. I could run and shoot, but George was big and strong. It all depended upon who got the fouls first. I had some of my best nights against George. I'm sure we respected one another.

The Celtics used to run on the break, with Cousy passing the ball. A lot of our game depended upon whether I could get a couple of fouls on George or not. I would much rather play against Minneapolis when he was on the bench. But it didn't always turn out that way, particularly in Minneapolis.

I fronted him as much as I could. But George could be playing against anybody in the league, and it didn't matter. If he caught the ball and had you behind him, he was going to get a good shot off. He'd come around with that left arm high − and I say this admiringly − it was just like a battering ram. If George got that position on you, you were in trouble. You had to fight to try and get the ball. You had to fight to keep the ball from coming to him. If he got the ball in any position, obviously, leading the league [in scoring] as many times as he did, you were going to be in trouble.

We used to say, if you can get a step on a guy like George, you had a chance. I was quick, so I'd get by George and drive to the basket and have a fairly open shot. But I would actually stop and wait for him to get close to me before I went up for the shot. I really didn't care if I made the shot or not as long as I could draw a foul on him. He was that dangerous.

If George was going to foul me, I was going to get two shots, anyway. But getting the foul on him was easily as important as getting the basket, because if you could get two fouls on him early, John Kundla would take him out of the game. We had a good enough team that Kundla didn't want George fouling out. So if you could get him in enough foul trouble, he'd spend a reasonable amount of time on the bench. When George was on the bench, the Lakers weren't nearly as effective.

෫

The time was soon to come when the Celtics' speedy transition game would be the dominant style in the NBA. After I had retired and the Lakers' dynasty had ended, Boston's fast-paced style − plus Bill Russell's defense − made the Celtics the next great thing in the league, playing in twelve of thirteen championship series from 1957 until 1969 and winning all but one. But in the 1953-54 season, the Lakers were still the defending champions, and we were still playing our methodical control game of size and power. As a result, the rulemakers continued to mess with it.

On March 7, 1954, the league decided to experiment with the Laker domination by raising the 10-foot high baskets to 12 feet. We were playing an exhibition game against the Milwaukee Hawks at Minneapolis Auditorium; just by coincidence, I am sure, the league decided to raise the baskets by 2 feet for that particular game. Any idea who that maneuver was aimed at?

The experiment was a disaster. If the rulemakers were aiming to change the complexion of the game, they succeeded, but the changes were terrible. As a rebounder, your timing was off. You would go up for the rebound that would normally come down in a certain amount of time, and it would take longer. You ended up stretching for the ball when your feet were hitting the ground. Our timing was thrown off, and a number of the guys got hurt.

Clearly, the rulemakers were trying to take away what they saw as an advantage for the big man by making it tougher to hit a short layup or hook underneath. But in this game, the big men adjusted. It was the little guy that got hurt. As I told *Minneapolis Star* writer Bill Carlson at the time, the 12-foot hoop "stinks. If they were trying to do something for the small man, they better think of something else. It just makes it tougher for them. The basket just makes the big man bigger."

Even though I missed 12 of 14 shots from the field, the game was still dominated inside by the Lakers' big men: myself, Mik (who led the scoring with 17) and Pollard. We didn't score as much as we might have ordinarily, but the Lakers still won, 65-63. Once again, a rule change aimed at the big man had fallen short. Try as the rulemakers might to legislate against it, size had become — and would remain — an integral part of the game of basketball. The short men had their place, but it wasn't firing away at a basket strapped near the court ceilings.

⟶

SLATER MARTIN: Our front-line players were fabulous rebounders. You couldn't beat them — there ain't nobody in the league that could beat them. They kept making rules to get Mikan out from the free-throw lane. They widened it and widened it. They even thought about raising the height of the basket. We played a game with a 12-foot

*basket. Couldn't even reach the damn thing. Couldn't shoot at it. If they
ever move that basket, it will set back the game of basketball thirty years.
Don't make any difference how tall people are getting, if you shoot an outside shot, it rebounds to midcourt. They'll never change that.*

ଔ

Another experiment that season involved Philadelphia coach
Eddie Gottlieb. The Warriors were playing a Brainerd Minnesota
team in exhibition, which gave Gottlieb an opportunity to try out
his idea for solving the foul situation. Gottlieb's plan was to save
up all the foul shots until the end of each half and then shoot them
all in what he called "innings." What resulted was an even worse
parade to the foul line than any that had been seen before. According to Carlson's *Minneapolis Star* newspaper piece, it resembled "a
game of throwing baseballs at wooden milk bottles, just like at the
fair."

The fans, like the players, did not appreciate either experiment.
So the league officials had to go back to the drawing board, while
the Lakers had to readjust to a 10-foot basket. That 12-foot basket
screwed us up for about a week. The proof happened four days
later, when the New York Knicks came to town and won their first
game on the Minneapolis Auditorium floor in nineteen tries. We
were definitely not ourselves.

The Lakers had made a roster change in the 1953-54 season that
affected me directly. That summer, we signed a young center from
the University of Kansas by the name of Clyde Lovellette, whose
28.4 points per game average in his college career had helped the
Jayhawks win the 1952 NCAA title. The 6-foot, 9-inch Lovellette
had spent a year playing in AAU competition before coming to the
Lakers and had also helped the United States Olympic basketball
team win a gold medal in 1952. He had quite the hoops pedigree
and was brought in to be groomed as my successor.

Lovellette came in at the right time. My eight-plus years as a pro
had started to take their toll on my body. I started the 1953-54 season with some knee problems, and the aches and pains acquired
under the NBA hoops were becoming harder and harder to shake.

But it wasn't only the pain of fierce competition in a brutal game
that had caught up with me. I believe the wear and tear of travelling around the country for nearly a decade was also getting to me.
From my years as a barnstorming youth, crammed into hard bus

seats and bouncing along the backroads of the Upper Midwest, to the "luxury" of cramped Pullman cars rattling through the hills and valleys of the Northeast between Chicago and New York, my twenty-nine-year-old body could certainly feel it.

Travel was always an issue back then, whether we travelled by bus, train or plane. Mostly, however, we went by train. When you're twenty-two years old, you don't think about the travel. It's just a game, a lot of fun to play. We had to travel on the train, and that's just the way it was. But after a while, it starts to wear on you.

For a guy my size, train travel lost its fun quickly. On the Pullman cars, the bunks weren't long enough to fit a fellow as tall as I was, so sleep was at a premium. I always tried to bunk with Slater Martin on the train, because he wanted to sleep on the upper bunk in the Pullman, and no one else wanted to sleep in the uppers. I had to sleep in the lowers, so I could put a suitcase at the end of the compartment to rest my feet on. The trains didn't have compartments long enough to fit me.

Sometimes, we'd be on the road, traveling by train for a week or more at a time. Try sleeping for a week on a Pullman car when you don't fit in the damn bunks. We learned to catch some sleep under a variety of circumstances, even sitting up for eight hours at a stretch. But the opportunity to get a good night's sleep was almost non-existent. Of course, we didn't know any better.

Minneapolis was the westernmost city in the NBA for many years, so we travelled more than most teams. And it just plain took a lot longer to get from one place to another back then. Frequently, we'd hop on the train right after a game, travel all night to Chicago, and then all day the next day to New York or Philadelphia or Rochester or Syracuse. We'd get off the train that evening and go over to the arena and play a ballgame.

C8

VERN MIKKELSEN: Travel made the game tough. In some regards, our travel affected us to where you almost ended up being a zombie, without really knowing it. After the first month of the season, you were playing in a stupor.

The league tried to schedule games with some continuity to them. But every owner wanted the prime dates in his own house, which I don't blame them for. Saturday night was the prime night for the Rochester Royals and Syracuse Nationals, and Sunday night was ours. We would finish a game about 10:30 p.m. in Rochester and then flag down the New York Central or the Pennsy coming through Rochester from New York City on its way to Chicago. Getting on the train after a tough ballgame, we usually didn't have time to shower, which people on the sleeping cars didn't appreciate.

We kind of hoped for overtime games. Then they'd be forced to fly us home, because we had to get home for the game on Sunday night.

After catching the train out of Rochester, we'd ride all night to Chicago, get in there at 7:30 or 8:00 a.m., go across town to the LaSalle Street Station, and catch one of the trains from Chicago to Minneapolis. That was another seven-hour train ride. We'd get in to Minneapolis at four or five in the afternoon, go right to the Auditorium, and play again that night.

ᏣЗ

It was brutal, it really was. People might wonder why we didn't fly, but there just wasn't the money in the league at that time. A lot of the owners were struggling financially. If a team made money, it was usually in the playoffs. The owners had to be very careful with their expenses, and it cost a lot more to fly than going by train. So we took trains. It's an easy decision to make when you are in management.

Teams did fly more frequently in later years, but early on management only used planes when they could get the teams to the game no other way. The other advantage trains had is that they were extremely reliable. You couldn't risk flying and forfeit a game if there was another conveyance that could get you there. That was a league rule at the time. So we'd go by train in order to make the games.

Sometimes, if the schedules were such that two teams were playing together in two different places, management would try to save money and fly both teams together. With two teams on the same planes, especially the planes of the early 1950s, that wasn't a luxury, either.

ᏣЗ

ARNIE RISEN: One of the first times we flew, we were playing Minneapolis in Rochester, somewhere during the 1949-50 season. They played a lot of doubleheaders at the time to boost attendance in the big cities. What would happen more times than not, two teams like Rochester and Minneapolis would be playing a doubleheader in Philly and then play each other the next night in Rochester or Minneapolis. So, quite frequently, the team owners would charter a flight for the two teams together.

That night, both teams got on the plane, with all the guys, the luggage, and a few cases of beer and the like. We were so heavy, we all had to go to the front of the plane to take off. The plane had to get up in the air before we could go back to our seats to sit down.

Once we got up in the air, on this particular flight there was no heat. We pretty near froze our tails off. We were in a storm and bouncing around with lightning striking all around us. Just like you see in the movies, with the plane bobbing up and down around the clouds, thunder claps and lightning all around.

[Back then,] you took the only flight available because you had no choice, and that was that.

CR

The traveling didn't lessen in 1953-54 because neutral-site games had become the order of the day in the NBA. In the past, teams played exhibitions in neutral cities as part of doubleheaders so that team owners could fill their arenas with an entire afternoon of entertainment. But now, the NBA was playing in whatever city they could get a guarantee of a decent gate. These weren't exhibitions, but rather actual league games played on the road for both teams — serving to bring the growing league to more fans around the country. The NBA was trying to capture a national audience, you see. Over the course of my Lakers career, we played in 38 cities, from Baton Rouge to Winnipeg and San Francisco to Raleigh.

The tough part about it was that, as a championship team, the Lakers were in high demand. I was, too, since I was the league's most visible player. Sometimes I'd head into a town before the rest of the team, to give the local media a chance to get their questions out of the way before a game. It helped to bring the league publicity, but it sometimes meant extra travel for me.

Of course, my fame had its share of advantages, as well. My popularity made me a celebrity around the country, and my size and glasses made me recognizable wherever I went — especially in New York.

CR

DICK ENROTH: Mikan really was a celebrity. Everywhere he went, his size made him immediately identifiable. In Washington, D.C., cab drivers would roll down their windows and yell, "Hey, Mikan."

One time in New York, Mikan, Kundla and myself went to Lindy's

for cheesecake after a game in Madison Square Garden. Milton Berle
was there, and he was at the height of his career in television. He came
running up to Mikan, wrapped his arms around him, and said, "Mike,
where you been? I've been looking all over for you."

George was a humble man despite his popularity. I used to room
with him on the road, and he never once asked me how many points he
had scored. He once said, "You're really fortunate to have five really
good friends." That was because of all the hangers-on [he encountered].

ᏣᎦ

Back home my face was recognizable, as well. It was also prof-
itable. Despite the struggles the NBA went through to get recognition in its early years, professional basketball players were still good
for endorsements. That practice began a long time ago in professional sports. I did endorsements for a variety of products — everything from Beech-Nut gum and GE televisions to Mennen de-
odorant and Northwest Airlines. I even had a comic book written
about my career.

I guess my boyish good looks made me appear honest and my
glasses made me look knowledgeable, which translated into a good
sales pitchman. Michael Jordan makes a bit more money off his
endorsements, but I did sell a few products in my day. Luckily, I
didn't have to sell anything on the basketball floor — my court demeanor was always a bit more intense.

Perhaps the most memorable product endorsement was the one
I did for Snoboy apples. I had a real nice contract with them, and
we always had the apples around the house — my kids loved them.
Well, in February of 1954, Pat and I were to be interviewed by Edward R. Murrow for his *Person to Person* show. It was an honor —
I was the first person from the Upper Midwest Murrow had chosen to interview. It was also a bit of a technical marvel at the time,
since I remained at home in Minneapolis for the interview. Re-
mote telecasts are routine nowadays, but back then it was a lot
different. Technicians planned for days to get our house ready; it
took almost twenty of them to set up the cables, cameras, speakers,
microphones and what-all they needed. The show even had to ar-
range to get an extra transformer from the power company to handle
the electrical demands of the shoot.

The interview itself went well. I gave Murrow a tour of our
house on camera, while he sat in New York and asked me questions. At one point in the show, I joined my two oldest boys, Larry

and Terry, and their mom, snacking on some apples in the family room. We had prearranged with Murrow to ask the boys what the name of the apples were, something the two tykes had done many times. When it came time for the scene, Edward asked them what kind of apples they were eating. Right on cue, Terry responded, "Red."

It gave Murrow a huge laugh, but I'm not sure how pleased the Snoboy people were.

All that stuff was fun and it would later help me make the transition from the game to my retired life, but in 1953-54 I was still playing and the game was what mattered to me. That year, the Lakers were playing just as hard as we ever did, no matter what town we found ourselves in. We had a title to defend.

Thanks to Lovellette behind me, my minutes that year were reduced from 38 per game to 33, but my points dipped as well, dropping from 20.6 in 1952-53 to 18.1 in 1953-54. I still plugged the middle fairly well all season, maintaining my rebounding average of more than 14 per game. I wasn't done playing despite, as old Mark Twain once said, "the rumors of my demise."

Many basketball scribes wanted to write us off that season, predicting the end of the Lakers dynasty, but our play would not allow it. Neither would the fans. We were still the team to beat and therefore the team to watch. We found ourselves on television quite a bit that year, and it wasn't for endorsements. NBC television had recently purchased the broadcast rights to NBA basketball, and it televised selected contests. Unfortunately, the camera magnified the problems that pro basketball was experiencing. Viewers were able to see just how rough the game was, and referees were told to clamp down on the "hockeylike" atmosphere. The unfortunate result was a kind of downward spiral in which fouls were closely called, games became free-throw shooting contests and the audience began to lose interest.

This sort of thing came to a head on March 20, 1954, in a nationally televised game between New York and Boston. The three-hour, five-minute contest produced a final score of only 79-78, thanks to a fourth quarter that took 45 minutes due to excessive fouling. The national audience didn't even see the outcome because the network, fed up with all the free throws, pulled the plug. They must have figured that no one wants to watch a bunch of players stand around while someone shoots free throws.

The NBA had other problems, though, and finances was chief among them. Before the season started, the financially strapped Indianapolis Olympians dropped out of the ten-team league, causing an imbalance at playoff time. With five teams in the Eastern Division, but only four teams in the Western, the NBA had to figure out a new playoff system. What it came up with was a three-team round-robin setup for the first round.

The Lakers made it to the playoffs with the best record in the league at 46-26, but the new round-robin playoff scheme afforded no advantage to the two division winners, Minneapolis and New York. In the Western Division, we survived the first round by winning two games (one each against Rochester and Fort Wayne) and advanced to meet the Royals again in the divisional finals. Rochester had gone 1-1 in the opening round, while Fort Wayne had lost both games, and only the top two teams advanced.

In the Eastern Division, New York finished 0-2 in the first round and was eliminated, giving way to Boston and Syracuse, who had finished the regular season tied for second place. In the first-round playoffs, the Nats had gone 2-0 while the Celtics were 1-1. It was a strange format that received plenty of complaints and unfortunately prevented yet another title series between Minneapolis and New York. There would be no high life in New York City after this NBA final series.

On March 24, 1954, we faced off against the Royals in the best-of-three game Western Division finals, after having just beaten them to advance to the second round. That's what such a cockeyed play-off setup had wrought. As players, we weren't too worried about it, but Kundla's already weak stomach — he had an ulcer — was doing flip-flops. Kundla knew the dangers of playing back-to-back games against the same team. It happened every year in the play-offs, but not in different rounds. Once you've beaten an opponent and moved on, it's tough to mentally prepare for them again. On top of that, the losing team is sure to make adjustments. The second round could be over before we knew it if we weren't mentally ready.

But we were ready. In the first game, played at Minneapolis Auditorium, there was no fear of overconfidence because we played like champs. We beat the Royals 89-76, with me and Pollard splitting 51 points. In addition to my 28 points, I pulled down 21 rebounds and played a nice game at both ends of the court.

"That was the one I've been afraid of," said Kundla at the time. "I haven't been able to sleep for two nights worrying about it. We're in good shape now with that first victory."

Many people thought we would end the series with the next game in Rochester, even a dispirited Les Harrison, the Royals' coach. But the Royals always seemed to have a little extra when it came to games with the Lakers. They fought back to tie the series with a 74-73 win on their home floor. I had a chance to win that game — with four seconds left, I took a shot that skimmed off the rim and was rebounded by Bobby Wanzer to seal the Royals' victory.

The series then headed back to the Minneapolis Auditorium, where we had yet to lose a playoff game. But the feisty Royals' play would keep our confidence in check. The Royals battled the final game to the finish, with tension high for both teams, before they went down in defeat 82-72. The Royals never played harder than they did that day, and we threw everything we had at them. I scored 15 of my 17 points in the first half until I got into foul trouble. Lovellette then came in off the bench to score 11 of his 16 points in the third quarter. But the Royals' Arnie Risen was the real star, tossing in 24 points against me and Clyde.

A foul called on the Royals in the waning seconds salted the Laker victory away. With fifty-one seconds to go, we were ahead by three and stalling to keep control of the ball. At that point, the officials called a deliberate foul on Rochester's Alex Hannum, and I received two free throws, making them both for a 76-71 lead. The Royals never came any closer, but they did get close to the referees after the game, complaining about that deliberate foul call and others. But their complaints fell on deaf ears, and the Lakers were on to another NBA final series. The Lakers had nothing but praise for their ever-tough rival, however.

The 1954 NBA finals pitted us against the Syracuse Nationals, the team we had defeated for our first NBA title in 1950. We might have been expecting the Knicks, who had had the best regular-season record, but it was the Nats who survived the Eastern round-robin playoffs and were ready to do battle.

I say survived because the Nats were walking wounded when they met us on the Minneapolis Auditorium floor on March 31, 1954. The Eastern playoffs had left them battered and bloodied, with forwards Dolph Schayes and Earl Lloyd both with broken hands and guard Paul Seymour with a broken thumb. All three wore casts, but all three still played. Despite what would seem like a disadvantage for Syracuse, the series went the full seven games, thanks to the "bandage brigade," as they became known. That series was a little war of its own.

In game one, the usually fast-paced Nats played a slower, methodical game, which threw us off our stride for the first half. We rallied in the second half, however, and cruised to a 79-68 win. The Lakers had four players in double figures (myself, Skoog, Martin and Lovellette). That win kept our Minneapolis Auditorium streak going — we had never lost a playoff game there over the previous six Lakers seasons.

The streak finally went down in game two, but not without a miracle. That game started out as a defensive struggle, with a half-time score of only 28-27. In the third quarter, the Nats, behind the shooting of guard George King, used a 16-1 run to build a 10-point lead going into the fourth. But with tough play underneath the basket, we battled back into the game. With ninety seconds remaining, King drove underneath and I went up to block his shot, but unfortunately broke his wrist. King left the game to join the other members of his team "cast" party.

With just eighteen seconds remaining, I tied the game at 60, but the Nats were not finished. Paul Seymour raced up court and, with seven seconds on the clock — still enough time to work closer for a good shot — he launched a 43-footer that hit nothing but net. The crowd was stunned that he would take such a shot and even more amazed that it went in and won the game. Seymour was later asked why he took the long shot. Paul simply replied, "I was open."

The Lakers weren't stunned for long, taking game three in Syracuse by a score of 81-67. I led the field in scoring that night by knocking down 30 points and grabbing 15 rebounds before the largest crowd (8,719) to ever watch a game in Syracuse's War Memorial Auditorium. I almost joined the bandage brigade myself when I stepped on another player's foot and twisted my ankle. Fortunately, the ankle was OK and I returned to the game. Syracuse's injured performed better, but they still had some healing to do.

Four nights later in game four, Syracuse showed an indomitable spirit by once again tying the series with an 80-69 win. It was Seymour again, the hero of game two, who scored 25 points to lead the Nats to victory — his points all came inside the 43-foot mark, however. Unfortunately, with their win came another casualty, as guard Billy Gabor suffered a knee injury. He would miss the next two games.

The fifth game was also played in Syracuse and went to the Lakers by the score of 84-73. It was won on the boards and across the board, as our team pulled together to get the win and a 3-2 lead in the series. Dolph Schayes, cast and all, improved to the tune of 17 points for the Nats, but Slater Martin guarded the red-hot Paul Seymour and held him to only 16 points this time. Mik led the way with 21 points for the Lakers, and we headed back to the Minneapolis Auditorium, where Syracuse had won only once — just one week before.

The Nats had another miracle up their sleeve for game six, though, playing again in close defensive style. In the closing seconds, they found themselves with both the ball and a tie game (63-63). Nats coach Al Cervi had a rookie backup center named Jim Neal in the lineup to take the final shot in the pivot. (Perhaps Neal was there because he wasn't wearing a splint.) With three seconds to go, Seymour passed awkwardly, and the ball wound up in Neal's hands nowhere near the basket. Not knowing what else to do with it, Neal shot from 27 feet away and hit the game winner, his only basket of the game. I'd scored 30, having a fairly decent night, but it wasn't enough.

The series thus came down to its final game, played on April 12, 1954, in the Minneapolis Auditorium. Once again, the Lakers proved they were champions. Led by the leaping Jim Pollard's 21 points, we beat Syracuse 87-80 to win our sixth title in our seven seasons of existence as a franchise.

For me, it was seven championships in eight years if you count my full season with the NBL's American Gears. A great way, I thought, to end my career. In fact, I thought about it throughout that summer. Then, on September 24, 1954, just three days before the new season would begin, I surprised the basketball world and retired from the game at the age of 29.

Basically, I retired because I wanted to spend more time with my family. I had three young sons, one six years old, one five, and one just two. My years of barnstorming around the country had kept me away from them — and my wife, Pat — too much. It's

George Mikan and Howard Cress at Reid H. Fay film studios filming a commercial spot, circa 1955. *(Courtesy of the Minnesota Historical Society)*

hard to be gone from your family for weeks at a time, especially when they're so young. I was also interested in getting my law career going, and it seemed like the right time to put the ball away.

But once you've got basketball in your blood, it's hard to get away from it. Two seasons later, I was talked out of retirement to play 37 games of the 1955-56 season. Pollard had retired, and the Lakers were struggling that season. They asked me to come back, so I joined them for the second half of the season. In my first game back, on January 14, 1956, I made the first shot that I took, and it brought the Minneapolis Auditorium hometown crowd of 7,100, a season high, to their feet.

It was exciting to be back, but it was also very difficult. I played myself into shape and ended up averaging 10.5 points and 8.3 rebounds per game. Despite what the critics might say, I ran right along with the shot clock that had been installed the previous season. My return was enough to help the Lakers start climbing in the standings, even though we ended the regular season with our first losing record ever, 33-39. It was still good enough for a second-place tie, however, and we made it into the playoffs. In the divisional semifinal round, we were beat by the St. Louis Hawks, two games to one — losing the final game, 116-115.

Fans and critics alike said that I shouldn't have come back that last season, and if you judge success only by winning the championship, then maybe they're right. But they forgot one thing, and that is my love for the Minneapolis Lakers and for the game of basketball.

When the Lakers said they needed my help, I did a lot of soul-searching. I was already playing a transition game of sorts in my post-basketball life, making an adjustment that was somewhat difficult. Coming back for one season was, I felt, the right thing to do. I never looked back in regret; never have I felt that it tarnished my career — I believe my record is too strong for that.

When I think about how much I've loved the game of basketball, from the time I was a kid in my backyard to my final game on March 21, 1956, in Minneapolis, I know I made the right decision. Basketball is in my blood — it got in there with my family and everything else I cherish. Leaving the court after the final buzzer doesn't mean the game leaves you.

❧Part IV

Working in the Front Office

Attorney George Mikan was admitted to the Minnesota bar — sworn in on October 14, 1952, with 138 other lawyers. *(Courtesy of the Star Tribune/Minneapolis-St. Paul)*

⋘15⋙
Law and Politics

When I retired from the Minneapolis Lakers in September of 1954, I was more than ready for life after basketball. In 1952, I'd passed the Minnesota bar and joined with Frank Ryan and John Kain to form the law firm of Ryan, Kain, and Mikan. During the summers of the last few years of my playing career, I had practiced law with them, preparing to support my growing family when I was done playing the game.

I enjoyed working as a lawyer and had long prepared for the day I would become one. But in the same way that I practiced law while I still played basketball, even when I left the game and changed the focus of my life, basketball was never too far away. Like a shadow, basketball has always followed me throughout life, lurking just a few steps behind. By retiring, I wasn't trying to separate myself from my playing career, but I was trying to move on. And as I was to find out over and over again, moving away from the game has been important to my own maturity, even though basketball has not always been willing to let me be.

On October 5, 1954, just eleven days after I retired, I surprised the sports world again by getting back into basketball — this time in a management capacity. Lakers owner Ben Berger made me the team's new general manager to replace Max Winter, who was retiring to focus his efforts on bringing professional football to the Twin Cities. It was an exciting new challenge for me, but strange all the same, to be in basketball and not tossing in hook shots down on the court.

At the same time, I continued working with Ryan, Kain, and Mikan as a corporate and general practice trial attorney. All my experience juggling jobs at Mikan's Tavern and the Ruberoid as a youngster in Joliet came into play in this period of my life. I was busier than ever, but loving it.

185

Those two jobs were joined by a third in January of 1956 when I returned to the Lakers as a player. Following my second retirement that March, I went back to my other full-time occupations, but that, too, was short-lived. Later that spring, my life took quite a different turn. I went from the dark and smoky arenas of professional basketball to the dark and smoky back rooms of the political arena.

For some time, the Republican Party had been trying to convince me to run for the 3rd U.S. congressional seat of Minnesota. Located in western Hennepin County and covering the southern and western suburbs of Minneapolis, the district had been controlled for decades by the Democratic Party, in particular, by then-Representative Roy Weir, who had the strong support of the unions and had held the seat for more than twenty years. The Republicans liked me for my name recognition, my background in law and my strong desire to succeed at my endeavors. They warned me that it would be an uphill battle, since Weir had never won by less than 15 percent in any race. But with me just stepping off the court, and my numerous championships still in people's minds, they thought I just might be the guy to unseat him.

I resisted the offer for a while. I had quit basketball to spend more time with my family, and this congressional race would make huge demands on my time. My wife, Pat, who always supported me in everything I wanted to do, was not too excited about this foray into politics. She, too, wanted me around more often — besides, Pat was a Democrat.

Still, Pat stood behind my eventual decision to run, which I thought at the time would work out well for us. The people in the Republican Party who were pushing me to throw my hat in the ring had promised me a lot of connections — and potential clients — after the election was over. I thought it would set up my law practice just right. I talked the matter over with my partners at the law firm, who also supported my decision, and my current clients were referred to other lawyers.

On June 7, 1956, at the age of thirty-one, I announced my congressional candidacy. A volunteer committee was formed, and I was quickly off and running. There were some things about campaigning that came to me very easily, like public speaking and attending meetings. In my basketball career, I had been honored at my share of testimonial dinners and had given a fair number of speeches. I felt comfortable with the public appearances.

But what I really didn't enjoy about campaigning was the long number of hours spent alone on the road. In basketball, I had always traveled with a tight, close group of friends who were battling together toward the same goal. Now, I felt like I was out there alone, fighting against a huge, rarely visible opponent — the Democratic Party. It was a different feeling for me. I was in new territory as a politician. I couldn't rely on my old fundamentals to pull me through the tough spots, and I had never been taught the fundamentals for this new game.

The hours were long and so was the road. Once, coming back alone from a meeting in Braham, Minnesota, I fell asleep at the wheel of my car and drove into the ditch. "Great," I thought. "That's all I need is a nice accident about now." From that point on, I would never ride alone.

I finished well ahead of the field of seven contenders in the Republican primary in September of 1956. Now, my only challenge was to take on the incumbent.

I challenged Weir to a lot of debates, but he never showed up for any of them. As a little comic relief at press conferences and political gatherings — and a nice bit for the media — I'd put a chair on the stage with me and prop a big picture of Weir on it, so that when the press or members of the audience would ask me a question about him, I'd point to the picture and say, "Talk to Roy." It was a picture of him in a bathing suit down in Florida, which my campaign was using to show how unconcerned he was about running against me.

Because he had a long history of wins, Weir never took me seriously as an opponent, despite my good reputation — and his, which was less than stellar. The rumors were rampant about his supposedly decadent lifestyle. It occasionally came up in the campaign, but I ran a campaign of good politics. More than that, I ran on a promise of getting things done for everyone, not just the special interests. "Let George do it," read our brochure. My message was that if the people would give me a chance to find out exactly what they wanted, we'd work toward that end. I wanted government to take care of the majority of the people and not just a few. With our aggressive campaigning, I believe we started getting that message across.

"Mike and Ike think alike" was the campaign slogan George used in his 1956 bid for a U.S. Congressional seat. Here he campaigns with President Dwight D. Eisenhower during Ike's Twin Cities' visit. *(Courtesy of the Minnesota Historical Society)*

President Dwight Eisenhower was running for re-election at the time. When he came to Minnesota on a campaign trip, we spent some time campaigning together. I took advantage of my wife's nickname for me and coined a slogan that read: "Ike and Mike, they think alike."

Finally, near the end of the campaign, Weir showed up for a debate and I got a chance to meet him. I remember going to the television station to greet him for the first time face to face. I had been told a lot of incredible stories about his lifestyle, so I had certain expectations about what he would be like. Well, here comes this little guy, immaculately dressed in a tie, shirt and beautiful suit. We shook hands and went inside for our debate. When the debate was over, Weir says, "George, I like you. If I weren't running, I'd vote for you."

All those stories people told me went right out the window. I thought he wasn't a bad guy, certainly not the horrible person he was being painted to be. To me, Weir seemed like a nice guy to know, congenial. I should have known better than to listen to the stories. It's always better to make up your mind about someone based on your own impressions.

Soon, my impressions about politics and the people behind it would be changed, as well, and not for the better. That October — a time when in the past I'd been preparing to defend another basketball title — I went racing around the state of Minnesota, trying to win a U.S. congressional seat. On November 6, 1956, when the votes were finally all counted, I had lost the race by less than one-half of one percent of the vote. Close, but no cigar, as they are wont to say.

Losing the congressional race was a tough defeat for me. Except for one NBA title, it was the first time I had been defeated for anything significant, and it was especially hard to have put all the work into it and to still have come up short. But at least Pat was happy to have me around again.

The race had been a very interesting process. I learned a lot from it, and as promised, I made some exciting contacts. From Eisenhower — who appointed me to his National Youth Council — and Ike's vice president Richard Nixon — who was as excited to meet me as I was him — to countless other national leaders and congressional candidates, I met some of the most powerful people in the country. Those were moments I would always remember.

But there were also moments I would never forget, as well, such as the six months following the election. As I took up my floundering law career after the defeat, I waited for the work promised me by the Republicans as enticement to get into the congressional race. It was not to happen. My phone did not ring for six months.

I felt betrayed when the promised work didn't come through. It was a crushing blow, both emotionally and financially. I had been a star during the campaign, but now that the "game" had ended, they apparently didn't need the star anymore. The party dropped me from the game like I had fouled out — not only banished to the bench, but out of the arena altogether.

What was worse, though, is that I had used all my money to finance the campaign. In the succeeding months, I had to sell all my life insurance policies to keep my family afloat.

There would be no second campaign for me in 1958, contrary to what you might expect after such a close battle the first time. In 1960, the Republicans put up Clark MacGregor, and he beat Weir handily. As in my basketball years, I had laid the groundwork and opened the door for others, although this time I didn't get to precede them through the door. I've since learned that this is the nature of politics (and life), but for a thirty-two-year-old fresh off the court, who had been sheltered by his stardom and never experienced such abandonment, this was a tough lesson to learn. The experience was as blunt as the time I got stiffed out of a promised tip when I was a child back at Mikan's Tavern.

I had never begged anyone for anything, though, and was not about to start then by asking the Republican Party for help. I proceeded to check out my options: I had my law career, which was not flourishing as I'd hoped, and I was still general manager of the Lakers. But I also had four children — a fourth son, Michael, was born in 1956 — and so I needed more. I needed to get back on my feet.

In February of 1957, a situation with the Lakers that had been brewing for some time came to a head. The Lakers were having financial trouble, and Ben Berger, the majority owner, had received a serious offer to purchase the franchise from two businessmen in St. Louis, which would mean moving the team out of town. The Lakers were still in my blood, and I offered to mortgage my home to help keep them in town. My offer was rejected because Berger had signed an agreement to sell only to a group or civic organization. But Ben wanted to keep the Lakers here, as well — his sales agreement with the St. Louis pair would go through only if a local group didn't come up with enough money to purchase the team by March 13.

That spurred a drive in town to sell stock in a corporation that would buy the team. With twenty-four hours to go on the deadline, a group of 117 people and organizations finally pulled together enough money to buy the team from Berger and keep the Lakers from leaving town. The group of stockholders paid $200,000 (with $50,000 retained for operating expenses) for the Lakers.

I had been general manager since 1954. Sid Hartman had assisted me in my first couple of years, but he resigned his control of operations in 1956, after the Lakers were unable to trade for the draft rights to Bill Russell. After years of putting people in the seats of arenas around the country, being general manager meant that it was my job to fill them in Minneapolis. Unfortunately, the team's former biggest draw was practicing law — it was two months into the 1954-55 season before we drew a crowd of more than 2,000 people. At the very least, being general manager was an ironic spot for me to be in.

But the Lakers had done all right the first season after I retired. They ended the 1954-55 season with a 40-32 record, the third best in the entire league. In the playoffs, they beat Rochester in the first round, but in the division finals they were eliminated, three games to one, by Fort Wayne. It was a good enough season's end to keep the fans coming.

Unfortunately, though, before the 1955-56 season began, Jim Pollard announced his retirement. Sid and I tried to fill the void with existing players like Dick Schnittker and Ed Kalafat. We also drafted shooter Dick Garmaker, who'd held eight scoring records at the University of Minnesota. But nothing worked. The Lakers got off to a terrible start and recorded their worst-ever loss, 119-75, on November 11, 1955, at Boston. It was soon after that when rumors started to surface that I would return as a player.

But my return didn't help fill the team's coffers significantly. The Lakers' money woes continued throughout the 1956-57 season.

When Berger sold the team to local investors in 1957, it was part of the deal that I be maintained as general manager and made part of the ownership group. That situation didn't last long, however.

Bob Short had been elected president of the board of directors for the owners' group. The first thing that he wanted me to do was fire coach John Kundla.

"No way," I told Short. "I played for John for ten years. I'm not going to fire him. You want to fire him, you fire him." John was my friend as well as my coach, so that was one duty I refused to do.

Instead, I suggested that the owners talk to Kundla because I felt that he might want to retire. John had suffered stomach problems for years and his ulcer was getting worse, along with the team. So someone from the owners talked to Kundla, and John said he wanted to be general manager.

"That's perfect," I said. "You've got your GM." I hadn't been overly keen on the job, so I was glad to step aside for Kundla. Unfortunately, I was even less excited about being coach, and that's the job the owners had slated me for next.

I never wanted to be a coach. But the Lakers were in a bind, and I didn't want to see them do poorly. The owners put a lot of pressure on me, telling me that I had to coach to maintain the continuity of the team. So I agreed to coach for the 1957-58 season on the condition that I would be able to choose my own personnel to play. They said, "Fine."

It was anything but fine. Soon after taking the job, I left town to give a talk in Raleigh, North Carolina. When I got off the plane there, I was paged by Charlie Johnson, a sportswriter for the *Minneapolis Tribune*. He asked me, "How did you like the trade?"

"What trade?" I said. Johnson then explained that Kundla had traded Ed Kalafat, Clyde Lovellette and Walter Dukes for Ed Fleming, a 6-foot, 4-inch guard, Art Spoelstra, and a third player. None of them was as good as the players they'd been traded for. I was so disgusted that I planned to tell the Lakers management that I didn't care to coach any more — they had traded all my team away. My thought was, "If you're going to trade players, get blue chip for blue chip." It was a very bad trade.

When I came back off the road, I met with the management. They said, "You can do it with these guys."

"You've got to be kidding," I said. "You don't need Mikan as a coach, you need Jesus Christ, because you need a miracle."

After that, John cut our training period down to one week, rather than the usual two, to save money. I had to try to get the players in shape in one week. I knew that was impossible.

From the front line to the front office. George is named general manager (above left), shown here with outgoing GM Max Winter and team owner Ben Berger. Soon he returns to the court as the Lakers coach, but only for a short time — much like his brief appearance in the game pictured above right. *(Courtesy of the Star Tribune/Minneapolis-St. Paul)*

As the 1957-58 season began, we were getting ready for a trip out East to open up against Boston and the phenomenal Bill Russell, who was in his second season. Facing Russell at center, we had Jim Krebs to start and Larry Faust coming off the bench. In Boston, I went to the press conference before the game, where about thirty reporters were covering the game. They started asking me how we would do against Russell that night.

"I think we'll do very well," I said. "In fact, tonight we're going to have Jimmy Krebs and Larry Faust play against him. Between the two of them, they'll score a hell of a lot of points." I think I said 50 at the time.

"But," I added, "we'll never win the game because we don't have enough strength."

When we went into the locker room before the game, I showed Krebs and Faust how to turn tight on Russell and take him into the basket, and they were very successful. We got our points, but we lost the game.

After that horrendous start, we went on to lose a lot more games. I tried to put a system in, but I had very little time to train the players. I was extremely frustrated — it was a very upsetting time in my life, and it probably showed in my oncourt demeanor. During one game at the Minneapolis Auditorium, my response to a referee's call got me ejected from the game. I spent the rest of the game sitting in the balcony, talking by phone with Kundla, who'd come in to take over.

I coached the Lakers to a record of 9-30, last place in the NBA's Western Division, before Kundla and I traded places again on January 15, 1958. After about two months behind the bench, I was sent back upstairs. Kundla coached the rest of the 1957-58 season, without bettering my mark to a great degree (10-23) — he discovered that we just didn't have the horses to get the job done. Even though I didn't have enough time to work with the players, I felt that the things we had tried to do were starting to pay off. But I was removed without getting to take a full crack at it, and my brief NBA coaching career came to a swift end.

That also marked the end of my career as a general manager. I received a three-page telegram from Bob Short explaining that he and Frank Ryan would run the team from there on. As a result, my share in the ownership, which was tied to my working with the team, went back to Short and the other owners. I never really owned the stock in the team — it was given to me in name only to entice other potential buyers to sign on. When I left, my stock ownership, such as it was, reverted back to the ownership group.

Still, my involvement in the Lakers' management had been a success on one level. I had — for the time, at least — accomplished my original goal in rejoining the organization, which was to make sure the team stayed in Minneapolis. And in 1958, it was still there.

From the Lakers, I tried to go back to my law practice, but it was still suffering from my congressional run and had pretty much run dry. I had to find something quickly — my family's needs did not disappear while I looked for work. But a new career soon came my way when I was offered a position with Bache and Company, a Minneapolis-based stocks and bonds trading business. I began learning the trade of stockbroker from the ground up, determined to make a good life for my family. It was not my ideal job, but it paid the bills, which was the most important thing at the time. I hoped that it would lead to something down the road.

In 1959, I was once again reminded of my basketball career when I received one of the greatest honors of my life. That year, the Naismith Memorial Basketball Hall of Fame was opened in Springfield, Massachusetts, the birthplace of the game of basketball. I was inducted into the Hall as a charter member, one of only fifteen individuals and two teams to be so honored. It was a great honor, surpassed in my career only by receiving the title of Mr. Basketball for the first half of the century, which I received in 1950.

Over the years, the Hall of Fame has meant a great deal to me. I have spent a lot of time working with the Hall and lobbying to get some of my old teammates and opponents inducted. Most recently, I saw my efforts rewarded when John Kundla and Vern Mikkelsen were inducted in 1995. It has been a labor of love.

Speaking of labors of love, Pat and I expanded our family during this period of time, adding a daughter, Tricia Ann, in 1959. Our second daughter, Maureen, would be born in 1963. To have our first daughter born in the same year as I made the Hall of Fame made for one of the better years in my life. With these two new additions, it became even more important to get my post-basketball career going, and that's what I was determined to do.

Meanwhile, things were not looking up for my old compadres at the Lakers. There were increased financial demands on the owners, and as some of the smaller owners couldn't pony up the extra funds, they were left with selling their shares to those who could. In a short time, Bob Short became the majority owner.

Even a surprising season in 1958-59 didn't help. In 1957-58, the team had finished in last place with a 19-53 record, which entitled it to the first choice in the next year's draft. In the 1958 draft, the Lakers selected the incredible Elgin Baylor, then a junior at Seattle. The 6-foot, 5-inch Baylor took the team on his shoulders and got it to the playoffs, despite a 33-39 record. The Lakers made it all the way to the finals in 1959 before losing to Boston in four games. This winning season did bring fans back to watch the Lakers, but it wasn't enough to keep the team in Minneapolis.

On April 28, 1960, Short, ostensibly facing bankruptcy, announced that he was moving the Lakers to Los Angeles. I was no longer a part of the organization, but I was very unhappy at the news, as were Lakers fans all over the country. The whole purpose of the Berger buyout had been to keep the team in Minneapolis, and now that was completely for naught.

Suddenly, the Minneapolis Lakers didn't exist. The team was abandoned, left behind by someone with other plans. (When Short sold the L.A. Lakers to Jack Kent Cooke five years later, he made nearly $5 million on the deal.) I had already experienced that sense of abandonment once, so I knew how to deal with the feelings. But I was never invited out to Los Angeles for anything with the Lakers, and I'm still not sure what to think of that.

Years later, writer Roland Lazenby captured the feelings of a lot of us ballplayers who built this team, this dynasty, from its infancy, and today don't even have our records and stats included in the Los Angeles Lakers Media Guide. In his book *The Lakers: A Basketball Journey*, Lazenby tells the story of how in the mid-1980s an employee of the L.A. Lakers organization discovered our old trophies sitting, dusty and in pieces, in a storage area in the bowels of the Los Angeles Forum. Inexplicably, the trophies were then thrown away, but fortunately someone retrieved them from the garbage bin. They've since been restored and put on display in a private collection somewhere in L.A.

"Can you imagine that?" Lazenby quotes John Kundla as saying, "That's unbelievable. That hurts."

According to Lakers owner Jerry Buss, today's Lakers consider their history as starting in 1960, when the team moved to Los Angeles. Their attitude seems to be that what took place with the Lakers in Minneapolis belongs to Minnesota.

"Or perhaps they belong to no one," writes Lazenby. "They are pro basketball's forgotten team, a dynasty without a city. . . the old Lakers belong to no one in particular. Time and basketball have slipped by, leaving the basketball they played in another age, one that few remember. And even fewer understand."

I hope you, the reader, can begin to understand now.

The Mikan children. The boys (from l to r): Terry, Larry, Mike and Pat. The girls: Maureen and Tricia Ann. *(Courtesy of George Mikan)*

∽16∾
The New Frontier

People sometimes criticize basketball because — so they say — the points are cheap. In the best seasons, pro basketball games typically eclipse the 200 mark in total points scored. A well-played basketball game dwarfs the number of points scored in hockey, soccer, baseball and even football. Yes, it's easier to score in basketball (the game has something called free throws, for Heaven's sake), and the good players score baskets often. But, while I'm a big proponent of defense in any sport, particularly basketball, people who make that criticism of the game miss a very important point. Scoring points is entertaining.

A long-distance basket gets the crowd off its feet sooner than a midcourt steal any day of the week, just like a powerful slam receives more cheers than a blocked shot. The object of most games is to score, and the more you do it, the more success you will have — and the more your fans will appreciate it. What's not to like about scoring points?

Even more, though, those critics miss another point about the high-scoring game of basketball — one that is more subtle than a Shaquille O'Neal rim-wrecking jam. More than many sports, basketball has a discernible ebb and flow in which each play builds upon the next. A tough layup off a rebound on one end of the court can quickly lead to a fast break on the other. A foul and missed free throw can create the smallest opening for a team to climb back into a game and eventually recapture the lead. Momentum can change in an instant and return back again after another stellar play. But each play and point builds toward that final shot, for that final score that determines who wins and loses. If, as some people say, you can tune into the last two minutes of a basketball game and basically "see the game," they have missed the preceding drama that brought the game and the players and the fans to that point. They may have caught the final score, but they missed the game.

Just as basketball has an ebb and flow, so does life — certainly my life did after my career with the Lakers ended. Basketball had brought me to the heights, but it had also created in me a person not totally ready to deal with life after the cheering stopped. After years living in the limelight, slightly pampered, certainly paid attention to, I was now living the life of a private citizen trying to support an ever-growing family of six — and believe me, when you have kids of all ages, from teenagers to a new baby, that takes a lot of support.

When I played basketball, my income was fairly certain from year to year. Now, though, I was out there on my own, trying to figure out how the life of an ex-celebrated jock should be run. Back then, we didn't have the huge contracts that basketball players have today, so the life that greeted me flush in the face after my basketball career ended was real and full of tough questions. And I had to answer them, without the benefit of a coach.

When the Lakers left Minneapolis in 1960, I was well into my career as a stockbroker with Bache and Company, and I still had my hand in the law business. But it was not enough for me or my family. Like my parents back in the Great Depression — both running the tavern, my dad selling coal and moonlighting as a justice of the peace — I knew that my days of working just one job to support my family were gone. So I patched together a number of things to make ends meet.

I took advantage of the opportunities that came my way. At the same time that I was learning the ropes at Bache, I became involved with several other businesses, some having ties to my old sporting career. First, I became sports director for the U.S. Rubber Company, as well as spokesman for its new product, Pro Keds tennis shoes. I traveled around the country promoting the new basketball shoe, an endeavor that is second nature to pro basketball players of today, and brought in some decent money for my family.

While working with U.S. Rubber, I made one of the more interesting acquaintances of my life. I had travelled to Kansas City with the basketball team from Gustavus Adolphus College (of St. Peter, Minnesota), which was playing in the NAIA tournament. The Gusties' coach, Gus Young, was a close friend of mine, and he asked me to come with him and the team to meet former President Harry Truman. I was thrilled at the opportunity to go see Truman because I had always admired him. We met him at his home in Independence, Missouri, talked with him and took pictures together. He was a delightful guy — politics had not soured his personality.

During this time, I also had the occasion to meet former heavyweight champion Jack Dempsey, the man who was named Mr. Boxing for the first half-century at the same time that I was named Mr. Basketball. Dempsey and I became great friends, and I always visited his restaurant every time I was in New York. I would meet many people in my life, both during and after basketball, and it was always interesting for me to meet someone else who has been in the public eye, who has seen some of the life I have.

In addition to working with U.S. Rubber, I took another side job with Wilson's Sporting Goods. Working in promotions, I travelled the country putting on basketball clinics and promoting Wilson products. Both jobs kept me in the public eye and helped me make plenty of contacts. With all the travel and hand-shaking and autograph signing, I couldn't help but think that this was leading me to something new. All the while I was learning the stock brokerage business, I was picking up other skills and making a lot of contacts. I felt like things were moving forward again in my career.

One of my clients at Bache was a businessman by the name of Connie Schmidt, who had a business partner by the name of Bill Erickson. Erickson, an attorney, and Schmidt were putting together an investment group and asked me to join them. The group was called Consumers Financial Corporation and we invested in a number of businesses, namely insurance companies, together. While I had met Erickson years before during my congressional run, this association led to a strong friendship that would become a big part of my life.

Consumers Financial was a big success and helped, as did all the other work I was doing, to get me back on my financial feet after the congressional run. Although my work kept me busy, I was still around home more than during my basketball days and could spend more time with my family. But just as I never passed up an open shot at the bucket, I rarely passed on a good business opportunity — and an opportunity was heading up the court.

In 1966, my old boss Max Winter, who was now the general manager of the Minnesota Vikings NFL franchise, approached me with an interesting business opportunity. At the time, Max also owned a travel business called Viking Travel, which was being run by some of his relatives. Six months earlier, there had been a tragedy. Viking Travel was handling a trip for Thermo King, a Minnesota business that makes refrigeration units for tractor-trailers, when a plane carrying many of the company's employees (and Max's relative) crashed in Japan. Max was devastated and at a loss about what to do. He offered to let me buy the business, so that spring, I became the owner and operator of George Mikan's Viking Travel.

I left Bache to run the travel business, and it became my primary livelihood for the next twenty years. I continued with my other business endeavors, but my life soon became centered around the travel business, and my business career had finally hit its stride. For those two decades, George Mikan's Viking Travel became one of the bigger names in the Upper Midwest travel business — of course, my basketball reputation had something to do with that. Finally, after a rough post-basketball period caused by my choice to run for Congress — against Pat's better judgment — I had recovered financially and was really heading forward in my career. Pat had always supported me, and she weathered this rocky period as well. Pat has always been the strong backbone in our lives together — my only problem was not listening to her enough. But we made it through together, with six kids and just about as many business ventures.

So that's how things stood in the mid-1960s. I was running George Mikan's Viking Travel, continuing my law practice, representing both the U.S. Rubber Company and Wilson's Sporting Goods, investing with Consumers Financial, and simultaneously acting as director or member of the boards for many of the organizations that we invested in. In addition, I was doing public speaking for charities and civic organizations. I had successfully bridged my basketball career into a very busy and promising business career. Amazingly enough, that bridge — through business contacts I had made — would lead me right back to basketball.

And guess what Pat thought about that.

৫১৭৪০
Commissioner Mikan

In the mid-1960s, for the first time in my life, I was too busy to be involved in basketball. I had a thriving business going in George Mikan's Viking Travel and plenty of projects on the side to keep me occupied — not to mention my wife and six children. So in 1966, when I was first approached to become commissioner of a proposed new basketball league called the American Basketball Association (ABA), my answer was, "No."

All the same, the idea of forming a new league to challenge the NBA intrigued me. Over the years, I had seen enough professional basketball leagues pop up and then die to know how risky such a venture could be. Yet I truly believed that there was room in this country for another basketball league. The NBA was good, but there was a lot of potential for growth that was not being tapped.

By 1966, the NBA had expanded to twelve teams but it was not going great guns, even though it no longer had much competition. Abe Saperstein's new American Basketball League, which had been launched in the fall of 1961, had folded on the last day of 1962, only a season and a half after it began. The AAU was also fading in popularity. There was college ball and some minor-league action, but the NBA was standing alone at the top of the pro leagues. Yet it was not attracting fans in droves. In terms of nationwide popularity, professional basketball was still running a distant third to professional baseball and football. Only one game a week was televised nationally.

Another factor that made me think there was a chance for a new basketball league to survive was the example of professional football. The upstart American Football League had taken on the established National Football League and in 1966 had succeeded in forcing a merger between the two, which ultimately strengthened the game. It appeared to be only a matter of time before such a maneuver would happen in professional basketball.

Commissioner of the American Basketball Association, George Mikan (right) answers questions at a press conference announcing the new league in New York on **February 2, 1967.** *(Courtesy of AP/Wide World Photos)*

I first heard a proposal for a new basketball league from Connie Seredin, a promoter from New York who had been working on creating a new league. Seredin pestered me to become his league's commissioner, but I kept putting him off.

About that same time, Bill Goff, an associate of mine through an insurance company I was investing in, mentioned that his neighbor out in California, Dennis Murphy, was also trying to put a new league together. It must have been a good idea, since there were two guys, one on the East coast and one on the West, each trying to put together a new basketball league.

Murphy called soon after, and I hooked him up with Seredin. They had several meetings and merged their efforts, and then I had the pair of them haranguing me about the commissionership. An article at the time in *Sport* magazine had listed a number of reasons why I should be commissioner of the NBA, and Murphy referred to it often in trying to cajole me into taking the position with his league.

I was very busy, but I was listening. "Once you get your investors and money in line," I told them, "then you come and talk to me." I didn't want to risk my current business endeavors — much less my reputation in the sport of basketball — on a fly-by-night project. Given the instability of earlier attempts at new leagues, that was a reasonable response. So as the group kept meeting, signing on owners and creating franchises, I continued working on my numerous other projects. I kept an eye on how the ABA was progressing, but I maintained my travel business. I was convinced that this new league needed me more than I needed it.

I finally agreed to be the first commissioner of the ABA about ten minutes before the February 2, 1967, press conference that announced the formation of the league. I was holding strong to my demands for a three-year contract because I didn't need the job and I would have walked if my conditions weren't met. My friend Bill Erickson, who would later become the ABA's general counsel, acted as my representative in the deal. Bill and the team owners were still hammering out the details of my contract even as the press conference was being put together. As soon as they worked out the agreement, I signed the contract and then I went out and led the press conference.

That press conference was quite the affair. It was in a big New York hotel, and there were about fifty media people there. We were giving away the red, white and blue basketballs that would become the trademark of the ABA. There were also young women in hot pants serving drinks. The whole thing needed some leadership, so as soon as I got to the microphone, I laid out very clearly for the media why the ABA had come into existence and exactly what they would see in the new league.

&

BILL ERICKSON: There could never have been an ABA without George Mikan. There were two gaggles of promoters and rich potential sponsors for the league — one on each coast. Both had come to George for consultation on starting a league: Connie Seredin from New York and Dennis Murphy from Los Angeles. George introduced them to each other and put the groups together to form the league. [As commissioner,] he gave them instant credibility, just being who he was.

&

Just because I was cautious in becoming commissioner of the ABA didn't mean I was reluctant. My dad had always told me that when you take on a job, do your best so that you can leave it with no regrets. That was my plan for the ABA.

I dove into my new job head first, setting out with the premise that, while there were only twelve teams in the NBA, there was a heck of a lot more basketball talent pouring out of the colleges around the country. I was determined to provide a quality vehicle for these athletes.

The owners believed that, like the AFL in football, the ABA could eventually either overtake the NBA or force a merger — and then they would make money back on their investment. In either of those scenarios, the league would be considered a success.

It was a strange conglomeration of people that had gathered for the initial ABA meetings, when the franchises were first being established. Most of the wannabe owners were promoters connected to monied investors. But almost everyone there came from a business background — only a couple of guys had any experience in basketball. At some point in the meetings, we had to weed out the promoters with big ideas but little cash from the serious investors with deep pockets. It was money that was going to get the ABA off the ground, not publicity.

&

BILL ERICKSON: Early meetings of the owners were a funny combination of the original promoters and the millionaires that the promoters had brought in to form the league. The only thing these two groups had in common was a general lack of knowledge of basketball — both the game and the business. It did not take long for the rich owners, all businessmen, to separate the promoters from the league. The owners threw their support to Mikan, because they found out quickly that he knew basketball.

℘

My experience in the game helped me to get things done in the formation of the ABA. The owners came from business backgrounds, not basketball, so when it came to proposing ideas and making decisions, a lot of them had to defer to me.

One of the most important things I did as commissioner was to hire referees. I wanted the best in the business because I knew that to ensure a good competitive ballgame you needed competent, knowledgeable refs. The best referees were working in the NBA, so that's ultimately where the ABA got them. Our league raided the NBA of its refs, offering them more money than they were currently making. The ABA had the reputation of being a wildcat league of rogues and rowdies, but I knew that if ABA games were officiated well, it would add legitimacy to the league. The game is always the most important thing.

Next in line of importance was the entertainment value of the new league. Back when I was playing, the game was all that mattered, but I recognized that in order for the ABA to compete with the NBA and survive, our game had to entertain to attract a new fan base. The NBA itself was only just surviving, and I felt we needed to differentiate ourselves from our rival in order to establish ourselves as a separate entity in the fans' minds.

It was out of this line of thinking that I came up with the idea for the ABA's signature red, white and blue basketball. It was the first and biggest battle of my involvement with the ABA, but on this front I was not going to be denied.

For me, the concept was simple, if not personal. I couldn't see the NBA's old brown balls from the second deck of those dark arenas where the teams played. Perhaps it was my poor eyesight, but the damn thing would get lost for me. I felt that if people could not see the ball go through the hoop — the essence of the game — they wouldn't be coming back to watch another one real soon.

I researched the ball problem both in the arenas and on television, and in both places the old balls were too hard to see. I decided on red, white and blue because this was the American Basketball

Association and those are the country's colors. And once I saw the ball in use, I knew we had a winner. On TV, the ball left a slightly discernible trail of color when it tracked through the air. When it spun through the hoop, it was fun to watch. Women and children loved it, and those were the people we wanted to attract to the game.

After we had the new colored balls produced, we did some market research with kids. We brought some kids into a sporting-goods store and let them choose the kind of basketball they wanted. Every single time, they picked the ABA ball over the brown one. Every time. According to *Loose Balls*, Terry Pluto's 1990 book on the ABA, more than 30 million of those red, white and blue balls have been sold. They were wildly popular.

It was a little tougher selling the ABA owners on the ball.

δ

BILL ERICKSON: No one knows the hassles that went on over the red, white and blue basketball. George knew it would not only be attractive to the fans and work well for the players, but it would become an identifying mark for the league. He received opposition to the ball because people said it was too slippery, the colors would make it too hard to play with, it was not traditional, and all kinds of other silly reasons that were later seen as such.

δ

The red, white and blue ball was a focal point of criticism and ridicule, particularly by the NBA. Sometimes, change comes hard. But that ball was a great success for the ABA, and years later, it still exists. Today, the red, white and blue ball is used in the three-point shooting contest held each year at the NBA All-Star Weekend. In that contest, when the red, white and blue ball goes through the hoop, it is worth more points than the other balls. I couldn't have given it a greater compliment myself.

Under my commissionership, the ABA produced a number of innovations to the game — many which were later adopted by the NBA and are still in use today. Along with the ball, my biggest passion in shaping the ABA was adopting the three-point play, which had never existed in the NBA. I remembered that Abe Saperstein had used the three-point play in his ABL, and I thought that it would be good for the ABA, as well. I always considered the three-pointer the home run of basketball. Nothing excites a basketball crowd like a long shot — just like a round-tripper in baseball. The three-point rule opened up the game and allowed the smaller guy another chance to contribute. Every time a small guard arcs one of those long bombs, the crowd watches it intently for the entire flight.

Another innovation I brought to the ABA was encouraging dunking, both during the games and as entertainment. When I played with the Lakers, most of us could dunk the basketball but it was frowned upon in games, so we only did it in practice. As commissioner, I recalled the way fans had cheered while watching the dunks during our pregame warm-ups, and I thought it would be a good way to attract more fans to the ABA. Not only did we allow dunking in ABA games, but we had players doing spectacular dunks during the pregame practice. Later, there were staged dunking contests during intermission as part of our halftime entertainment.

The concept of halftime entertainment itself was another lasting change that the ABA brought to professional basketball. We wanted to draw as many people into the games as possible, and new fans, too, people who might otherwise not have gone to a game. That's why we had slam-dunk contests, cheerleaders and other halftime events. We didn't want the fans in the stands to ever be treated to any dead spots at a ballgame. In today's NBA, that has become the nonstop "ambiance" that you experience throughout the time you're in an arena. People walk away from a game feeling like they have been entertained.

Dunking helped put the ABA on the basketball map and was also instrumental in spreading the fame of one of the ABA's most outstanding stars, Julius Erving, Dr. J. Today, the slam-dunk contest has been incorporated into the NBA's All-Star Weekend, where it is one of the biggest attractions. I used to love to watch the NBA's 5-foot, 9-inch Calvin Murphy race up the court and leap at the basket for a dunk. The crowd would go wild, like they do for Michael Jordan today, whose stats would be a little different without the dunk.

Speaking of statistics, mine would look different today, too. Back in the first couple decades of the NBA, only the basic stats were kept. At the ABA, we made some changes in the stats, thanks to our public relations director, Lee Meade, who also became the league statistician. Meade was the former sports editor for the *Denver Post*, and as ABA statistician, he set out to create a whole new stat sheet. We figured we could make a better product for sportswriters to use in writing stories and thereby generate more publicity for the ABA.

On his new stats sheet, Lee collected numbers that hadn't been recorded before, such as the number of steals, individual turnovers, blocked shots, team rebounds and the differentiation of rebounds — offensive versus defensive. Today's players base their salary demands on some of these statistics, and Lee was the first to keep track of them.

Another innovation in the ABA was a red light behind each basket that went off when a basket was scored. It was based on the idea behind the goal light in hockey — something to alert the crowd when a basket occurred. In the old dark arenas in which we played, that was pretty essential. In today's game, the light behind the basket indicates a stoppage of play. But a light of any kind behind a hoop first appeared in the ABA.

I had a 30-second shot clock installed in the ABA, as opposed to the 24-second clock in the NBA. It wasn't done just to be different; rather, it was done for the same reason we made any change in the ABA — because it was good for the game. I believed that a 30-second clock would give the offensive team a little more time to set up a second play. Too often, I felt, the offensive team comes down the court and finds its initial offensive salvo thwarted. The player with the ball then sees the clock ticking down to nine seconds, and he begins to panic. With another six seconds on the clock, he would have time to call another play rather than cast up a desperate prayer. The 30-second clock put more coaching back into the game.

My critics would love to believe that my reputation for lack of speed was the reason I favored the longer shot clock, that the NBA's game was too fast for me. But the irony of it was that the ABA was played at a very fast tempo. The entire feel of the league, with its long shots and slam dunks, was one of uninhibited emancipation. The players played with an abandon that seemed to say, "Here is my shot at the big time — I'm going for it." ABA players flew up and down the court, playing to stay in the league, playing to win and playing to entertain the fans.

The ABA started play in the fall of 1967 with eleven teams: the Pittsburgh Pipers, Minnesota Muskies, Indiana Pacers, Kentucky Colonels, New Jersey Americans (later the Nets), New Orleans Buccaneers, Dallas Chaparrals, Denver Rockets, Houston Mavericks, Anaheim Amigos and Oakland Oaks. Over the nine seasons that the ABA was in existence, these teams would change names and cities with a frequency that was amazing. At the end, the Pacers and Colonels would be the only two of the original teams to have retained the same city and team name.

Rather than teams, it was individual players who really made the ABA what it was. The ABA was identified by the players' exuberant playing styles and hard-living personalities. And it was in the recruitment of players where I feel I made my biggest contribution to the ABA. We wanted to make the ABA a players' league but also to develop our own stars out of it. That is why I allowed players who had been banned from the NBA to have a second chance in the ABA. Chief among them was Connie Hawkins, a great player who had been in the ABL and with the Globetrotters but was now spending his basketball career on the playgrounds of New York City.

Connie had been banned from the NBA for his alleged involvement in a college basketball point-shaving scandal in 1961. But we investigated his case and discovered that nothing had ever been proven, not in his case, or in Doug Moe's, or Roger Brown's. I thought they all deserved a second chance, and in the ABA they came back to the game with a vengeance. The fact that Hawkins went from the ABA to star in the NBA later in his career proved that he should have been playing in the pros all along.

Connie was one of the ABA's first stars, but there were more to come. Julius Erving, Moses Malone, George Gervin, Larry Brown, Artis Gilmore, and the list goes on. All these people got their start in the ABA. They became stars because we specifically worked on developing them as stars. Once the league got itself established, we started to promote our players. That kind of intensive player promotion had never been done before. However, it's been done with fervor ever since.

On July 14, 1969, after my second season as commissioner, I left the ABA. There was much talk — then and now — that the reason I left was my much-celebrated failure to sign Lew Alcindor (who later changed his name to Kareem Abdul-Jabbar). The story goes that I had a $1 million check in my pocket when I met with Alcindor to negotiate, but that I did not offer it to him. Instead, so this version of events goes, I was saving that check for a second round of talks, which never happened. One part of this story is untrue — Alcindor did see the check. (In fact, I still have a copy of it.) But I don't think that meeting is why he rejected the ABA for the NBA. I felt then — and still feel — that Alcindor had committed himself to the NBA before we even met, and that I didn't have a chance either way. I can't prove that, nor do I care to. Alcindor made his own decision, and he went on to a great career in his own right.

The real reason I left the ABA was because I refused to move the league office from Minneapolis to New York, which is where the owners had wanted it right from the start. For the first two years of the league, I ran the ABA out of an office right down the hall from George Mikan's Viking Travel. That was about the only way I could have done both jobs effectively, which I did. I kept running my travel business, even when I was at my busiest with the ABA.

But the ABA owners kept insisting that the league office should be in New York, to go head-to-head with its competition. I knew that would be a mistake. To move to New York would have been tantamount to entering the lion's den. The NBA owned the media in New York, and as a result the media there ignored everything we did. We would get a couple inches of press in New York, compared to columns and columns of copy that the NBA generated. We couldn't win.

To prove my point, I drove to Ely, a small town in northern Minnesota near the entrance to the Boundary Waters Canoe Area. From there, I issued a press release on the ABA. That release was picked up all over the country; it generated more copy than we ever saw out of New York City.

I tried to compromise, suggesting we move the ABA offices to California, so that the league could still maintain its own identity. But that didn't satisfy the owners. They wanted New York and nothing else, so they lost me. I left on my own conditions — the league bought out the remaining year of my contract — and I happily returned across the hall to my travel agency.

I left the ABA confident in the fact that I had accomplished what I had set out to do, which was to get the league established and make it viable. The ABA survived for seven more seasons as a place for players to get a chance to play professional basketball. In 1976, when the ABA merged with the NBA, the league had become a complete success. I look at the NBA today, and I can see our mark all over it, from the three-point shot and halftime shows to the exciting style of play and marketing of players into megastars-stars. I know that the NBA today has more of the ABA in it than just the four teams that took part in the merger. I see the spirit of the ABA in every NBA game I watch.

I'm happy to see that, as ABA commissioner, I made yet another mark on the game that I love, helping to make basketball the great sport it is today. I did my job and have no regrets.

⚮Part V
The Mikan Legacy

George joins Bob Kurland (left) and Wilt Chamberlain at the Basketball Hall of Fame. *(Courtesy of George Mikan)*

ᘓ18ᘔ
Playing in Overtime

I can remember exactly what it felt like in 1971 when I was named to the NBA's Silver Anniversary team. This was just two years after I'd retired as commissioner of the rebel ABA, which was picking up steam and seriously competing with the NBA. I was thrilled by the award and also relieved that the NBA had not forgotten me. An older athlete occasionally wonders if anyone remembers — in my case, as the ABA grew stronger, I often wondered if the NBA wanted to forget me.

They didn't. In celebration of its 25th anniversary, the league had asked former NBA All-Stars to pick ten players, regardless of position, for the Silver Anniversary team. I was honored to be included alongside some of the greatest players in the game. Many of these were my former foes — Paul Arizin, Joe Fulks, Dolph Schayes, Bob Cousy — but others, like Bill Russell, Bob Pettit and Sam Jones, were great players who came after my time. It was a great feeling to step onto the court on January 12, 1971, at the ceremonies during the 21st All-Star Game and receive that award.

After I left the ABA, I had gone back to George Mikan's Viking Travel and concentrated my energies on building up that business. And I became quite successful at it. Throughout the 1970s and most of the 1980s, I dabbled in a number of business ventures but worked the travel business as my main vocation.

With my wife, Pat, as the hostess at my side, the Mikans became world travel hosts for thousands of people in the Upper Midwest. Pat and I travelled throughout the world for George Mikan's Viking Travel, building a solid business with a reputation as a top-notch travel agency. I was proud of the work we did and enjoyed it very much. It was a wonderful experience to travel the world and take in good times with a lot of people.

I met a wide variety of people through our travels, from the neighbor-next-door folks to the famous — once, I golfed with Willie Nelson in Hawaii and Arnold Palmer in Florida. But our travels also gave many of my fans the opportunity to meet me. And that was one of the greatest joys of my travels and my life — I have always loved people. Wherever we would go, I would receive requests for autographs, and I never failed to oblige them.

Sometimes, my reputation would precede me into a town and I would end up on the local radio or TV, doing interviews and talking with the press. Occasionally, I thought that I wanted to be left alone, but then I would remember an experience that reminded me that being a retired basketball player was not so bad.

On this particular trip, we had landed in Tel Aviv, Israel, with a travel group and were in the process of going through customs. The city had been bombed the day before, so the security personnel were exercising extreme cautionary measures. The customs officers took my baggage and started rifling though it, one of them taking my shaver apart.

Another Israeli customs agent walked up to the one searching me and asked him, "What are you doing?"

"I'm looking for plastic explosives," he responded.

"Don't you know who that is?" the first agent asked. "That's George Mikan. I saw him play in the Garden."

I was quickly hustled through customs after that.

The travel business served me and my family quite well. It saw my kids through college and provided Pat and me with a nice life. It even saw us through a tragic fire that enveloped our home in 1970. My daughter Tricia awakened us at about three in the morning to a fire that forced us to abandon the house. The fire started in the furnace room and gutted the house, taking with it a number of my newspaper clippings and other basketball memorabilia. But thankfully, no one was harmed, and we were able to rebuild.

I ran George Mikan's Viking Travel until 1986, when I acquired my real estate license and went into the real estate business, working as a consultant to people trying to buy and develop properties. I brokered deals throughout the Twin Cites area, from downtown Minneapolis skyscrapers to a proposal for the old Met Stadium property. I had gone from the very mobile travel business to a much more stationary line of work, but I still found it interesting, both in

George joins his old teammate and former Minnesota Vikings coach, Bud Grant, on a 1989 hunting trip and compares prey. George had the tougher shot, anyway.

(Courtesy of Sports Illustrated)

the people I met and the deals I worked on. I still deal in real estate to this day.

My real estate work took a small detour in the late 1980s, however, when I took some time out to develop another "property" that was near to my heart. The NBA had announced that it was expanding by two teams in 1988 and two in 1989. In Minnesota, a contingent of state politicians and prospective franchise owners was formed to bring professional basketball back to the state of Minnesota, and I was approached to chair their committee.

It had been almost twenty years since professional basketball had been played in the state. (Two ABA teams had played there briefly — the Minnesota Muskies in 1967-68 and the Minnesota Pipers in 1968-69.) But most importantly, it had been almost twenty-nine years since the NBA, in the form of the Lakers, was in town. I was very interested in becoming part of the team that would return professional basketball to the fans of Minnesota.

I was approached by then-Minnesota Governor Rudy Perpich and by Marv Wolfenson and Harvey Ratner, the local entrepreneurs who would become the original owners of the Minnesota Timberwolves. The group liked my reputation in business, my status as a former pro basketball league commissioner, and the fact that I was still in good standing with the NBA — I had been named to the NBA's 35th anniversary team in 1981. Governor Perpich and his people figured that my credentials would make me a credible presenter when the Minnesota delegation put its case for an expansion franchise before NBA commissioner David Stern.

Those of us on the committee put in more than a year preparing our presentation. I was now a 40-year resident of Minnesota and could speak quite well of the state's — and the Twin Cities' — attributes. On April 3, 1987, we took our presentation to the league, and the expansion committee recommended that the state be awarded a franchise, the Minnesota Timberwolves, to join the league with Orlando for the 1989-90 season.

It was a great day for Minnesota, reentering the NBA after so many years, just as the league was experiencing a peak of popularity. In the late 1980s, the NBA was strong, basically carried on the backs of Magic Johnson, Larry Bird and Michael Jordan. The Timberwolves would have their start grabbing onto the tail of a growing sports giant, taking off on the exciting ride that is the NBA today.

For me, Minnesota's acquisition of the Timberwolves franchise was a victory of immense pride and personal satisfaction. Back in the 1950s, I had tried my best to keep the Lakers in Minnesota because I knew what a great sport basketball was and how much I loved the game. I never wanted to see the Lakers — or professional basketball — leave Minnesota, so I was excited to have helped bring the NBA back for all those young fans who had never experienced the pro game. The thrill of the achievement energized me, and I believed that I was ready to get back into the business of basketball yet again.

Unfortunately, that didn't happen.

Timberwolves owners Marv and Harv (as they were known around the state) had promised me a meaningful position with the Wolves once we acquired the franchise. In New York, at NBA headquarters, the owners saw how effective I was as the committee chair, and they valued the credibility my name would lend to the organization. I brokered the agreement that the franchise made with Ogden Corporation, the organization that runs Target Center, home of the Timberwolves. That deal was another demonstration of my viable talents for the new team.

But Marv and Harv installed Marv's son-in-law Bob Stein as president of the Timberwolves, and Stein didn't share the owners' feelings about me. Wolfenson and Ratner gave Stein, a lawyer and former University of Minnesota and Kansas City Chiefs football player, complete control of operating the franchise, and he decided not to hire me in any capacity.

I saw that outcome coming long before it ever happened, however. On April 22, 1987, when the NBA board of governors voted to award us the franchise, Harv, Marv, Bob and I were in New York to hear the results. After the announcement, everyone was gathered in a meeting room. We were talking with Commissioner Stern when somebody came into the room to tell us that the press was outside waiting for some comments. Reporters had afternoon papers to fill, and they wanted some quotes on the new franchises for their stories.

Marv turned to Bob Stein and told him to go out and talk to the press. He did, but he came back in the room about thirty seconds later.

"They don't want to talk to me," Stein said. "They want to talk to George Mikan."

George is flanked by former Minnesota Governor Rudy Perpich as they announce plans to submit an application for an NBA basketball franchise in Minnesota. In 1989, Mikan's committee brings the Minnesota Timberwolves and professional basketball back to the state. *(Courtesy of UPI/Corbis-Bettmann)*

I could tell by the look on Stein's face when he gave us this news that my days with the Timberwolves were numbered. That was one I lost for winning.

Frustrated and disappointed as I was, I could understand Bob Stein's decision on one level. Stein was the organization's president, and it was his team to run as he saw fit. I know I would have contributed, but my reputation would have probably attracted attention away from Stein like a lightning rod. I don't see it as ego on Stein's part so much as him having difficulty finding a meaningful position for me that would not supplant the team's president. What basketball president in his right mind would want to hire a person under him who has already been a basketball great, a general manager of a team, a member of an owners' group and a commissioner of a league? Such a president would be setting himself up for a fall, I suppose. I've been known to be "forthright" with my opinions from time to time, so I can understand Stein not wanting to invite this headstrong Croatian under his roof. It probably wouldn't have worked.

That's not to say that being rejected didn't hurt, however. It took me some time to accept the fact that there was nothing for me at the Timberwolves. I pulled back from basketball for a time, just to understand it. I had loved being part of bringing the team to Minnesota, and I hated not being a part of putting it together once we got it. The Wolves franchise was the joining of basketball and Minnesota, two things that I love — I was at the wedding, and I thought I should have been there for the marriage. The truth is, however, that my time hadn't passed; it was just someone else's time arriving.

I did land on my feet, old and rickety as they might be, after that disappointment. Like a good pivot player, seeing one option not open, I pivoted and selected another. My success in bringing an expansion franchise to Minnesota led to more consulting work on the acquisition and relocation of other sports franchises.

Franchise relocation. Such an experience would not seem to lend itself to a nine-to-five, over-the-counter, get-'em-in and get-'em-out type of everyday job. But in the sports business of today, you'd be surprised. Since 1987, I have worked with several groups of people who were either looking for a new expansion franchise or trying to attract an existing one. And the work was reasonably lucrative.

Now, before sports fans across the country start trying to blame me for the instability of their favorite teams, I need to say that I never tried to drum up business for the venture. I have always been approached by people or groups already well into the process of trying to acquire or move a franchise. It's a long and involved process that doesn't always pan out; my job as a consultant is to help the participants navigate the process. The process is interesting to me because it's important to locate franchises in places where they would survive and thrive. It's better for individual teams and for the game in general if the teams are financially viable — Heaven knows, I saw enough of the converse in my day.

I eventually invested my time and money in some fledgling sports franchises of my own: currently, I'm involved with a couple of roller hockey franchises that have played in Chicago and Minnesota. Interestingly enough, I got invited into the roller hockey league by my old ABA buddy Dennis Murphy. Murphy has a great deal of experience in the acquisition and movement of franchises, from the ABA to the World Football League to the Indoor Roller Hockey league, both of which he helped found. I guess some guys just can't get the thrill of setting up leagues out of their system.

I still count the Minnesota Timberwolves as my biggest success in the franchise relocation field, and I'm happy that the Wolves are now surviving and thriving. The team almost didn't make it, however. In 1994, after only five years in existence, the Timberwolves were sold to new owners in New Orleans. (Believe me, I was nowhere to be found in that transaction.) Fortunately for the state, the NBA's board of governors rejected the sale, and owners Ratner and Wolfenson instead sold the team to an owners' group headed by Minnesota businessman Glen Taylor of Mankato, Minnesota. Taylor bought the team to keep it in Minnesota, and the Timberwolves' fortunes have been turning around ever since.

The sale of the team to Taylor has benefited me, as well, for I have finally found my way back to Minnesota basketball. In 1995, I began working with the Timberwolves organization, providing a connection to the state's championship basketball history. The new ownership has recognized the value of allowing me to contribute my wealth of basketball history and knowledge. My involvement with the Timberwolves connects their young and exciting team to the rich and grand tradition of the Minneapolis Lakers. It completes a circle of Minnesota basketball — and of my professional life — in a way that I find rewarding.

George and Pat Mikan in suburban Minneapolis, 1989. *(Courtesy of Sports Illustrated)*

But the era in basketball history that I represent is important to more than just Minnesota. My playing days with the Minneapolis Lakers, the NBA's first dynasty, are a big chunk of the history of the game. My popularity in the 1940s and '50s helped give the fledgling league a viability it needed to become the NBA of today. My dominance as a player led to some of the rules changes that created the modern game. Some basketball writers consider me a foundation cornerstone of the NBA. Well, the surface of this particular stone might be a little weathered now, after fifty years of NBA seasons, but I'm still proud to be recognized for doing something I truly enjoyed — playing basketball.

When the NBA celebrated its 50th anniversary in 1996-97, I was honored to be named to the NBA's 50 All-Time Greatest Players list, along with a group of incredibly talented players. I enjoyed all the hoopla that went along with that — who wouldn't?

But what a greater honor it is to simply be remembered. To have one's life — for whatever reason — be part of a continuing memory, to be a life worth thinking about. That is truly an honor. And for that, I thank all of you.

↫Epilogue

The NBA on Mikan

Michael Jordan, a man with a good chance to be named Mr. Basketball of the second half of the twentieth century, was asked if he was familiar with the career of George Mikan, Mr. Basketball of the first half-century. Jordan jokingly responded that he was too young to have known about Mikan: "They didn't have television when he played the game," Jordan said.

Jordan was kidding, of course, since the two are among the biggest names in basketball history, and both serve as nice bookends to the 50 years of basketball the NBA celebrated in 1996-97: the biggest star that was and the biggest star that is. But Jordan's comments are more telling than one might imagine, since there are a lot of basketball players and fans who are not cognizant of the contributions of Big George. And that's surprising.

Fifty years is hardly a blink of the eye in baseball lore, but in basketball it seems to be the equivalent of a triple-overtime game with no scoring and a lot of commercial timeouts. In other words, a very long time. Anything before Magic and Larry in the 1980s is considered by some to have been played with peach baskets. But that is hardly the case.

As this book has endeavored to show, George Mikan was the first superstar of the league and his numbers bear that out. Still, it is hard to believe that basketball fans might be unfamiliar with a player with such a long list of honors and awards (see Appendix II). But thanks to the league's recent focus on its history, more basketball fans are finding that out.

Either way, the facts remain, and through the years, Mikan has made more than a name for himself, both with the players who played when he did and those who followed. During his career, two quotations were often repeated when talking about Mikan.

225

They are:

"Mikan ran the whole show. He was an athlete despite what some people say about his bulk, and nobody ever had better offensive moves under the basket. When George played, he owned that lane."

— Larry Foust of the Fort Wayne Pistons

&

"George Mikan is six-foot-ten. He couldn't have been greater if he was ten-foot-six."

— Oscar Fraley, former UP writer

Here's what others have said about George Mikan since then:

The Team

JOHN KUNDLA: George was unbelievable. I never had any trouble with him. He was brought up fundamentally sound by Ray Meyer. He was coachable; he would listen. I didn't teach him anything to speak of. He played defense, he played offense. And he knew if he didn't get the ball, he couldn't score. But he was a team ballplayer, and he knew when they pressed us to come out high, he'd pass off and he had a lot of assists the same way. But he was easy to coach, very coachable. And all the players knew this and they knew that he brought championships.

&

VERN MIKKELSEN: George had more desire than other players, that probably would be the defining nature. Other players were good athletes but they didn't have that burning desire to win which carried George throughout his competitive career. Those of us who played with him as teammates, recognized this real early that as far as George was concerned we couldn't get beat and we were going to win the game.

He was the ultimate player you could ever hope to have as a teammate. Every team has a leader, the strong player, and then there are the role players. We were all very, very satisfied in taking our positions as role players because we knew this combo was going to win for us. And George was never a selfish player. He was a dominant player and knew that he could get the job done.

But he was very, very quick to hand off praise and accolades to the other players, saying he couldn't do it alone. And obviously he couldn't. Somebody had to get the ball into him. We did it and we did it very well. Once he got it, he did what he was supposed to do with it — he put it in the hoop.

He's also a very gracious man. George was the first person to ask anybody along with him. He was catered to by a lot of people. He still attracts people very readily. Back then, he was Bird and Magic and Jordan all wrapped into one and he was invited to the nicest restaurants and people's houses, and he always insisted that his teammates go with him.

We were in Tri-Cities, playing the Blackhawks on New Year's Eve in 1949 or '50, and there were some very wealthy people there and they invited George out after the game. They were having a New Year's Eve party and George accepted the invitation and after the game we were getting dressed and he said, "Hey, c'mon guys, we're going to a party." Can you imagine the hostess? She invites George and here comes 10 guys over six feet tall walking into her house. I could still see her over in the corner just chewing out her husband something fierce. But George thought, "If I go, my teammates go." He didn't care.

It was great, and we ended up having a marvelous time getting to know the people, nice people. The hostess finally decided it wasn't such a bad deal after all. We weren't very rowdy and we didn't eat or drink too much. But George insisted that we were going — if he was going, we were going.

ಲ

DON CARLSON: George was one of the greatest basketball players that I ever played with. As I looked at other players during my time, there weren't any who could do everything that George could do. We [the Lakers] had certain plays on offense that we set up for different guys, and George would watch to see who was open and who wasn't. He wasn't selfish at all — he just handed the ball off, and you found yourself getting a nice easy layup off of it, off of his big body.

ಲ

SLATER MARTIN: It was pretty easy playing with George Mikan. All you had to do was give him the ball. You just had to throw it to George, and he could do just about anything with it. He was a good solid player, a real competitor.

He made me a better player because I learned how to pass the ball to him and learned how to cut behind him and get the ball back and screen, the whole thing. He taught me a jillion things.

But, overall, he was a hell of a competitor and hell of a basketball player. He knew how to win. He was a great free-throw shooter. He'd get to the line if there was one second left, he'd make the free throws to win the game.

ಲ

BUD GRANT: George was a great offensive player and he got up and down the floor as good as any of the big men at the time. So in order to counter that, other teams had to get big men who could move up and down the floor like George and become a part of the offense. George changed the game. The evolution of basketball had a lot to do with the way he, Mikklesen and Pollard played — everyone had to meet those standards.

I have played with and coached many great players. And I've seen and coached against some of the best. But I'd have to say that George Mikan is the greatest competitor I've seen or been around in any sport.

ℰℴ

THE COMPETITION

ED MIKAN: George and I were very competitive. We fought and scrambled and everything else. I tell George that I made him famous because he had nobody else to practice on, so he practiced on me. I had a couple of free-throw records and Chicago Stadium points records, but I basically played in George's shadow. But I was always proud to have as great a player as he was for a brother. It never bothered me in any way.

ℰℴ

ED MACAULEY: Every time I was around George Mikan, he was very pleasant. Pleasant is a nice word to use for people. I think when you're pleasant to people that comes from your heart. Some people are nice when it fits their needs, but every time I was around George he was always very pleasant. He was outspoken — you put him in a crowd and with his legal background, he wasn't afraid to express his opinion on anything. But generally, he was just a nice guy.

ℰℴ

BILL RUSSELL: I didn't get to see him very much. But with George it was more how he carried and conducted himself. An extraordinarily fine gentleman, and I just found him awesome. When I met him, he was one of the most generous people in terms of his conduct toward kids that I had met at the time.

I met him in California when the NBA was playing an exhibition game there. I was in high school at the time [and people were scouting me for the pros]. George was just so kind to me — all the other people I had encountered had not been as gracious as he was. I think he was the most gracious person I had met outside my family at the time. I wanted to play on the Lakers because of George Mikan. I was greatly impressed.

When he came out to California to meet me, that was the first time I thought about playing pro basketball. Although there was no reason I should have been thinking that at the time, because I wasn't very good. He was a real inspiration — one of the men I respect in the history of the NBA.

I've seen bits of him playing on film. All my teammates at Boston had played against him, and they had overwhelming respect for him. He established the way the center position was played when he played. That was the standard by which players who came later were judged — judged by George Mikan. He was probably one of the most competitive players to ever play the game. He would go out and compete every night. If you beat the Lakers, you had to beat them — they didn't lose to you.

His legacy is one of a quality player and quality individual in establishing the NBA as a major league. I always look to him as a guy that brought prestige and dignity to the league. I love George Mikan. I think he's great.

℘

BOB KURLAND: George was by far the most dominating center in his day. There were other guys who were better centers, better post players, but George had the ability to play with his back against the basket, and as he moved across the lane (before it got that wide), particularly in college, he was a very effective scorer and a good rebounder. He was a good passer, strong and had good stamina.

What we know about post play today and what existed in those days are two different things. Strength and weight were not that essential in those days. Footwork and positioning and a little finesse was probably the most important thing and George had all those abilities.

℘

BOB PETTIT: In my opinion, Mikan would have been a great player in any era. And the reason I say that is that if he played today, he would play differently. None of us would play the same way. But he had the desire and drive inside of him that would not have settled for anything less than being the best.

When he first started, he was not real good to start with, and it was because of the time and effort that he put in practicing and working that he made himself into a super basketball player. And that would have happened today. Guys like George Mikan would have been a superstar in any era. Simply because he had that desire and drive to make himself a great player.

℘

ARNIE RISEN: George was great. The only advantage I had [over him] was that I got up and down the court a little faster. Everybody thought George was slow running the court. He wasn't as fast as some *of us, but he was very quick. I don't think there was anyone else in the league that I played against, as a big man, that was quicker than George. His hands were quick, and he had quick movements in the pivot despite his size — which I'm sure helped him a lot.*

ဆာ

RED AUERBACH: *Mikan was a giant among men. There weren't many guys who could stand up against him physically in those days. This is what made him outstanding. He was a little more mobile than people thought he was, and he knew how to put the ball in the hole. He knew how to use his weight properly.*

ဆာ

BOB COUSY: *George was a pain in the ass. Simply because the Lakers won all the time in those days. He was so dominant physically. In those days of a six-foot lane, George would just come down and position himself. That made it a little more difficult to trap down. Nowadays, you can trap down more easily because you have less distance to travel to get from whoever your defensive assignment is down to the big man.*

In those days, you had to travel a little bit farther to get to him and George didn't waste a lot of time before he shot. He obviously wasn't in the mold of today's Hakeem Olajuwons and Patrick Ewings. I guess Shaquille O'Neal comes closest to him today in how he played the game. There was nothing fancy about George's game, he was just literally overpowering.

ဆာ

THE MEDIA

HERMAN MASIN: *Nobody could stop George Mikan. He was unstoppable. He was playing with a six-foot lane under the basket and there was no one as big with his athletic ability. He put his left elbow in your face as went up to the basket, and I swear he broke more jaws than anyone. Then he'd throw that single-pivot shot. He was athletic, had a great feel for the game. He turned very well in the pivot toward the basket.*

ဆာ

DICK ENROTH: *George was a tremendous competitor. I used to do a pregame show and I asked Johnny Logan, who was an Indianapolis basketball player, "What do you think of Mikan?" And he says "Mikan and four Coke bottles could beat you." That's how much respect they had for him.*

George was confident, but he never really talked about himself. He'd smile at you. A pleasant smile. He knew he was good. He knew he could do it. I don't think there ever was a time he didn't think he would win. And his team won much more often then they lost.

&

SID HARTMAN: As competitive an athlete as I've ever seen or been associated with. He was great. He had a great pivot shot, a great rebounder. He played 150 percent every game. He could play today, in my opinion, with some of these centers they got playing today. Maybe he wouldn't be as quick or agile as David Robinson, or somebody like that, but there's no doubt in my mind that he could play today and be as good as any of them.

He's one of the top players in the game — without a doubt. He helped make the league. He was the Michael Jordan of the late 1940s and '50s. That says it all, doesn't it?

&

THE NBA TODAY

KEVIN GARNETT: Anybody who doesn't know who George Mikan is, is not a basketball fan. Mikan was the first dominant big man. We [the Minnesota Timberwolves] honored him on opening night [1996], and he stopped by the bench and he told me, "Keep your enthusiasm — be yourself. Just keep doing what you're doing, and you'll be one of the great ones." Coming from him that's quite a compliment, since he's already considered one of the greatest to ever play the game.

&

CHARLES BARKLEY: He was probably the first really true big man who ever played the game. I have a lot of respect for him, I have a lot respect for all those guys who opened doors for us.

&

CLYDE DREXLER: George Mikan gave tall guys, who were all considered awkward at that time, a reason to be proud and stick their head up. Tall guys are often stared at, especially when they're school-aged. But he gave that tall guy a purpose — to play basketball. He gave them the strength to go on without feeling like a freak — to know that there are some other tall guys out there. And that it's something to be very proud of and not ashamed of.

When I was coming up, the tall guys were always looked upon as freaks of nature. They were stared at and people would just gawk, and they would always ask you, "Do you play basketball?" So it gave that tall guy an identity, and I think George Mikan was the first guy to really create that aura.

৪১

KEVIN McHALE: *I think the best players from each era can play in any era. People ask if George Mikan could play today. Absolutely. If he started playing now, he would be exposed to the game, playing AAU ball, and doing everything the guys are doing now. Of course, he could play.*

[Similarly,] I would not be the same player playing in that era [the 1950s] as I was in the era that I played. Just because of the exposure to the changing game. Those guys set the table for us to play a little differently in our era. I doubt that thirty years from now people will be saying that Michael Jordan couldn't play in that era. But the game will shift a lot. The game is evolving, ever evolving.

৪১

SHAQUILLE O'NEAL: *At first, I didn't know who George Mikan was. I'd never seen him play or anything, but I heard from my coach at LSU, Dale Brown, that he was a great player. Brown used to make us do the Mikan Drill. I think I shot 125 hooks in 60 seconds.*

George Mikan was the first great big man. And the Lakers have had a great tradition of centers. Their outcome was great, and I hope when I'm done playing that my outcome with the Lakers is great, too.

৪১

DAVID STERN: *George Mikan is the first dominant big man in the game, the first NBA star. That is the way he has always been known, and I've seen nothing to deter from that description.*

All the great teams throughout the history of the league have constructed their teams around great centers — a tradition of dominant centers that has Olajuwon connected to Jabbar to Chamberlain to Russell — and Mikan is at the start of that tradition.

It's important, given the national and international scale on which the game is expanding, to understand the context from which it originates. The recent focus on the first fifty years of the NBA has brought that to the fore. Looking back at the past fifty years is like looking at a family tree. And George Mikan is the trunk of that tree.

Appendix I:
Selected Bibliography and Sources

Readers may be interested in the following books about George Mikan, the Minneapolis Lakers, the ABA, or the 1940s-50s era in basketball:

Mr. Basketball: George Mikan's Own Story, by George Mikan and Bill Carlson. Greenburg Publisher, New York, 1951.

The History of the Lakers: Basketball's Original Dynasty by Stew Thornley. Nodin Press, Minneapolis, 1989.

Lakers: Collector's Edition by Joseph Hession. Foghorn Press, San Francisco, 1994.

The Lakers: A Basketball Journey by Roland Lazenby. St. Martin's Press, New York, 1993.

Coach by Ray Meyer with Ray Sons. Contemporary Books, Chicago, 1987.

The Golden Game: The Hot Shots, Great Moments and Classic Stories from Basketball's First 100 Years by Billy Packer and Roland Lazenby. Jefferson Street Press, 1991.

Kings of the Court: Legends of the NBA by Alan Minsky. MetroBooks, New York, 1995.

Loose Balls by Terry Pluto. Simon & Schuster, New York, 1990.

Tall Tales by Terry Pluto. Simon & Schuster, New York, 1992.

This book includes information from original newspaper articles published in the *Minneapolis Star, Minneapolis Morning Tribune, Chicago Tribune, Chicago Herald-American, Joliet Herald-News, Rochester Times-Union,* and other newspapers of the times.

Interviews for this book were conducted with the following individuals:

Red Auerbach, Boston Celtics head coach, 1950-1966

Charles Barkley, Philadelphia 76ers, Phoenix Suns and Houston Rockets forward, 1984-present

Don Carlson, Minneapolis Lakers forward, 1947-50

Bob Cousy, Boston Celtics guard, 1950-63

Clyde Drexler, Portland TrailBlazers and Houston Rockets guard, 1983-present

Dick Enroth, Lakers broadcaster

Bill Erickson, former general counsel of ABA

Kevin Garnett, Minnesota Timberwolves forward, 1995-present

Harry "Bud" Grant, Minneapolis Lakers reserve forward, 1949-51, and Minnesota Vikings head coach 1967 - 1983, 1985

Les Harrison, Rochester Royals owner and coach

Sid Hartman, Minneapolis *Star-Tribune* sports columnist

Michael Jordan, Chicago Bulls guard, 1984-present

John Kundla, Minneapolis Lakers coach, 1948-59

Bob Kurland, Oklahoma A&M center, 1942-46

Ed Macauley, Boston Celtics center, 1950-56

Karl Malone, Utah Jazz forward, 1985-present

Slater Martin, Minneapolis Lakers guard, 1949-56

Herman Masin, charter member of the Basketball Writers Association of America

Kevin McHale, former Boston Celtics forward/center, 1980-93, and current Minnesota Timberwolves vice-president of basketball operations

Ray Meyer, award-winning coach of the DePaul University Blue Demons, 1942-84

Ed Mikan, brother of George Mikan and Chicago Stags center, 1948-54

Patricia Mikan, wife of George Mikan

Vern Mikkelsen, Minneapolis Lakers forward, 1949-59

Shaquille O'Neal, Orlando Magic and Los Angeles Lakers center, 1992-present

Bob Pettit, St. Louis Hawks forward/center, 1955-65

Arnie Risen, Rochester Royals center, 1945-1958

Bill Russell, Boston Celtics center, 1956-1969

David Stern, NBA Commissioner, 1984-present

Gene Stump, DePaul guard, 1945-47

Jerry West, former L.A. Lakers guard, 1960-73, and current L.A. Lakers general manager

George displaying some of the hardware collected during his days on the court.

(Courtesy of AP/Wide World Photos)

Appendix II:
Mikan's Records and Awards

BASICS

Position: center
Number: 99
Height: 6 feet, 10 inches
Weight: 240 pounds

CAREER HIGHS

Single game points: 61
Single game rebounds: 36

CAREER HONORS

1950 — Earned the title "Mr. Basketball" after being named by
Associated Press poll as the best basketball player in the
nation for the first half of the twentieth century

1959 — Enshrined in Naismith Memorial Basketball Hall of Fame,
charter member, as a college player

1970 — Voted to the NBA's 25th Anniversary All-Time Team

1980 — Voted to the NBA's 35th Anniversary All-Time Team

1996 — Selected one of 50 Greatest Players in NBA History as part
of NBA's 50th Anniversary celebration

COLLEGE HONORS (DEPAUL UNIVERSITY, 1941-46)

All-American first team, 1944, 1945, 1946
Player of the Year (awarded by Helms Foundation), 1944, 1945
NIT All-Star team, 1944, 1945
NIT Most Valuable Player, 1945
NIT Hall of Fame, 1981

DePaul's leading scorer: 1944-45 (23.3 ppg), 1945-46 (23.1 ppg)
Number 99 retired at DePaul, January 26, 1990

RECORDS STILL HELD AT DEPAUL

Single-game scoring — 53 points March 21, 1945, vs. Rhode
Island (NIT)
Most field goals in a single game — 21 March 21, 1945, vs. Rhode
Island (tied with Stanley Brundy and Mark Aguirre)
Best scoring average as a junior (1944-45), 23.3 points per game

MIKAN AT DEPAUL

Scored 1,872 points in 98 games, a 19.1 average
Averaged 18.7 points as a sophomore, 23.2 points as a junior
and 23.1 points as a senior
Scored 20 or more points 43 times
Scored 30 or more points 12 times
Scored 10 points or fewer only 11 times
Scored in double figures in 30 consecutive games
Led the DePaul team in scoring 68 times
Scored 22.5 percent of DePaul's points in 1942-43; 31.1 percent
in 1943-44; 37.6 percent in 1944-45; 37.2 percent in 1945-46
Scored 120 points in three games in the 1945 NIT, including 53
in the March 21 game against Rhode Island

DEPAUL IN THE MIKAN ERA

Compiled an 81-17 record
Scored 5,754 points and allowed 4,156 for an average margin of
victory of 16.3 points

Season	Record	Margin of Victory	Postseason Play
1942-43	19-5	50.7 - 39.4	reached semifinals in NIT
1943-44	22-4	60.1 - 40.2	reached finals in NIT
1944-45	21-3	61.8 - 43.7	NIT champions
1945-46	19-5	62.1 - 46.4	none

PROFESSIONAL HONORS (1946-56)

Season	Team (League)	Games	Points	Avg.
1946-47	Chicago American Gears (NBL)	25	413	16.5
1947-48	Minneapolis Lakers (NBL)	56	1,195	21.3
1948-49	Minneapolis Lakers (BAA)	60	1,698	28.3

1949-50	Minneapolis Lakers (NBA)	68	1,865	27.4
1950-51	Minneapolis Lakers (NBA)	68	1,932	28.4
1951-52	Minneapolis Lakers (NBA)	64	1,523	23.8
1952-53	Minneapolis Lakers (NBA)	70	1,442	20.6
1953-54	Minneapolis Lakers (NBA)	72	1,306	18.1
1955-56	Minneapolis Lakers (NBA)	37	390	10.5

Note: Mikan played the last few weeks of the 1945-46 season with the Gears. Mikan did not play in the 1954-55 season.

Led team to league championships: 1947 (Gears in NBL)
1948 (Lakers in NBL)
1949 (Lakers in BAA)
1950 (Lakers in NBA)
1952 (Lakers in NBA)
1953 (Lakers in NBA)
1954 (Lakers in NBA)

Voted to the All-NBL first team: 1947 (Gears), 1948 (Lakers)
Voted to the All-BAA first team: 1949
Voted to the All-NBA first team: 1950, 1951, 1952, 1953, 1954
Voted NBL Most Valuable Player: 1948
Led league in scoring: 1946-47 with 16.5 ppg (Gears in NBL)
1947-48 with 21.3 ppg (Lakers in NBL)
1948-49 with 28.3 ppg (Lakers in BAA)
1949-50 with 27.4 ppg (Lakers in NBA)
1950-51 with 28.4 ppg (Lakers in NBA)

Led NBA in rebounding: 1953 with 14.4 rpg

SINGLE-GAME CAREER BESTS

61 points, January 20, 1952, against Rochester (two overtimes)
22 field goals, January 20, 1952, against Rochester
45 field goals attempted, January 20, 1952, against Rochester
19 free throws, March 4, 1952, against Philadelphia
21 free throws attempted, March 4, 1952, against Philadelphia
36 rebounds, March 4, 1952, against Philadelphia

CAREER BESTS

1,932 points, 1950-51
678 field goals, 1950-51
576 free throws, 1950-51
28.4 ppg average, 1950-51

1,028 rebounds, 1953-54
218 assists, 1948-49

ALL-STAR GAME APPEARANCES

Played in inaugural NBA All-Star Games for the West team, 1951, and in subsequent All-Star Games: 1952, 1953, 1954

Voted NBA All-Star Game Most Valuable Player in 1953 with 22 points and 16 rebounds

Averaged 19.5 points and 12.8 rebounds in four NBA All-Star Games

POSTSEASON APPEARANCES

Scored 2,141 points (23.5 ppg.) in 91 postseason games

WORLD PROFESSIONAL BASKETBALL CHAMPIONSHIP APPEARANCES

Played in two World Professional Basketball Championships: third place with the Chicago American Gears, 1946; put in 100 points over four games for a tournament record

First place with the Minneapolis Lakers, 1948; put in 40 points in one game for a tournament record

Won the World Professional Basketball Championships' Most Valuable Player award both years (the only player to ever win it twice)

MISCELLANEOUS

Mikan is one of only four players in NBA history to both lead the league in scoring and in the same year lead his team to a league title. Mikan did it twice, scoring 28.3 ppg. in 1948-49 and 27.4 ppg. in 1949-50. The other three players are Joe Fulks (23.2 ppg. in 1946-47), Kareem Abdul-Jabbar (31.7 in 1970-71), and Michael Jordan, who did it four times (31.5 in 1990-91, 30.1 in 1991-92, 32.6 in 1992-93 and 30.4 in 1995-96).

Mikan is known as a high scorer, but he was also an unselfish passer. In one season, 1948-49, he both led the league in scoring (1,689 points) and led his team in assists with 218 or 3.6 assists per game. This is a rare feat for a high-scoring center.

About the Authors

George L. Mikan lives in Minnesota with his wife, Pat.

Joseph Oberle is publications manager for the Minnesota Timberwolves NBA basketball team. He and his wife, Lora, live in Fridley, Minnesota, with their three children, Seth, Tessa and Paige. Oberle has also written *Diary of a Mad Househusband*, a humorous account of his time as a stay-at-home parent, and *Anchorage*, an educational book for children about the Alaskan city.